A SURVIVOR'S
EDUCATION

A SURVIVOR'S EDUCATION

Women, Violence, and
the Stories We Don't Tell

JOY NEUMEYER

PublicAffairs

New York

PublicAffairs
Hachette Book Group
1290 Avenue of the Americas, New York, NY 10104
www.publicaffairsbooks.com
@Public_Affairs

Printed in the United States of America

First Edition: August 2024

Published by PublicAffairs, an imprint of Hachette Book Group, Inc. The PublicAffairs name and logo is a registered trademark of the Hachette Book Group.

"Six Lectures in Verse, Lecture IV" from *New and Collected Poems: 1931–2001* by Czeslaw Milosz. Copyright © 1988, 1991, 1995, 2001 by Czeslaw Milosz Royalties, Inc. Used by permission of HarperCollins Publishers.

The Hachette Speakers Bureau provides a wide range of authors for speaking events. To find out more, go to hachettespeakersbureau.com or email HachetteSpeakers@hbgusa.com.

PublicAffairs books may be purchased in bulk for business, educational, or promotional use. For more information, please contact your local bookseller or the Hachette Book Group Special Markets Department at special.markets@hbgusa.com.

The publisher is not responsible for websites (or their content) that are not owned by the publisher.

Print book interior design by Amy Quinn.

Library of Congress Cataloging-in-Publication Data

Names: Neumeyer, Joy, author.
Title: A survivor's education : women, violence, and the stories we don't tell / Joy Neumeyer.
Description: First edition. | New York : PublicAffairs, 2024. | Includes bibliographical references and index.
Identifiers: LCCN 2024004110 | ISBN 9781541702790 (hardcover) | ISBN 9781541702882 (ebook)
Subjects: LCSH: Neumeyer, Joy. | Intimate partner violence—United States—Case studies. | Women college students—Violence against—United States—Case studies. | Campus violence—United States—Case studies. | Sex discrimination against women—United States—Case studies.
Classification: LCC HV6626.2 .N4737 2024 | DDC 362.82/920973—dc23/eng/20240416
LC record available at https://lccn.loc.gov/2024004110

ISBNs: 9781541702790 (hardcover), 9781541702882 (ebook)

LSC-C

Printing 1, 2024

While here, I, an instructor in forgetting,
Teach that pain passes (for it's the pain of others),
Still in my mind trying to save Miss Jadwiga,
A little hunchback, librarian by profession,
Who perished in the shelter of an apartment house
That was considered safe but toppled down
And no one was able to dig through the slabs of wall,
Though knocking and voices were heard for many days.
So a name is lost for ages, forever,
No one will ever know about her last hours,
Time carries her in layers of the Pliocene.

—Czesław Miłosz, from "Six Lectures in Verse, Lecture IV"

AUTHOR'S NOTE

The names of everyone connected to the investigation of my case have been changed. The story, however, is real. Depending on who you ask.

CONTENTS

PART 1

Prologue: A Magic Mountain   3
1. The Idea of Knowing   13
2. Deep Play   23
3. The Red Sun   31
4. "Es schwindelt"   41
5. The Captive Mind   55
6. Drop by Drop   65

PART 2

7. Targeted Risk   81
8. Due Process   89
9. The Flood   109
10. Sweet as Always   121
11. Other Voices   131
12. The Real Daniel   149
13. Preponderance of Evidence   161
14. The Hammer   171

PART 3

15. Mastering the Past   181
16. Public Peril   195
17. No Major Problem   207

18. Patterns   219
19. War   231
20. Lessons in Forgetting   243
     Epilogue: A Long Time Ago   259

     Acknowledgments   *261*
     Works Cited   *263*
     Index   *285*

A SURVIVOR'S
EDUCATION

Part 1

PROLOGUE
A MAGIC MOUNTAIN

THE FOG HANGS LOW AS I SLIP OUT THE DOOR AND ONTO ARLING-
ton Avenue. It could be any season or year. In the Berkeley hills
there is no winter or summer, spring or fall. Plants bloom in January,
and micro-down jackets guard against the chill that descends with the
creeping mist. Like a California reincarnation of *The Magic Mountain*,
Berkeley's hills seem to stand outside time. Thomas Mann's hero, Hans
Castorp, arrives at a Swiss sanatorium for a brief visit but invents a fever
that allows him to stay for seven years. He discusses love and death at
deliriously high altitudes, far from the war that will soon break out below.

After working as a journalist in Russia, I came here to study Europe's
past. When my plane from Moscow landed in San Francisco, I stepped
out into balmy temperatures. Across the bay in Berkeley, I smoked weed
and smelled angel's trumpet flowers, their orange blossoms bursting with
nocturnal perfume. I never wanted to leave. While sitting in seminars,
I sometimes stared at the redwood trees outside the window and wondered at my good fortune. Theory is gray, Goethe's Mephistopheles tells
a student in *Faust*, but the tree of life is green. Silver fog and emerald
branches—Berkeley had it all.

Time, however, can only be suspended for so long. At the end of the
novel, Castorp comes down from the mountain and into the trenches.

It could be any season or year, but it is fall 2016, and I'm walking home
from the Halloween party I attended last night as Hamlet. I have a black

3

coat over my shoulders and a plastic skull in my hands, decapitated from a skeleton I bought at the CVS on Telegraph. Peter, the philosophy grad student I'm dating whose house hosted the party, dressed up as Donald Trump, a red baseball cap shoved over his straw-blond hair. With barely a week left until the election, "President Trump" still sounds like a novelty costume for polite men hoping to get in a few off-color remarks before political correctness is restored.

At the party, Tame Impala had thumped from the speakers as Peter bobbed his head to the bass in "Brand New Person, Same Old Mistakes." I half-assed my line about poor Yorick and danced. Beyond a cluster of smokers on the house's front step lay the onyx eternity of the bay at night.

"Academia isn't a job, it's a vocation," one of them was saying as he took a drag on his hand-rolled cigarette. "Like the priesthood."

A woman with the round, blank eyes of a doll nodded back at him.

I didn't know anyone there and started drinking, first a little, then a lot. After my prolonged absence Peter came to find me in the bathroom, asked if I was okay, and left to rejoin the party. Later, I was lying on his bed, traces of vomit encrusted on my clothes, when he reappeared and began touching me.

"I want you so badly," he said.

I was impressed by the unfailing precision of his grammar; even while pawing for a drunken fuck he managed to use an adverb.

The next morning, my head feels as blurry as the houses in the mist. I'm moving slowly on my high-heeled boots as I walk by front yards brimming with rose bushes and lemon trees. Now it is mostly senior faculty who can afford to live in the hills. A professor who's been teaching at Berkeley since the '70s once had our seminar over for dinner and martinis at his hillside mansion, while his younger colleague warned us that he had a place in the lower-rent suburb of El Cerrito and no invitations would be forthcoming. Peter is lucky: the father of one of his philosopher friends taught at Berkeley years ago and bought this house. The professor left his old copies of Kierkegaard in the living room.

I feel my phone buzz in my pocket. It's Daniel, my fellow PhD student and closest friend.

"I got so drunk I don't remember how I got home," the message reads. "Never drinking bourbon again," I reply.

"I'm never drinking period."

I walk under live oak trees past Indian Rock Park, the boulders where my friends and I sometimes watch the sun go down over the bay with a pizza from Cheese Board. Daniel attended another party, held by historians in our program, and is reporting on who threw up where. He tells me that the best costume was worn by a grad student who came as the French philosopher Michel Foucault. I tell him about a drunken speech I made to Peter in which I declared that if you don't care about other people's feelings there's no point in living.

"Hmm well there is truth to that," Daniel writes.

I ask if he's in the department. He is, and I agree to stop by.

I continue down the steep decline of streets with botanical names— Rose, Spruce, Vine, Cedar—and onto campus. Heading toward the Campanile, the faux-Venetian clock tower whose bells mark the procession of hours, I pass Doe Library. There is always a man in tattered jeans pacing around the library's marble entrance. He looks like Robert Redford, with strawberry-blond hair and a tanned face. I can't tell how old he is or how long he has been there. As students walk by, he seems to gaze through them, toward a troubling vision only he can see. Just up the hill stands the neoclassical residence of Chancellor Nicholas Dirks, who has recently come under fire for using university funds to build a fortified fence around the property after protestors vandalized it. The additional security measures, which came amid a massive budget shortfall in the UC system, included the installation of an escape door near his office.

I open the door of Dwinelle Hall, where Daniel is waiting for me in the History Department library. I find him sitting in a corner that holds the bookshelves of a professor who, while riding his bike on campus one day, was hit and killed by a truck as it was backing up. Daniel is reading with a highlighter tapping between his fingers. He looks up at me in my Jim Beam–stained overcoat and blurred mascara.

"Well look who it is," he says with a smile.

I sink into the armchair across from him, relieved at the sight of his face. He tells me that at the historian party he fell face-first onto the sidewalk, knocking off the devil horns he'd been wearing.

After we conclude our dissection of the previous night, I walk back outside and onto Sproul Plaza, the concrete expanse that was the epicenter of the Free Speech Movement in the mid-1960s. In the decades after FSM, state funding for public education in California plummeted. The number of tenured faculty remained stagnant as the ranks of highly paid administrators grew, while the university poured funds into vanity projects like a new aquatics center. In 2011, students affiliated with the Occupy movement staged a sit-in to protest a tuition hike and layoffs. But the neoliberal transformation of Berkeley, like that of other American universities, was already complete. As the campus corporatized, the tech industry exploded, leading to a housing crisis that has spilled over into the East Bay. Some students pay huge sums to rent a room on the city's lower-altitude south side, while others go without regular shelter and sleep in cars or on couches.

Sproul empties onto Telegraph Avenue, the main artery that runs from the edge of Berkeley's campus to downtown Oakland. Though the '60s are dead, their spirit lives on in the sights, sounds, and smells of the surrounding blocks: the vinyl racks at Rasputin and Amoeba; the chanting Hare Krishnas who process to the shake of a tambourine; the funk of urine and marijuana; the dreadlocked gutter punks with their drowsy dogs; the Marx-Engels Readers on display at Moe's Books and the empty windows of Shakespeare and Sons, a used-book emporium that will soon be replaced by a third-wave coffee shop; and the hand-painted signs at People's Park. The latter was created in 1969 when activists turned a vacant lot owned by the university into a community garden. A standoff over land use culminated in "Bloody Thursday," when dozens of people were shot and one killed. Governor Ronald Reagan declared that "once the dogs of war are unleashed, you must expect things will happen, and people will make mistakes on both sides." Although these days the park is mostly taken up by a homeless encampment, a mural continues to honor its utopian spirit. Depictions of police brutality give way to a lone woman sitting under a tree. The branches above her turn into a technicolor whirl of naked figures who hold hands and dance in a circle, free from clothing and time. The fog has fully dissipated by the time I reach my building at the corner of Telegraph and Dwight Way, an ashen construction that stands above a tattoo parlor, a liquor store, a hat shop, and a Taiwanese hot pot place.

A couple of weeks earlier, I woke up in Peter's bed to the sound of a video that a friend had sent him—Trump talking about grabbing pussy. Peter laughed nervously, just as he had when we watched Trump pacing around Hillary Clinton on a big-screen projection of the debate in the History Department. Peter, who grew up on a tobacco farm in Ohio, reinvented himself as a hipster who attends techno parties in abandoned warehouses and buys Japanese condoms you can "barely feel." After chatting on OkCupid, we first met up for beers at a dive bar in Oakland. We headed out around midnight. He hopped on his bike with an impartial "I'll be in touch" and rode off, leaving me to find a bus stop alone.

Peter's apathy toward me has been obvious from the moment we met. But I'm sick of online dating—the infinite drinks and hookups that never turn into anything lasting, the erratic communication as we all weigh our other options—and cling to his company like the raft of the *Medusa* (which, notably, didn't get most of its shipwrecked passengers to shore, while the survivors resorted to cannibalism). During a run with my friend Hannah on the Fire Trail, a dirt path in the hills with a scenic view of water and sky, I report that while I'm unsure whether Peter and I have an emotional connection, if we become exclusive one will definitely appear. As Hannah's Prius winds around the bends back down to south Berkeley, we sing along to Dolly Parton with the windows down. After parking in front of my building to drop me off, she turns toward me.

"Would you ever consider going out with Daniel?"

I demur. "We're so good as friends. And would he even be interested?"

"I think he doesn't think you would give him a chance," she says as I get out and close the door.

A few days after the Halloween party, on his birthday, Peter dumps me by telling me that I make him feel empty inside. After he leaves, I eat one of the brownies I baked for him and dispose of his present—a lotería card with a watermelon on the front and a cringe-inducing inscription from me on the back ("May you let the juice of life run down your chin"). I quote Peter's parting words in a self-pitying phone call to my mom.

"Oh honey," she says. "He's not worth your time."

There's one man I know who does seem worth it, who always walks me home when we hang out at night and whose eyes light up whenever he looks at me. I call Daniel about the breakup and he comes over to my apartment. We walk up the hillside to a running track that looks out over the lights across the bay.

"Life goes on," he tells me as we walk around the asphalt oval. "Now to spend it with people who value and look forward to your company."

Daniel and I are close in a way that exceeds friendship. One night I send a text with a wink face asking if he's on a date.

"Sort of," he replies. "But always loyal to you."

He tells me that meeting me was a blessing; I call him my partner in crime and say it feels like we're one person. During our constant strolls, text exchanges, and dinner dates, Daniel airs his exhaustion with the "beigeocracy"—his term for the dominant whiteness of our department and the world at large—and his feelings of inadequacy and isolation over being a first-generation academic of color. Though he won mentors and fellowships that took him all the way to graduate school, he likes to say that he is "a burden in the world of others."

When some of our peers in the program swap stories about how they wore awkward braces as teenagers, Daniel stays quiet, and tells me later they don't know how lucky they are that their parents could afford orthodontics. I'm a WASP who grew up in the suburbs, but a shared streak of social observation brings us together. We're as skeptical of the chancellor's fence as we are of the tales of humble origins that predominate in our circles. Though the majority of our peers come from relatively well-off backgrounds, it's common to play up any claim to underprivilege as a form of social currency—a self-presentation encouraged by the "diversity statements" we were asked to include in our graduate school applications.

We skewer Berkeley's social codes but strive to abide by them. Though we all look up to our mentors, Daniel venerates them more than anyone else. He likes to say that one of his advisors is a king to his serf: "All I can do is either beg for mercy or a quick death." On bad days, he says he wishes he were an iron statue that could be melted down.

"Since that is not an option," he says, "I'm just gonna stuff my face."

We eat our feelings all over the East Bay: Great China on Bancroft, Zachary's Pizza on Shattuck, Black Bear Diner in Emeryville, Jack in the Box on Telegraph, In-N-Out Burger in Alameda. No comfort food is beyond the reach of my 1991 Geo Prizm, which ferries us away to forget our problems with the help of animal fats.

I try to counter his despair with gentle optimism.

"Being sour has its place," I tell him. "But so does being happy. And I want you to be happy. Sometimes."

He says that no one can understand the path he has trod.

"I will support you in all things," I say, "even if my own understanding is limited." Though I counsel him to have faith (and try therapy), I'm also drawn to his melancholy, which seems more real than humblebragging or virtue signaling. We repeat the mantra that neither of us will let the other go down.

Despite its rising fees and bloated bureaucracy, Berkeley still feels like the enchanted realm that all of us were hoping to find in academia. The university provides us with top-notch health insurance, steady if inadequate stipends, and free food at campus events. In seminars, lectures, working groups, and drinking sessions, we learn to ask more incisive questions and refine our answers. We commit the historiographies of entire continents to memory while spending hours debating the definition of fascism. The conversation never stops as we buy three avocadoes for a dollar at Berkeley Bowl, ride bikes to each other's houses, grade papers, down beers, shoot hoops, perform our own sort of circle dance through centuries of thought. I'm particularly interested in death—the practices surrounding it and the stories that different societies have told to make sense of it. Daniel calls me Lady Death and sends me intriguing representations of mortality, like a funeral scene he finds in a painter's memoir. Sometimes our talks turn to gender. He tells me about a discussion session he taught on Rudyard Kipling and other colonial writers in which he steered students' conversation toward "masculinity and the burden of appearing dominant."

"White men were offended and progressives didn't like victimizing colonizers," he reports.

"That's a rare one-two punch," I joke.

In trying to explain our varying views of the past, the historian E. H. Carr once invoked the image of a mountain. "It does not follow that because a mountain appears to take on different shapes from different angles of vision," Carr wrote, "it has objectively either no shape at all or an infinity of shapes." Though our accounts must approximate some kind of truth, the possible forms they can take are more expansive than Carr allowed. For surrealists such as René Magritte, a mountain could be collapsed into the shape of an egg. Historical prophets like Karl Marx argued that what humans think is a mountain is really a volcano, ready to erupt at a moment's notice and upend the world they think they know. We are all the imperfect historians of our own pasts whose recollections are colored by our present knowledge and desires. I can strive to represent life on this campus by the bay as it was before and after my personal world exploded, but the view will remain partial and subjective. When I show a friend the above pages about Berkeley, she says that she remembers it much differently.

Perhaps the most unsettling vision of history was created by the German philosopher Walter Benjamin in 1940, writing about an image by the artist Paul Klee. The "angel of history" that Benjamin sees in Klee's print gazes in horror at what came before as his wings bear him ceaselessly into the future. The past, in Benjamin's framing, is not a mountain or a volcano, but an ever-rising trash heap. The angel is doomed to look backward, comprehending what has occurred when it is already too late. Hegel coined a similar thought with his phrase that "the owl of Minerva flies at dusk." Insight, in other words, only comes in retrospect.

Daniel and I roll our eyes at talk of angels and owls. We are postmodern readers who know that all symbols are arbitrary and snarky twentysomethings who regard most received wisdom as suspect.

"He uses the owl of history line, I can't deal," I text him when I come across a reference to Minerva in a book I'm reading.

"Tell him that owl is dead and stuffed," Daniel replies.

Now, writing from the perspective of a future when I realize how much I didn't know then, I am struck by how these images capture the desire to understand what cannot be undone.

In a seminar I took on twentieth-century Europe, we read a book about the buildup to World War I. Its author points out countless moments when things could have turned out differently. Even the conflict's immediate trigger, the assassination of Franz Ferdinand, almost didn't occur. The archduke's motorcade was supposed to go down a different street, but no one informed the driver. Through the final moments, when Kaiser Wilhelm cabled his Russian cousin Nicky that Germany was mobilized for war, there were choices with consequences. After hundreds of pages of diplomatic breakdowns, missed opportunities, and dreams of violence, the historian reaches his conclusion: that the European monarchs and those who served them were "sleepwalkers," stumbling bleary-eyed into a conflict that would leave twenty million people dead.

The same currents ripple through individual lives. Looking back on those final days before I started dating Daniel, I wonder: Could what was about to happen have been avoided? What should I, could I, have seen about a man I was so close with I thought we were one? How might all our fates be different if our perception were clearer? In *The Stranger Beside Me*, true crime writer Ann Rule recounts her slow realization that her close friend Ted—a charming man who answered calls with her at a crisis line, talked her through her divorce, and escorted her to her car at the end of each shift—was also the serial rapist and murderer Ted Bundy. Rule sifts through her memories for anything she might have missed and comes up empty. The only thing she can think of is that her dog always growled at him.

After leaving Daniel, I initially felt most comfortable around people whose professions made them closely familiar with how humans are often not who they claim to be. When I met with a social worker or a legal aid lawyer, I didn't have to explain how someone could undergo a metamorphosis from one moment to the next, or why I had tried to forget the hideous shapes I'd seen. They'd observed it so many times before; they already knew. According to a Russian saying my PhD advisor liked to quote, "the soul of another lies in shadow." Psychoanalysts argue that we are strangers to ourselves, while some sociologists claim that all behavior is contextually dependent. Marxists maintain that individual subjectivity is a "bourgeois fiction," and that what we mistake for the self is really the window dressing of class. Even so, we are compelled to find clues that we can arrange to make meaning—to discern the shape of the mountain.

The first time I look through my text messages with Daniel from before our relationship began, I don't find any hint of what would happen next. When I sort through them once again, certain things appear more significant: his resentment over his status as an underling in the world of others and fixation on the male "burden of appearing dominant," my longing to feel needed and promises of limitless support. Our dynamic reminds me of a photo that a friend once took of us. My arms are wrapped around Daniel's waist as my face looks up at him from a sideways tilt, shining with a delirium touched by danger. We are both on the verge of tipping over, but I hold on anyway.

The closest I can come to a warning that I think I should have recognized, a road sign that pointed the way to a different future, appears in an extended late-night text conversation. Daniel is telling me about his father, who left when Daniel was a child.

"I only have one image of my dad. His fist. Not his face," he types.

"I'm sorry you remember him that way," I reply. "Or to be more exact, I'm sorry he made you remember him that way."

He writes that his dad would periodically hit him, "to the point where life was pain and reconciliation." He admires those who "turn all that pain and all that suffering into something beautiful and die." I urge him to carry on living and find some kind of peace. But the memory of his father will not be forgotten.

"How much of him lives in me?" Daniel asks.

At the time, neither one of us had an answer. The owl, as usual, flew too late.

1

THE IDEA OF KNOWING

IT WAS AN ORDINARY AFTERNOON IN POMPEII WHEN ASH STARTED falling from the sky. The watercolor lava pouring out of the volcano's top is the same shade of scarlet as the velour upholstery of our couch. My mother turns the page. The people of Pompeii, I learn, were frozen in the same spots where they had hidden or tried to flee, some of them paralyzed in a protective crouch.

"What happened to them next?" I ask my mom when we finish the book.

"They died," she says.

"What do you mean, 'died?'"

"Well, that was it. They were gone."

I imagine the boundless smog hanging over Vesuvius.

"Will you and Dad die?" I asked. "Will I die?"

"Of course. Everyone dies."

I bury my head in the couch and cry. There must be some way to bring them back, all those people who came before and were both like and unlike us.

Our next book is about mummies. These bodies were fully prepared for the end, with their desiccated organs carefully packaged in jars and their limbs accompanied by emblems to ensure their safe passage to the underworld, along with jewels and games to keep them elegantly attired and entertained. I wonder if they ever made it. At First Christian Church Disciples of Christ, we downplay the mysteries of the afterlife in favor of the mercy that Jesus showed on earth. My favorite story is the parable of the Good Samaritan, which we act out in Sunday school. My heart seizes at the thought of that poor traveler to Jericho who was robbed, beaten, and forsaken by passersby, until at last a kind soul took pity on him. I imagine marching up to the troubled wanderer in my Girl Scout uniform, dotted with patches that attest to my dubious skill at selling cookies, and easing his sorrows with a hug and a complimentary Thin Mint.

My induction into the heavenly fold took place in Lynchburg, Virginia, a town in the foothills of the Blue Ridge Mountains. Many of the world's smokers once rolled cigarettes with tobacco grown in Virginia, and much of that tobacco was processed in Lynchburg. The skeletons of factories where enslaved workers wrapped shriveled leaves into paper shells still stand along the James River waterfront. Across town, a massive red and white "LU" marks the territory of Liberty University, the Christian juggernaut founded by the televangelist and conservative culture warrior Jerry Falwell. Falwell gradually progressed from opposing racial integration to railing against abortion. By the time I'm growing up in Lynchburg in the 1990s, he's turned to outing the purple Teletubby Tinky Winky as a homosexual.

When I'm not at church, I alternate between watching Britney Spears and Christina Aguilera on MTV and retreating to dreamworlds of the past: the Minnesota farmland worked by my American Girl Doll Kirsten, the Spanish court of Isabella I of Castile or the kingdom of Nzingha, "Warrior Queen of Matamba" (as detailed in the Royal Diaries series), any place where women were something other than a taut stomach in low-rise jeans. Though my tenth-grade European history class can't pronounce the names written in the textbook's tiny print, and neither can our teacher—"Cardinal Rich, Rich-uh, Rich-uh-lee . . . oh, you know what I mean," she says with a laugh while admitting defeat—its tales of old regimes and revolutions offer an electrifying new set of possibilities. The highlight of my year is History Day, a competition that assigns students to turn a past figure or event into a presentation or performance. In my one-woman reenactment of George Sand, the gender-bending writer who rose to fame in mid-nineteenth-century France, I begin by meekly composing a letter to my husband, only to rip off my skirt (revealing pants underneath) and chomp on an unlit cigar while declaring that my true love is the pen. I don't quite have the guts to defy convention and embody a different future, but I like imagining what it was like to be someone in a faraway time and place who did.

I find the most radical alternatives in Russia, a country whose history, language, and culture I begin to study in college. A sprawling kingdom of peasants overthrew the tsar and transformed into an industrialized superpower that defeated Hitler and threatened to pulverize its capitalist nemeses, only to collapse within the span of a single lifetime—I can't conceive of greater expectations or a harder fall. I'm most interested in how revolutionary dreams play out in individual lives. The summer before my senior year, while working as a research assistant at the Library of Congress, I come across several boxes of letters sent to the editor of a Soviet newspaper in the 1960s. While deciphering the handwriting with my intro-level Russian, I uncover surprisingly personal confessions. A childless engineer wrote that she felt judged and rejected for not being a mother; an impotent worker at a tractor factory described how "the thought of my incompleteness follows me everywhere." I draw on the letters to write a senior thesis that crafts a dutiful argument in line with recent historiography. But my analysis feels flat compared to the sources, with their intoxicating mixture of intimacy and distance. I would never know more about their authors than what they left on a piece of paper that wasn't meant for my eyes.

After graduating in 2010 I get a Fulbright grant that allows me to move to Moscow for a year and supplement my project with archival research and interviews. When it ends, I decide to stay on in Russia and get a job as a reporter for an English-language newspaper. Over the next few years, my articles keep turning to the past—the gay cruising routes of late Soviet Moscow, a Stalinist mass grave that has yet to be exhumed. I interview a sculptor named Nikolai, who cast Lenins, proletarians, and cosmonauts for public spaces across the Eastern Bloc. At the end of our conversation, Nikolai invites me to come back to his studio and pose for a portrait. I agree.

Nikolai is ninety-five years old, with gray hair that falls to his chin. I am twenty-five with a pixie cut that I am not quite pulling off. After a few moments of painting, he starts to grunt with displeasure.

"Why are your breasts so low?" he asks. "Can't you make them any higher?"

I blush and try sitting up straighter. He orders me to tighten my bra straps.

"Higher! Higher!"

I hoist them up as far as they'll go, and he begrudgingly proceeds. After an hour we're interrupted by his wife, who urges me to have some of the bread she's just taken out of the oven. I look over at the painting-in-progress and see a woman in yellow against a blue-green background. She looks vaguely like me, except for one key detail: she doesn't have a mouth. I assume it will be filled in at our next sitting.

A few days later, I'm in the newspaper office when my cell phone rings. The paper has just published my profile of Nikolai, a two-page spread about his life and work as a court artist, and I wonder if he's calling to invite me over again. But it turns out that the sculptor, accustomed to turning mortal workers into marble gods, doesn't like losing control over how he's represented any more than I did.

"You pig!" he yells. "I want to punch you in the face."

He doesn't explain what his problem is with the article before hanging up. He takes his revenge by leaving my image unfinished, with an empty space where the mouth should be.

I never get used to the weight of depicting someone else in words, or the shameful sting I feel whenever they're dissatisfied with their portrayal. Writing about the dead feels safer and more substantial, unveiling how and why things came to be rather than attempting a facsimile of life as it is. On a visit to the estate where Vladimir Lenin died, I attend an exhibition of plaster death masks made of the early Soviet elite. As I look at the final facial expressions of politicians, poets, and secret policemen, I remember the mummies of ancient Egypt, and wonder why modern people who aimed to build heaven on earth still created relics of those who left it. I read everything I can find about Soviet art and rituals but crave more knowledge than I can glean from a Google search or library trip. Getting a PhD would give me the time, training, and funding necessary for more extensive research and longer word counts.

Berkeley was where my college mentor went to graduate school and where the most interesting researchers I meet in Moscow are studying. I never seriously consider going anywhere else. "I am ready to embark on formal training in the study of history and to teach students about the culture that continues to haunt and fascinate me," I write in my admissions essay. "I feel that Berkeley is truly the best place for me, and I can't wait to make it home." I receive a fellowship offer of $27,500 a year and an invitation to admitted students' day.

After listening to a panel of faculty and grad students answer questions about the program, the new admits are invited to a nearby hotel bar for beer and snacks. As I approach the standing tables, my eyes falling greedily on a platter of macaroni-and-cheese bites, I hear a hesitant voice.

"Hey, are you Joy?"

I look up and see someone gazing at me with a shy smile. He introduces himself as Daniel. There's something about him that's both disarmingly vulnerable and reassuring, as if he were a friend I already knew and had missed. As we pick over the appetizers that are going cold, Daniel tells me that he's still debating between Berkeley and a couple of other schools. I urge him to join me here.

"Come on, won't you be my comrade?" I say with what I hope is playful charm as I sip a hoppy IPA that's going directly to my head.

He smiles again.

A few days later, after I've flown back to Moscow, Daniel emails me to let me know that he's chosen Berkeley, too.

"It was a tough decision but I think it was the right one."

──────

That August, I move into a studio apartment and start assembling Ikea furniture. Aiming for a hip, eco-friendly vibe, I purchase a creaky 1968

Peugeot bike from a man with a gray ponytail. I subsequently learn that his shop is known for selling stolen goods and that the bike's gearless wheels are powerless against Berkeley's hills.

I'm joined before the start of classes by my boyfriend Lars, a journalist I met in Moscow.

"You'll love it here," I tell him. "It's like Berlin!"

Lars is from Scandinavia and seethes at America's smug jingoism, inadequate bike lanes, and disregard for the poor. On his first night in town, we walk past people stretched out on tarps on Telegraph. Berkeley's homelessness crisis is guiltily ignored by the students, teachers, and staff hurrying back and forth from campus, who learn to avert their eyes at the sight of a moaning figure pushing a shopping cart down the sidewalk.

"This is nothing like Berlin," Lars says.

We will break up the following summer.

On the first day of Introduction to History and Theory, I sit down at a long, rectangular table, still hyperventilating after running up the stairs to arrive exactly at "Berkeley time," the unwritten rule by which everything starts ten minutes past the hour. Around fifteen graduate students (most in their first year, a few in their second) are pulling out laptops. The professor occupies an unassuming position on one of the rectangle's longer sides. He mentions that he used to work construction and presents himself as an outsider in the world of professional historians, which he calls "the guild."

The class begins with an icebreaker game that I will later inflict on my students as a teaching assistant: each person has to say their name and one fact about themselves, then repeat the names of everyone who has gone before them. Like the nonhierarchical shape we sit in, it creates an atmosphere of camaraderie as well as mutual surveillance, a vague anxiety that our ignorance (about a particular name, monograph, time period, or way of talking) will be exposed.

Once the introductions are over, we proceed to discussion.

"Why study history?" the professor asks.

"To create citizens," someone suggests.

"Citizens of what? The nation-state? The globe? The cosmos?"

The professor explains that in the discipline of history, "the most vicious form of struggle" is "boundary construction"—determining what is included and what is left out. According to recent scholarship on the Anthropocene, for example, humans must overcome geographic, social, and chronological divisions in order to see ourselves as a species and recognize nature as an actor with agency. (I have never heard the word "Anthropocene" and make a mental note to Google it.) This class, he says, will historicize "the idea of knowing" itself. With each text we read, we will ask where history starts, where it ends, and what agenda is implied by the answers given.

For next week's session, we're assigned to read Hegel's *Lectures on the Philosophy of World History* and his essay "Lord and Bondsman." According to Hegel, the lord (or master) sees the bondsman (slave) as an object for the satisfaction of his desires, while the bondsman lives only to serve. The bondsman liberates himself through a trial by death that forges an independent consciousness. His goal is not to subjugate the master in turn, but to achieve collective emancipation. This progressive unfolding of freedom, Hegel wrote, is world history. The professor notes that Hegel thought some peoples had history, while others (including indigenous Americans and Africans) did not and were therefore doomed to assimilate to the rising West. In his later years, he became an apologist for slavery in Europe's colonies. Despite Hegel's hypocrisies, his dialectic became an enduring template for those who thought the point of studying the world was to change it.

Marx, whom we read the following week, picked up Hegel's idea of history unfolding in a predestined arc and reframed the conflict between master and slave as class struggle. According to Marx, history was moving from feudalism to capitalism, and from capitalism to communism. Once exploited workers achieved self-consciousness, they would rise up and overthrow their oppressors, the bourgeoisie. In the ensuing kingdom of freedom, each person would contribute according to his ability and receive according to his needs. Private property would be abolished, and the state would wither away. Marx's vision of history converted desolation into hope—the worse things appear, the better the chances for change.

In another seminar, we learn how historians analyze specific phenomena without relying on an overarching theory. This class is taught by a kind professor with wrinkled shirts and a weary air. Upon discovering that we haven't heard of yet another essential book, historian, or event, he is fond of getting up to write on the board. In one of our first sessions, he jots down the name of Leopold von Ranke, the pioneer of positivist history. In the nineteenth century, Ranke helped create history as a modern discipline by moving it away from philosophy and closer to the natural sciences. Ranke, the professor says, thought that the historian's objective was to impartially understand a time in its own terms, "as it actually was," through the study of archival documents. On another occasion, the professor tells us about how the French Annales school brought a social scientist's eye to the study of the past, analyzing both long-term developments and short-term contingencies. The *longue durée* is the ocean, he says; the events are the waves.

This professor puts a premium on names, dates, and places and asks us to assemble them in a way that makes the past comprehensible. He invokes Karl Popper's falsification principle, which held that in order for an argument to be scientifically valid it must be possible to disprove. He talks about how to work with sources: the closer in time the material is to the actual event, he says, the more reliable it tends to be. Every week we write a review essay that critically assesses the books we've been assigned to read. In one of my reviews, I dismiss a historian's account on the grounds that it lacks nuance.

"Why do you prefer nuance?" the professor comments in pencil.

I don't really have an answer.

We practice building our own arguments in research and writing seminars. After signing up for one with my advisor, Alexander, I come in thinking I don't have much to worry about: after all, I've been writing professionally for the past four years. I quickly discover how little I know and how much more cautious I need to be. In the draft of my research paper, I state that a sculptor's heart "beat wildly."

"Be careful with such things," Alexander writes in the margins.

He warns me to make sure that my assertions match the evidence, to analyze my subjects without condescension or judgment, to be specific rather than generalize, to avoid trendy jargon, purple prose, and poetic license. At a couple of points in the draft, I repeat information from a popular history book that doesn't contain footnotes. While identifying the resulting errors in the margins, Alexander offers some advice:

"Generally beware of unconfirmed claims."

2

DEEP PLAY

DWINELLE HALL, THE HOME OF OUR DEPARTMENT, IS A CONCRETE behemoth on the slope curving up to the Campanile, composed of two separate buildings awkwardly sutured into one. The History Department occupies the first and second floors of the downhill side. They wrap around a courtyard that hosts events like the fall welcome reception, where grad students and professors make small talk while clutching sweaty bottles of beer. The dank first floor is the hub of grad student life, with an informal library, shared offices that are distributed among teaching assistants, and a lounge with couches and a microwave. Leftover food from a departmental event occasionally appears on the lounge's table, only to vanish within minutes. Most of our fellowship deposits go toward paying rent.

For the first three years of the program, PhD students take seminars in our first, second, and outside fields; mine are late modern Europe, early modern Europe, and anthropology.

Most seminars assign two or more books a week.

"My eyes may fall out of my head from reading," I email Daniel in September.

In the second year, students begin working as teaching assistants for undergraduate courses and take a master's exam. The third year culminates in the crucible of the program: "orals," a two- to three-hour test in which a panel of professors asks questions to which the graduate student should respond with mini-lectures demonstrating their prowess. Those who pass become "ABD," or "all but dissertation." They go off for a year to do archival research, then return to write, teach, and prepare for the academic job market. The minimal time to complete the PhD is six years, with the possibility of extension if the student secures more funding.

My cohort is awed by our own membership in a top-ranked department. Yet we are also aware of undergraduates' declining enrollment in history courses and the sharp downward slant in the graphs of the American Historical Association's annual jobs reports. The number of tenure-track positions nosedived in the wake of the 2007–2008 financial crisis and never recovered, in wild disproportion to the rising number of PhDs. We know that in the age of big data and keyword searches, our beloved archival odysseys—the slow turn of crinkly pages and microfilm dials, the careful mining of folders that occasionally produces gems— are derided as anachronistic. Some try to resist obsolescence by framing themselves as "global historians" rather than area specialists or practicing "digital humanities" through tricks like N-grams. Others trudge ahead with our geographic focus, language classes, and mildewed documents. We study change over time while crossing our fingers that it isn't coming for us.

Eager to start filling some of the vast holes in my knowledge, I audit European Civilization from the Renaissance to the Present, a large survey course for undergraduates. The professor, who has been teaching at Berkeley for over forty years, wears a tweed jacket and a fickle hearing aid. He says that this course's approach is cultural history, or "the history of how ideas, objects, places, sensations, institutions, and actions acquire meaning and potency in the world."

"There is an idea of power as coming from the end of a gun," he says. "But actually, it also comes through claiming legitimacy."

He notes that the sociologist Max Weber emphasized this idea in his writings on authority.

"It's not just coercion. You're listening to this lecture not only because I could fail you, but because I'm wearing a suit, and you're well brought up and know what's expected of you."

The PowerPoint behind him lights up with an oil painting of Charles V. The Holy Roman Emperor is mounted on a horse and clad in armor that indicates his wealth and influence; steel plating was already archaic in battle. The screen then shows a portrait of the monarch with his loyal dog, an image which signaled to his subjects that he possessed sufficient testosterone to subdue a beast.

"But the aura of legitimacy that supports power can also be lost," the professor says.

To illustrate this point, he plays a clip of the Romanian dictator Nicolae Ceauşescu in December 1989. Weeks earlier, the Berlin Wall had fallen, and massive protests began unsettling communist leaders across Eastern Europe. In late 1989, Romania's popular discontent appeared to have been contained. To confirm the regime's stability, Ceauşescu ordered a loyal street demonstration of the type that had been held routinely for the past several decades. In the video, he stands on a balcony, wearing a fur hat. The crowd below holds banners emblazoned with socialist slogans and pictures of Ceauşescu's face. As he reads his speech on live television, a noise starts to spread through the crowd. People are booing and rattling their keys. Ceauşescu pauses and looks up, confused. The noise grows louder.

"Hello?" he starts to shout, as if there were a bad phone connection. "Hello? Hello?"

Ceauşescu waves and tries to return to his prepared remarks, but no one is listening. The leader's control was gone. Several days later, he and his wife were executed by their own security agents.

The professor cites Machiavelli's observation that behind the mystical curtain of power stands a man putting on greasepaint. Authority is artifice, a set of tricks that gild inequality with the sheen of inevitability.

"It's not the great ruling because they have a natural right to rule, or because their power is granted by god, or something intrinsic to them," he says. "Power is made by ritual."

In a graduate seminar I take with the same professor, we read the anthropologist Clifford Geertz. In his 1972 article "Deep Play: Notes on the Balinese Cockfight," Geertz framed a sporting event in which roosters armed with steel spurs peck each other to death (to the delight of betting crowds) as a performance of status anxiety. The cockfight, Geertz wrote, is "a metasocial commentary upon the whole matter of assorting human beings into fixed hierarchical ranks." The spectacle thrills by revealing the hidden aggression beneath any contest for prestige, however polite it may appear. Women, like children, do not participate; the scepter belongs to men.

We scrutinize power relations elsewhere without directly acknowledging how they operate around us. Graduate students are transient figures, hitchhikers on the road to the ivory tower whose arrival is unassured. Unlike at some other universities, Berkeley PhD students have guaranteed stipends and belong to a union. But tenured faculty serve as gatekeepers who determine our access to a broader set of unevenly distributed resources. It is their recommendation letters that will secure us grants and jobs, their enthusiasm and stature that will boost our application to the top of the pile, their hesitation or inadequate eminence that will drive it toward the bottom. Some advisors are helicopter parents, eager to inquire about their graduate students' mental health and coach them on networking. Others tend to their own affairs while their advisees wait in vain for them to read the dissertation chapter that was emailed months ago or send the recommendation letter whose deadline has already passed.

Daniel and I say that our shared professor, Alexander, is the sun, while we are distant planets in his orbit. Alexander speaks in sardonic aphorisms that make everyone else look like they're trying too hard. A displeased word or frown from him activates our imposter syndrome, while an approving smile or adjective confirms our secret suspicion that we're really geniuses. Attentive without hovering, he punctually submits our letters and reads our drafts.

"Alexander's students always get jobs," several people assure me.

On a Thursday evening in September of my first semester, I walk up the hill toward the Campanile and under the pointed arch that marks the entrance to Stephens Hall. When Daniel and I accepted our admission offers, we were greeted by a volley of enthusiastic welcome emails from Berkeley's large and supportive community of graduate students. Once a month, we meet with a group that assembles to discuss an article or chapter in progress, sometimes authored by an invited guest. At today's meeting, the first of the year, we will dissect a dissertation chapter written by one of our own.

I enter the room and inhale the comforting aroma of melted cheese. Pizzas sprinkled with roasted corn and cilantro-lime sauce lie on a long table surrounded by chairs. On the wall hangs an enormous, outdated map of the Soviet Union. The orange and magenta sand of the Central Asian desert fades into lush taiga under the Arctic Ocean's azure crown. I put a slice of pizza on a paper plate, open a beer, and exchange a glance with Daniel. Too nervous to sit at the main table, we choose seats in the outer circle of extra chairs. As the conversation quiets down, we are introduced to the ritual that will anchor our years in graduate school.

We begin by going around the circle and saying our names, year, and what we study. Those who have been lingering in the program for what appears to be an unseemly amount of time laugh and pause before either coughing up a number or saying they've lost track. The graduate student whose paper is under discussion sits at the head of the table. After he talks for a few minutes about his dissertation, we begin the autopsy of his draft.

As the first grad student shoots up his hand to pose a question, I notice that he's shaking. In the same instant I realize that I didn't read the paper and have nothing to ask. I try to inconspicuously open my computer in my lap and scan through the Word document for ideas.

Another student raises a finger.

"Two things," he says. "The first is more of a comment than a question."

As the discussion unfolds, I don't recognize most of the authors and books being referenced but nod along as if I do. I ask something about gender and am relieved when my turn has passed. Alexander sits at the far end of the table with a bored expression, his arms folded across his chest and his chin resting in the crook of his thumb. When the graduate students have finished asking questions, he lifts his head and makes a penetrating remark that exposes the underlying problem we've all failed to identify, like a champion swimmer who completes a perfect dive after witnessing a series of cannonballs.

The discussion comes to an end and bonding time commences. Our faces flush as we sip Solo cups of $3.99 wine from Trader Joe's. Daniel self-protectively holds the plastic container next to his mouth. We stick close together. A few people step out to smoke cigarettes, officially banned from Berkeley's campus but occasionally enjoyed at the risk of fines. Someone has brought a guitar and sings songs by the Grateful Dead in a light falsetto. As we talk and sway to the music, the collective performance anxiety evaporates, and I savor the realization that these people will be my friends for life.

My eye catches a movement off to the side. Anna, another professor, is laughing as she lunges at her advisee, who presented his chapter today. He grabs her arm and pins it behind her back. They are both holding disposable cutlery.

"Knife fighting," someone whispers to me.

We watch the dance taking place before us.

"This is for not submitting your chapter on time," Anna says giddily as she makes a stabbing motion in her student's direction.

According to Geertz, what distinguishes "deep play" from the shallow kind is the stakes. Everyone is in over their heads: "they have entered into a relationship which will bring the participants, considered collectively, net pain rather than net pleasure." Though no blood or treasure is involved in the plastic duel, there's still something discomfiting about the game. The idea that a person could actually get hurt is unthinkable, but so too is the idea of stepping away.

The next year, our second in the program, Daniel and I are the co-organizers of a working group. It is now our task to write polite invitation emails, order food, buy alcohol, and wait until the last person has gone home for the night to wipe down the tables, turn off the lights, and recycle the bottles. We respond with the appropriate chagrin when we realize that we have drunkenly failed to complete these final tasks and the institute's coordinator arrives for work in the morning to a room smeared with pizza grease and wine stains. When Daniel walks me home at the end of the night, we linger at the corner of Dwight and Telegraph, not quite ready to say goodbye.

"Daniel and Joy are *friends*," Anna says, beaming, to a colleague at a conference we all attend the following fall.

In a seminar we take with Anna on the history of emotion, Daniel and I learn about the Enlightenment idea of sympathy as virtue. In the eighteenth century, weeping while reading sentimental novels like Rousseau's *Julie* was thought to cultivate refinement through fellow-feeling. Julie asks her lover to swear that "I will never cease to be your heart's confidante." On her deathbed, she passes away with a beatific smile.

Crying over literary characters fueled political change. According to one author we read, the leaders of the French Revolution expressed an optimistic faith in empathy as the foundation of a more just society. They championed the idea that power is vested in "the people," rather than a divinely sanctioned monarch, and that those people have equal rights founded in natural law. The young republic created a new calendar beginning at Year I, accessible fashion like "liberty caps," and egalitarian forms of address.

The emotional communion we study is what we're building together. Daniel starts to confide in me about things he says he's never told anyone else. He describes childhood friends and relatives who ended up in jail, his feeling that he only got into Berkeley because people feel sorry for him. I tell him that he understands things most of us don't and how much I admire him. He teasingly calls me "therapist Joy," but he doesn't stop talking.

As we progress through the PhD program, we start to catch more historiographical references than we fake and master the art of posing comments disguised as questions. Daniel speaks more in discussion and socializes afterward rather than brooding off to the side. In the summer of 2016, we both take a research trip to Eastern Europe. After spending the day reading in libraries and archives, we meet up in the evening to grab drinks, go to the theater, and watch soccer on TV. I comfort him when he and his girlfriend back in Berkeley break up, and he consoles me when my fling with a local guy falls apart. At the end of the summer, I send him the research paper I've been writing. I'm taking a nighttime stroll along a riverbank when I get a message saying he's finished reading.

"I love it," Daniel says. "Now I'll put on my pince-nez and read it dialectically."

I laugh, affection for him flaring inside me like the flashes of light on the black water.

"I wrote it for you," I text back.

By the fall of 2016, Daniel has become the closest person in my life. We develop an increasingly elaborate, occasionally morbid array of inside jokes and conversation topics. In early November, he texts me that he's struck by how strange the phrase "in the face of death" is.

"The idea that death has a face?" I reply.

"And that one 'faces death.'"

In our history of emotions seminar, we also learned about a more disquieting breed of sympathy. Certain eighteenth-century theorists argued that the dread of physical punishment had the power to forge more perfect men. This idea precipitated the French Revolution's turn to terror, which sent those who challenged the new order to the guillotine. Maximilien Robespierre, who had once condemned violence as despotic, now framed it as the essential armor of the republic. "Without virtue, terror is disastrous," he said. "Without terror, virtue is powerless."

3

THE RED SUN

THE "WORKERS' MARSEILLAISE," THE RUSSIAN REVOLUTIONARY anthem that Daniel and I read with Anna, was inspired by the French original. "Let's renounce the old world! Let's shake the remains from our feet!" it proclaims. "From the bloody dawn will rise the sun of truth and the brotherhood of man!"

In Russia, aspiring radicals from noble families dreamed of overthrowing the tsar. After failing to convert peasants to the cause, they turned to industrialized workers, relatively few of whom existed in the Russian empire at the time. Though Marx said that Russia wasn't ready for communism, his disciple Lenin thought that history could be given a push. Lenin's circle of revolutionaries decried their own privilege and worshipped books. They progressed from reading to holding rallies, robbing banks, and attacking officials.

Amid the chaos of World War I, Lenin decided to strike. In October 1917, he led a coup against the provisional government that had taken over from the flailing autocracy. In the civil war that followed, men who'd spent long years in prison and exile donned leather jackets and commanded troops. Lenin's Bolsheviks saw themselves as completing the work of France's Jacobins; like their predecessors, they decided to execute the monarch and eliminate their enemies.

Daniel and I are fascinated by the idea of building a better world by any means necessary. We want to be on the side of the people against power and are open to the argument that violence (under certain conditions) is justified. In their living room, Daniel and his roommate display a print of Louis XVI's decapitation on the Place de la Révolution in Paris. After falling from the guillotine, the king's severed head was held up to the crowd. "Long live the republic!" they cried. Our circle of historians calls each other "comrades," an affinity with our subjects that is only kind of a joke. Daniel and I love to speak Bolshevik.

"Put on your leather shell and execute the task," we tell each other by way of encouragement.

Together we read *Red Cavalry*, the short-story collection by Isaac Babel. Babel was born in Odesa and served in a Cossack unit on the Bolshevik side during their war with Poland in 1920. The hero of *Red Cavalry* is an intellectual much like the author, a man with spectacles on his nose and autumn in his soul. Though he's alienated from both the shtetl and the Bolsheviks' bravado, the latter holds a certain allure. In "My First Goose," he's captivated by the Cossack warriors' muscles and medals. When they laugh him off as a bookish weakling, he decides to assert himself by ordering the old woman whose house they are occupying to make him something to eat. After shoving her in the chest, he catches sight of a goose. He cracks the bird's neck under his boot, stabs it with his sword, and orders the woman to roast it for him. She complies. "The lad will do all right with us," one of the Cossacks says with a wink.

"Nerds are always into violence," Daniel observes.

In the wake of revolution, the grim reality of poverty, disease, and death only heightened hope in the paradise to come. In a 1921 painting, the artist Konstantin Yuon imagined the revolution as a new planet. Awestruck figures on bluish soil reach up toward gigantic red and gold orbs ascending in the sky.

Daniel and I don't share Lenin's conviction that the worse the better. We're enthralled by the Russian Revolution's atmosphere of pure possibility because it feels so remote from our country's political circus, in which corporations are people and the candidate who talks about draining the swamp is a corrupt tycoon seeking bigger tax cuts for the rich. Our favorite TV show is *Veep*, which depicts all of Washington as a self-interested cesspit. Like most of our friends at Berkeley, we supported Bernie Sanders in the primaries, even though we knew that his democratic socialism was doomed from the start. Daniel remembers how Bill Clinton's "welfare reform" made it harder for his family to get food on the table, and I rail against Hillary's support for the invasion of Iraq. We vote for her anyway because we have no choice.

"I want god to just show up and end this world now," Daniel texts me as I'm getting ready to bike to the polling station on November 8. "Can't take this fucking shit any longer."

That evening I pick him up to watch the election results at a friend's basement apartment in an East Bay suburb. We grow quiet as more and more states are called for Trump—too many. None of us saw it coming. The only ones vaguely prepared are a couple from the UK, who say that Trump's victory feels like Brexit all over again. Around midnight, an agitated Hillary supporter turns on a Bernie bro.

"This is your fault," she snaps, her eyes shining with tears.

He sits up and begins opining about how the Democratic establishment is rotten. His calm tone infuriates her further. Daniel and I walk out to my car past the house's turquoise pool, garishly lit up in the somber night.

"I can't," I keep saying pointlessly. "I just can't."

Our society seemed broken but stable. Suddenly it has also grown unpredictable.

Later that week I ask Daniel if he wants to do something to take our minds off things. He says he's planning to watch "whatever schlock is out" at the movies but warns that he's "extra mopey."

"Yes, that is possible for me," he adds.

"Why are you extra mopey?" I ask. "Other than the precipitous decline of Western civilization."

"Usually I get strength from the cheeriness around me," he says. "I didn't know how much strength I got from you all until dark clouds appeared."

"Yeah. I guess now's the time we curl up together in the basement while the tornado rips off the roof and carries away the cows."

After the superhero movie, we stand on my balcony and listen to the pounding subwoofers of the frat boys who rent the house below. In the pale light cast by the moon, I stare at the face I've been drawn to ever since I saw it. Daniel has been growing a beard, which I joke makes him look like John the Baptist in the wilderness. It matches his thick eyelashes.

"Can I ask you something weird?"

He nods.

"Have you ever thought about being . . . together?"

His face creases with confusion.

"It's never been like that with us," he says quickly.

"But what if it were?"

He pauses.

"You don't know how my moods can get, Joy."

"I do know. I know you better than anyone."

"But you . . . you . . . don't know how I can be," he says, searching for words I'm not fully able to hear. "With my last girlfriend, sometimes I would just walk out the door. Like, I had to remove myself from the situation."

His body is tensed, his eyes darting toward the balcony's screen door. His panic reminds me of the "fearful cat" drawing that we saw in Darwin's *Expression of the Emotions in Man and Animals*. Darwin saw emotion as a set of physiological reflexes that is innate and externally observable across species. Daniel and I preferred the sentimentalism of the previous century, the idea that emotions welled up from within through sympathy with another soul.

"You don't have to run away from me," I say softly, shifting closer toward the spot where he's leaning on the railing.

He steps away.

"I've gotta go."

After he leaves, I climb into my empty bed and stare at my poster of Francisco Goya's *The Sleep of Reason Produces Monsters*. A man lies face down at his desk, oblivious to the winged creatures swarming over his head.

■■■■■■

We sleep together a couple of days later after getting drunk at a friend's party. The next evening, we buy ice cream sandwiches on Telegraph and eat them on the grass outside Dwinelle. It's Sunday evening; campus is quiet. We don't talk about what happened, either that day or in the following couple of weeks.

In late November we fly to a conference in Washington, DC. My presentation goes badly; the pages I printed to read are out of order, and the airless hotel meeting room is packed with senior academics asking pointed questions that I don't know enough yet to answer. Daniel hugs me afterward and tells me that it was as polished as a job talk. He seems so sure that I choose to believe him.

As we say good night in my hotel room that evening, we come close to touching. He pulls away and moves toward the door, but this time his tone is more flirtatious than fearful.

"There's still some wheels that need to turn, Joy," he says with a half crescent of a smile as he walks out.

Everyone at the conference is on edge and prone to catastrophism. I serve as the chair on the panel of a friend of mine in which the discussant, a distinguished professor, tears into his paper as the defective product of a post-truth age.

"This pack of falsehoods and misinterpretations represents the irrational forces that brought Donald Trump to power," he says, his voice simmering with anger unrelated to my friend's actual presentation, an analysis of how a Russian Civil War hero was depicted in popular culture.

In the evening, Berkeley grad students and alumni progress from a reception in a hotel ballroom, to a nearby bar, to the floor of someone's suite, where we drink whiskey and make gloomy predictions for the future. Daniel and I realize that a celebratory alt-right conference is taking place in a different DC hotel at the same time. "Explains the amphibious cesspool figures on my plane," he says. I ask if he's read the recent *Hollywood Reporter* interview with Trump's chief of staff Steve Bannon: "He praises Dick Cheney and Satan in the same sentence."

"Needless repetition," Daniel replies.

I laugh. We pause.

"Shit has really taken a bad turn," he says.

At the end of November, we're sitting in the history lounge eating doughnuts when Daniel turns toward me, face glowing, and tells me that he's ready to be in a relationship. We're both euphoric. The rest of the world seems to be falling apart, but one tiny piece of it is coming together.

"Today should be a holiday in our revolutionary calendar," I text him later. "Even if there are no days."

"The rising of the red sun of sacrifice will let us know."

"Sounds ominous," I say.

The next morning, he tells me he dreamed that I was having an affair with his roommate Evan, another grad student in our program. Though I assure him that he's the only one I want, he starts getting nervous whenever I'm away from him. Daniel says that although he knows "retrospective jealousy" is foolish and petty, he feels sick at the thought of me dating other men before him.

"Knowing it's petty doesn't make it any less difficult," I say sympathetically.

I tell Daniel that I wish I could take his pain onto myself. He says he should be grateful that other people's stupidity gave him the chance to be happy.

"Before I used to feel like a light on a street no one walks through any more," he texts. Now "I feel like everything is on fire and I want it all to burn so I can build something new."

"I guess you have to be patient and let the embers die out," I reply.

"I know and I will."

We go to the History Department Christmas party, where the tweed-coated professor who teaches European civilization mixes cocktails as laughter and conversation echo off the hard floors. Daniel is pouring gin and tonics in the grad student library. Barely able to stand up, he drapes himself across me in one of the armchairs. We end up outside, in front of Dwinelle's glass doors.

"You're the smartest person I've ever met," he whispers, and gives me a deep kiss. Though people inside can surely see us, we're too enraptured with each other to care.

When we're both home for winter break, Daniel texts me that people there condescend to him because he doesn't have a job, a car, a wife, or a macho vibe. He regrets that while Lenin's comrade Leon Trotsky described sailing away from the past with a mighty push, he is forced to return a couple of times per year.

"Sadly, and sometimes [I] do mean sadly," Daniel writes, "I don't have the license for violence that he did."

Daniel says that being at home allows his mind to feed on itself and makes him more self-conscious about the differences between us. I tell him that I see him as my equal and want to understand him insofar as he'll let me. But the chasm between us in his head keeps widening. When he's not using Bolshevik terms of endearment, he calls me "the princess."

"I'm too much of a thick-skulled peasant to understand what you mean," he says caustically when I reference a poem he doesn't know.

He compares our friendship to the story of unrequited love in Fyodor Dostoyevsky's *Poor Folk*, a novel I haven't read. He explains that the protagonist, a humble copying clerk and social outcast, forms a close bond with a fallen young woman. Despite the hero's efforts to improve his station, she ends up leaving him for a richer man.

Sometimes I sense that Daniel is exaggerating the extent of his deprivation. He tells me that he's never been to an art museum, but I know that he must have: as an undergrad Daniel went on a study abroad program in a European city that has some of the greatest art collections in the world, and he must have gone to several then. He admits that he did.

"I thought so," I say lightly. "Well, let's go to one together sometime." After all, I reason, his lie expressed an underlying truth—he didn't have access to such places when he was growing up.

Daniel tells me he can't stop thinking about an evening a couple of months before we got together when he asked me out to dinner, and I turned him down because I was going on a date. I say I didn't know he was interested in me. He says how vulnerable he feels with me and how scared he is that I'll walk away.

"Our relationship was teleological," he finally concludes. "What brought us together and moments that foreshadowed our union are what matters; the rest is accident."

This appears to be the end of it: his jealousy has been extinguished, and our life together can begin. We look forward to reuniting in Berkeley with a bacchanal under the theme "decline and fall of the American empire."

A few days later, I wake up to an early-morning text from him. It describes a sexual dream he had about me and someone I used to date, followed by another message:

"I think we should take a break."

I volunteer to show how much I care about him by traveling to spend New Year's with him and his family. Daniel is delighted. On the way back to Berkeley, we drive past the airport. Daniel loves flying; whenever I'm about to take off, he asks me what make and model I'm traveling in and monitors my trip on FlightWire. I park the rental car near the runway so he can watch the planes. As they're borne aloft, I allow myself to hope that this really is the start of a bright future. On the highway we fantasize about the courses we'll co-teach once one of us gets a tenure-track job and brings along the other as a spousal hire.

"It'll be you who gets the job," Daniel says modestly. "I'm just riding your coattails."

Over break the History Department releases its winter newsletter, which begins with a statement from the chair. He offers some reassurance for this disorienting new age. "Truthful, evidence-based, reasonable and reasoned explanation of how the world got to be the way it is—this seems to be an endangered commodity, a scarce resource, in our world today," the letter concludes. "We in the History Department take pride in the fact that this is our specialty."

●

After the election some of our peers decided to fight back against Trump by joining the Democratic Socialists of America. Our friend Adam has already grown disenchanted. He says that the Bay Area chapter is repeating the mistakes of the Bolsheviks, establishing an arrogant centralized leadership that claims to represent the interests of the working class but is really focused on maximizing its own power.

"They're so sure they know best," he says exasperatedly as we walk down Telegraph.

Daniel and I listen but don't want to get too involved. In the coming semester we'll be preparing for our oral exams, a period when we're expected to read and develop answers to practice questions from morning until night. Daniel has a fellowship for students from disadvantaged backgrounds that allows him to focus on studying. I will also be working as a teaching assistant. Toward the end of winter break, we start stockpiling books in Dwinelle and arriving in the morning to claim the grad student library's most desirable spot, a two-person table secluded behind shelves.

For most of the day we read and exchange flirty texts. But if I reference a book he doesn't like, or an exam topic I'm not worried about that he says I should be—anything that challenges him—he scowls and storms off. He follows his exit with a damning text.

"I can actually taste the hate in my mouth," Daniel writes me one afternoon. "Taste[s] like aluminum."

I send worried messages asking if he's okay, and he either returns or we meet up again later.

At the end of break, we have dinner at Hannah's house with a couple of other women in our program. Hannah lives in an "in-law" apartment, a guest cottage behind a larger house that Bay Area homeowners rent out for extortionary sums. I bring my signature bacon and kale salad; Hannah has made fried polenta. After dinner, we're sitting around the table talking when the women disagree with something that Daniel has said.

"You've gotta admit they have a point," I say with a smile.

Daniel frowns. He silently rises and walks out, slamming the door behind him.

The other women exchange glances. One of them laughs uncertainly. I look down at my phone and see a message from Daniel:

"At the end of the day that's why you're like them, and not like me. And that's why we're done.

"I don't want to be with you anymore."

I go outside to find him. The only source of light is from a streetlamp a few yards away, and all I can see is the outline of his body in the shadows. As I get closer, he steps forward and shoves me with all his strength.

"How could you do that to me?" I ask after I catch my breath, tears flowing down my face.

He says he barely touched me and tells me to calm down. When I don't, he says that he's sorry. It will never happen again, and I must never speak of it. I nod, trying to understand. Of course it won't. I know him better than anyone.

He takes my hand and suggests we go back to his place around the corner. I'm still nodding as I follow him into the dark.

4

"ES SCHWINDELT"

LENIN, MY ADVISOR SAYS FROM THE LECTERN, WAS THE REVOLUTION'S leader, the ruthless ideologue against all things lukewarm. His second-in-command was Trotsky, "enormously confident and particularly brutal—or as he would put it, decisive."

I'm sitting in the front row of a dim lecture hall beneath bright lights. The spring semester has begun. Behind me are eighty undergraduates with laptops. Adam, my fellow teaching assistant, sits farther back in the tiered seats to monitor illicit social media usage. Daniel, who's auditing the class, is next to him.

"And so there they were," Alexander says. "The prophecy was fulfilled, and the real day had arrived."

Alexander speaks without notes or apparent effort. His lightly ironic tone makes it seem as if he'd been watching history unfold from the wings and knew all the players, whose struts across the stage he'd found intriguing if inept. Adam doesn't have to patrol the students too closely; most of their eyes are locked on the raconteur at the front of the room.

Alexander quotes Trotsky's recollection of a tender, surreal moment when Lenin turned to him in the days after the Bolshevik coup. "You know," Lenin said hesitantly, "from persecutions and a life underground, to come so suddenly into power. . . ." Searching for the right word, he switched to the German that they had spoken for years in exile.

"*Es schwindelt* [it makes one's head spin]," he said, making a circular motion with his finger.

The course encourages students to adopt the mindset of people at the time and consider the choices they faced. In discussion posts and exams, they are asked to write from different perspectives: a princess from St. Petersburg, a peasant from the Black Earth region. Alexander models this identification with historical figures by leading in-class thought experiments. Suppose we are tasked with implementing the cultural revolution in Berkeley. What to do with the History Department?

"We need to eliminate masked enemies," Alexander says. "There will be purges, of course, but of whom? How do we ensure that everyone acquires true consciousness?"

A student raises his hand.

"Make sure that everyone is a Marxist?"

"Well, everyone claims to be, of course," Alexander says. "But can you really take their word for it? We're wallowing in heresy and bourgeois equivocation here!"

The class decides to abolish geographical divisions and reorganize the department along class lines. We weigh additional measures, like removing distinctions among professors and conducting exchanges between the university and the factory floor.

In the vacuum of the lecture hall, as Alexander slips back and forth between the past and the present tense, time and space compress. My pen moves across the pages of my notebook, I feel Daniel's eyes on my back, the lights above my head flicker like chandeliers. When the lecture is over, Daniel and I walk out together past the Campanile and down the hill to Dwinelle, toward the mist swirling over the bay.

One morning that week, I'm tired from an argument we had the night before and text him that I'm struggling to get out of bed. A few minutes later, the buzzer rings: Daniel is at my door. He comes upstairs and sits me down on my blue couch that sags in the middle.

"I love you so much it scares me sometimes," he says.

He starts to describe another dream he had about me and someone I briefly dated, then gets up and runs out the door. Shortly afterward, he messages me that he stands by what he came there to say: that he loves me and wants to be together.

"It's a dizzying feeling, shifting from despair to elation," I text him. *"Es schwindelt."*

"I think we are cosmically having the love affair Lenin and Trotsky were supposed to have but never could," Daniel replies. "History got in their way; we were brought together by History."

He says he'll take me to Great China, our favorite restaurant.

———

In the wake of Lenin's death, Alexander says the following week, Joseph Stalin gradually maneuvered himself into the role of heir, promoting his allies and sending Trotsky into exile. After several years of disappointment and retreat, Stalin announced that the great transformation had finally come. He vowed to industrialize the Soviet Union and collectivize its agriculture at breakneck speed, obliterating the country's backwardness with blast furnaces and turbines.

Stalin's Five-Year Plan was a leap into the future and a fight to the death. Alexander assigns our students to read *The Education of a True Believer*, the memoir of Lev Kopelev, a Communist Party activist who was sent to the countryside to report on the collectivization drive. Kopelev described how he and his comrades forced farmers to give up their livestock and grain, in a campaign that caused hundreds of thousands of them to starve. Shirkers deserved no mercy. Stalin warned that class enemies were growing ever more devious. They wore masks and hid in the most unexpected places, from Kremlin offices to pig stalls.

"We believed him unconditionally," Kopelev recalled.

Stalin's plan broke with the more moderate economic policy of Nikolai Bukharin, the talented theoretician whom Lenin had called "the party's favorite." Under the party's ban on factions, however, Bukharin couldn't express open opposition. Stalin and the newspapers kept saying that the greatest danger was the new conciliators—including, implicitly, Bukharin. These men lost their positions and apologized for deviating from the party line.

"If you sin against the party and confess," Alexander asks from the lectern, "how do you gain absolution?"

Alexander reads from the transcript of a 1930 party meeting at which an official asked another top politician who'd come under attack, Mikhail Tomsky, to prove the sincerity of his confession. Tomsky admitted his errors but asked how long he had to continue apologizing, for "it is rather difficult to be in the role of permanent penitent. Some comrades seem to be saying: 'repent, repent without end, do nothing but repent.'" The hall broke out in laughter.

———

Daniel often asks me for details about my past relationships. My phone vibrates with questions when I'm teaching section, when I'm at the library, when I'm asleep. When we're together, he starts grilling me in the middle of an unrelated conversation:

"Where did you guys have dinner?"

"How many times did you have him over at your apartment?"

"How many times did you have sex?"

"Did you come?"

Sometimes I try to pacify him by answering. Other times I say how crazy I am about him, or tell him that those relationships don't matter, or point out that he had an online dating profile and love interests, too. He is never satisfied.

"And it continues," he says. "Your lies and mischaracterizations. Always sidestepping the question, making pointless excuses."

Daniel combs through his mental archive for evidence of my promiscuity and always comes up with an incriminating find. He recalls a night before the start of our first semester in grad school when we were playing the drinking game "never have I ever" with our cohort, and I raised my finger to cop to something he doesn't approve of.

"I realized I'll never be happy with you," he texts me when I walk away from him in the department library. "Go; maybe have another one of your wild sex acts you proudly told all of us when we first hung out."

One afternoon we have lunch in the Dwinelle courtyard on a bench under spindly tree branches. I'm eating an egg and cheese sandwich when

I notice that one of my long red hairs has fallen on his sweatshirt. I joke that maybe he wants to keep wearing it as a reminder of me.

"This hair has been on every man in town," he says, pulling it off and dropping it to the ground with disgust.

On February 1, when classes are done for the day, I meet up in Dwinelle with Daniel, Hannah, and our friend Rose. We're going to a protest against Milo Yiannopoulos, an alt-right provocateur with bleach-blond hair who was invited to speak by Berkeley's Republican student group. In his tour of American college campuses, Yiannopoulos issues gleeful tirades against feminists, trans people, Muslims, and whatever other targets are most likely to offend "liberal snowflakes." At the last minute, the university canceled the lecture, citing the risk of violent clashes. In an interview, Yiannopoulos says that Berkeley's protestors are "absolutely petrified by alternative visions of how the world ought to look and people with arguments and facts and reason that don't conform to the crazy social-justice left vision of the universe." On Twitter, President Trump threatens to revoke the university's federal funding.

A crowd of several thousand people has assembled on Sproul, chanting and carrying signs with slogans like "Solidarity trumps hate." We find a spot on the steps in front of Sproul Hall, which sparkles with rainbow lights. An exploding firework turns the plaza crimson. I smell something acrid and see flames on the ground. As police in riot gear instruct everyone to leave the area, a figure in a black face mask throws a rock at the window of the student union. Still standing on the steps, I lose sight of Daniel in the crowd.

That morning, Daniel had written me that he'd made an "awful discovery": his text message archive. "You know exactly what this is going to be used for," he tells me. I think I do. I assume that he will look through every conversation we have had over the past three years in search of anything I said about other men.

At the protest, I finally spot Daniel near the Wells Fargo on Bancroft, where someone smashed a window. He is hovering near the shattered glass, pacing around with an air of expectation. Though he has refused to speak to me all afternoon and evening, when I approach him and suggest we get going, he agrees.

After we walk up the groaning wooden stairs to Daniel's apartment, he unleashes the fury that he absorbed on Sproul. It's sickening what I did, he says, going around with those men. Another animal from Darwin's book flashes into my mind: the snarling dog, pupils dilating as it bares its teeth.

"You know they have a word for women like you, don't you?" I am sitting on the couch and he is standing over me. "A whore."

Daniel pauses.

"But you know what?" he says, his wrath cooling into the hate that tastes like aluminum. "You're worse. At least they do it for the money."

———

I awake with the sensation of a hand around my throat. As my eyes struggle to adjust to the light, the hand drags me sideways, up, out of bed. The head attached to the hand has Daniel's face. In his other hand he holds a belt. His eyes are emanating a frenzied rage. He calls me a whore and a liar, and orders me to strip naked so that he can beat me black and blue. There's an electricity in the air, an aura that I have come to recognize as the current of violence. When it comes, the world falls into shadow. It's like a solar eclipse, the moment you realize that someone you trust might kill you.

Suddenly, Daniel drops my neck and runs into the bathroom. He has taken the belt with him. I hear movement on the other side of the door. I open it and see that he has tied the belt around his neck. When I remove it, he collapses and starts crying.

"I need you," he says, looking up at me like a little boy, his eyes glossy with tears.

"Please don't hurt yourself," I whisper. "I love you."

All my concern has shifted to him. What he was doing and saying to me a few minutes before has vanished, as if it never happened at all.

When Daniel is around, the laws of physics are suspended. We might be standing on a street corner, or sitting in one of our apartments, when we enter a zone where objects lose their permanence. My books, phone, and glasses levitate and fall, my body slams sideways, fists smash near my face. We are on the new planet, the red sun is rising, I run toward it and fall to the earth with an ecstasy that might be horror.

I have always had it easy, Daniel says, while he has suffered. When he was alone, I was having the time of my life.

"You had your dates, your get-togethers, and your sex," he tells me. "I had nothing."

I know it's not true, but I question myself; maybe I really hadn't paid enough attention to him. Worst of all, the other people I dated before him at Berkeley were white men, whom Daniel says "always get what they want." I was abandoning him for the privileged few who flaunt their superiority in his face. Daniel tells me that on an evening last October when I was with Peter, he wanted to kill himself, and that because of my neglect he almost died. He has never told me this story before; I have no idea if it's real. But now he repeats it until I'm overcome with guilt. At first, he says he only thought about harming himself, but as he keeps haranguing me for my absence, vague ideation mutates into a full-blown suicide attempt. I apologize and say I never meant to hurt him—I didn't know. Daniel says my intentions don't matter; the damage has been done and now it's time to pay.

"You refuse to give me any empathy, ever," I write him on a night when I can't take it anymore.

"I am going to reserve my empathy for someone [whose] idea of suffering isn't dating a muscular man or having wine and a good fuck," he texts back.

Daniel frames himself as my defender against hostile members of our department: a guy in our program whom Daniel says called me ugly ("I explained that you just have an angular face—I personally find it beautiful"), another who supposedly branded me a sociopath ("You come off as overconfident, Joy, like you think you're better than the rest of us. You need to work on that."). He's always stood up for me, Daniel says, and all I repaid him with was heartache. Now that the two of us are together, he claims, people are starting to see how great I really am. I feel deeper and deeper in his debt.

Reality is a kaleidoscope. In one moment, my skin is turning purple beneath Daniel's fingers; a turn of the device, the colors whirl, now he's smiling and making me a quesadilla. I feel dizzy as I walk down his building's staircase and head back north up Telegraph, past the gas station, the Ethiopian restaurant, the Whole Foods, the middle school. The sun is rising again. Or is it setting?

At dusk, as the golden light fades over the bay, the birds on Berkeley's campus moan in a low, sorrowful sound. They are mourning doves, named for their grieving call. As I listen to their song, my heart pounds with the fear and shame of what evening might bring. If I apologize and do what Daniel asks, I think, maybe he'll finally go back to being the person I used to know.

Sometimes, for a few hours or days, he is. We hold each other under the gray comforter on his bed, an archipelago surrounded by stacks of books, and look through the swaying branches outside his window.

"I don't mean to understate the incredible support you've provided me over the years," he tells me. "It's the reason I fell in love with you."

My body softens; the world stabilizes.

Then it begins all over again.

At night Daniel tells me he is going to choke me to death. Holding my neck with one hand, he tries to raise my hand to his throat with the other. His fingers dig into my wrist as I struggle with him. The next morning, I put on long sleeves and try to forget—I have to go hold office hours.

As I'm making breakfast in Daniel's apartment, he tells me that he will bash my head in with a hammer so that my brains come out like scrambled eggs. I stare at the pan in front of me, swirling the yellow yokes as they congeal. I hear the words, but it's as if they had been spoken to someone else. I'm there, but I'm also not. *"Ia ne ia, loshad' ne moia,"* goes a Russian saying of denial—"I am not me, the horse is not mine." I remember it from the transcript of a Central Committee meeting in which Bukharin was accused of plotting against Stalin.

Alexander recounts how Bukharin begged for forgiveness and was allowed back into the fold, only to fall into disfavor once again. Since everyone had questioned the party in thought or deed, anyone could be charged with criminal activity against it. The only one above suspicion was Stalin, who embodied the spirit of history and whose judgment could never be questioned. He seemed to enjoy the cat and mouse game with the accused, Alexander says, and with Bukharin in particular.

When Bukharin's apartment was searched, Stalin called him to express outrage and take his side. The last time that Bukharin went to the Revolution Day parade on Red Square, he was already in disgrace and stood down below in the crowd. Stalin sent a guard to bring Bukharin to the top of Lenin's mausoleum—an honor reserved for top officials. At the time, the leader was already planning Bukharin's show trial.

"Bukharin lost the chess match," Alexander says.

After lecture, Daniel asks me to watch him play in a soccer game, then disinvites me by telling me to take my cheap displays of affection to another man. I try to slow my racing thoughts through reading. At Doe Library, I open "With Hegel to Salvation: Bukharin's Other Trial," an article on my orals reading list for Alexander. Upon his arrest, Bukharin initially vowed that he wouldn't tell lies about himself like his predecessors. But it was his word versus the party's, and the party could never be wrong.

While awaiting trial in his prison cell, Bukharin strained to remake his perception of reality to suit the objective laws of history. To help break his own will, he composed an essay in which the narrator chases away Mephistopheles, "the devil of solipsism." He also wrote letters to Stalin that atoned for any mistakes he may have committed and asked for the leader's pardon.

While reading, I compulsively check my phone to see if Daniel has texted. Finally, a message: he tells me that he's waiting for me outside the library. He says he left the game early because he loves me and doesn't want to live without me.

"I finally reached the point where I recognize that I am the problem," he says. "Only me."

"I love you, too," I text back. "I also care about your emotional health, which is ultimately more important than our relationship." I ask him to promise that he'll contact the student health center the next day to make an appointment with a therapist and suggest we wait to see each other until after he's called.

"I can't believe you," he says.

I say that I'll call, too, on my own behalf.

"Since you are also calling, this has pushed me to not do it," he writes. "No one makes me feel more pessimistic about the world I live in than you."

"The point is, I want to support you."

"You want a break from me? You'll get it. One much longer than you bargained for."

Who is he threatening, himself or me? I can no longer tell the difference.

Today's party line, the sin to which Daniel insists I confess, is wearing a charming mask to seduce men. In messages to Hannah, I call it the "love-hurt dialectic": Daniel initiates a rapprochement and presents himself as my protector, only to say he can never forgive me for fucking other men when he needed me.

"Why put up with this shit?" Hannah asks.

I can't explain how my mind is merging with Daniel's. He and I have always been on the same side of history, politics, the seminar table. If I've provoked rage in a person to whom I've sworn loyalty, then surely his criticisms must carry some degree of truth. I want to vanquish the devil of solipsism and show Daniel that I deserve his love.

In his last letter, written on December 10, 1937, Bukharin said he was ready to sacrifice himself for the common good, but asked for a sign of recognition that he had not really performed the monstrous acts of which he was accused (like trying to assassinate Lenin). Bukharin addressed Stalin as "Koba," the revolutionary nickname that evoked their shared past. His old friend never replied.

Stalin watched the trial from a curtained box above the courtroom. Bukharin pled guilty to crimes against the motherland while continuing to deny most of the specific charges against him. Stalin's prosecutor said that Bukharin was not a person but a thing, "a foul-smelling heap of human garbage" capable of the worst "hypocrisy and perfidy." In Bukharin's final plea in court, he bowed down before the party. Since the whole country stood behind Stalin, he said, there was no point in living if one was said to be against the leader.

"What matters is not the personal feelings of a repentant enemy," Bukharin concluded, "but the flourishing progress of the USSR."

Bukharin's self-abnegation did not bring mercy; he was shot anyway.

Daniel agrees to go to counseling.

"You are the most dishonest and artificial person I have ever had feelings for," he texts me. "I am going to seek help for myself in spite of you not because of you."

After Daniel starts therapy and antidepressants, things are better. We meet some friends from our cohort to play kickball by the edge of the bay, in a park that used to be a garbage dump. The sun glitters on the water as we run over buried pits of waste.

Soon enough, things get much worse. Daniel's mental health issues provide an indisputable new rationale for why he treats me the way he does and why I have no right to object. The interrogations begin again with renewed intensity. Daniel tries to trip me up and "catch me lying," to prove that I'm running around behind his back. Energy leaks out of my body from the effort of trying to convince him that I'm faithful.

On a Saturday night in April, we take a break from studying to have dinner on Shattuck. "I guess Saturday must've been date night for you, right?" he says as we're finishing up our stir-fried noodles. Though his tone is casual, I sense the onset of a rant.

"Tell me," he continues, "what was it about those guys that made you want to treat me like trash you could throw away? Was it their big strong arms wrapping around you?"

We walk back to Dwinelle through the eucalyptus grove, their silver leaves gleaming in the spring night. Daniel's soliloquy is reaching its climax; the electricity is zapping at our heels.

"You think you have the right to touch me after you've been in another man's bed?"

As we climb the concrete steps that lead into the History Department, Daniel is slightly in front of me. When we reach the top, he turns around and slams his hands against my shoulders. Suddenly I am tumbling backward.

I mount the stairs again, lightheaded with panic, and go inside to get my things. Another grad student studying for orals is reading under the fluorescent lights. He says hi and starts chatting about our upcoming exams. I try to act as if everything is fine, like the performative liar Daniel says I am. My phone buzzes with a message.

"Having fun without me?" Daniel asks. "I see the smile on your face."

He must be watching me through the window.

━━━━━

"Why did this happen?" Alexander asks at the end of his lecture on the Terror. "Was it rational? Did it have a purpose?" Some historians, he explains, see it as the revolution's final chapter. Others call it a tragic postscript or block it off as irrelevant.

One explanation for what occurred, he says, is Stalin's personality. Thanks to historians' research, we now know that the leader initiated the process, set its goals, and issued orders. Yet terror required so many other participants. After all, the Bolsheviks prided themselves on their willingness to commit violence, which they saw as legitimate.

"Terror also had its benefits," Alexander adds.

It offered upward mobility as younger officials took the places of the repressed. These were the functionaries who would keep the Soviet Union running for the remainder of its existence.

In section we discuss Arthur Koestler's *Darkness at Noon*, a novel inspired by Bukharin's plight, which Koestler reframed as the saga of a character named Rubashov. The students' desks are assembled in a circle. I stand in front of the blackboard, taking notes on their remarks in chalk. It's Friday morning; we are all under-slept.

"Did Rubashov deserve his fate?" I ask.

The students submitted discussion posts on this subject before class and are eager to speak.

"Definitely," one of them says. "He wasn't ruthless in the way that Stalin required. He was standing in the way of utopia. Like the professor said, 'If you want to get rid of something, kill it.'"

"Yeah, he had too many doubts," someone else agrees. "According to the party, a thought crime is just as bad as a physical crime. So from their perspective, he got what was coming to him."

"But the party was so convinced it was on the right side of history that it lost sight of its original goals and became paranoid," another student says. "Someone had to start questioning it."

We talk about how Rubashov tries to accept what is happening by dismissing his own life as insignificant compared to the collective cause determined by Stalin. Under the party line, there is no "I," only "we."

"So why does Rubashov tap the word 'I' on the wall of his cell just before he's executed?" I ask.

They don't get a chance to answer. The Campanile bells are ringing. Time is up, and Daniel is waiting for me.

5

THE CAPTIVE MIND

O N THE MORNING OF MY ORAL EXAM, THE FIVE PROFESSORS ON MY committee stare at me from across a wooden table. We should be in Dwinelle, but instead we're at Alexander's house in north Berkeley, under the orange lampshade that hangs in his dining room. Alexander helped me change the exam's location at the last minute so that Daniel wouldn't find me.

"What did it feel like to live in Eastern Europe during the installation of Stalinist regimes?" one of the professors asks.

I don't get what he's driving at. He feeds me the answer.

"How does Miłosz describe it in *The Captive Mind*?"

A short walk above us, on the crest of Berkeley's hills, stands a small house with a brown shingled roof. For almost twenty years, the Polish poet Czesław Miłosz lived there in obscurity, an experience he captured in a poem called "A Magic Mountain." He descended periodically to teach long-haired students he didn't understand—until one day in 1980, when the Nobel committee called to inform him that he'd won their prize for literature. Miłosz was best known abroad for *The Captive Mind*, his examination of how Eastern European intellectuals were seduced by Stalinism. It became a classic study of "totalitarianism," a framework steeped in Cold War narratives about the civilized West versus the backward East.

When I read the book during my first semester of graduate school, I had little patience for a writer who seemed like a reactionary. I thought that Miłosz's profile of communist doublethink—exemplified by the "Ketman," whose accommodating exterior conceals his inner reservations—overlooked how the "free world" also ran on two-faced conformity. We were living in a post-Fukuyama age, when trust in liberal democracy had dwindled while its slogans lived on. With President Obama deep into his second term and both parties unable to confront inequality or climate change, Miłosz's warnings about fervent conviction felt far away.

In the wake of World War II, Miłosz, like many of his peers, believed that only Soviet communism was capable of rebuilding the region from rubble and ensuring it wouldn't happen again. Yet he was disheartened by seeing his homeland turned into a "Stalinist province," and found a middle ground by working abroad as a diplomat. In 1951, when the culture of loyalty and subservience became too stifling, he defected to France (where he joined a non-communist left circle whose members included Arthur Koestler). There, while struggling with "the corroding effects of isolation" and pangs of guilt, Miłosz wrote *The Captive Mind*.

Through several anonymized character portraits, Miłosz showed how a combination of opportunism, exhaustion, and hope led Polish writers to swallow the pill of contentment in exchange for compliance. Some prospered, like "Alpha, the Moralist," a pious Catholic who became a celebrated Marxist. Others choked on their mixed feelings, like "Beta, the Disappointed Lover," an Auschwitz survivor and author of acerbic stories about life in the camp, who briefly wrote in a socialist realist mode before gassing himself to death.

"We are concerned here with questions more significant than mere force," Miłosz wrote. He observed how obeying orders creates a sense of purpose, and self-repression provides "masochistic pleasure." The Ketman does not simply pretend to assent. Like Bukharin, he tries to fuse the mask to his face and accept the spirit of universal reason as dictated by one man.

I know that by staying with Daniel, I'm submitting to misogyny. But I strain to see him as what he says he is—a victim whose violence is warranted and inconsequential in comparison to his own pain. Daniel conflates the collective good with his personal gratification; whatever actions he might take to achieve it are beyond reproach. I don't like it when he calls me a whore, but I do feel ashamed of how much energy I spent trying to please some of the people I dated. Though I know I'm not a "princess," I'm aware of how my membership in the beigeocracy afforded me easier entry into an academic world that reproduces the same power imbalances it dissects. I'm comfortable in my self-appointed role of compassionate ally, and I'm not sure how to disentangle the ideals I thought we shared from the man whom Daniel has turned out to be. So I collaborate with him in covering up and excusing what he is doing to me.

As the months pass, I share details with a handful of friends. We meet in secluded spots around campus where I don't think Daniel will see me, at least not right away: a picnic table by the Bear's Lair student bar, a bench under the main staircase in Doe, a patch of grass beneath a camphor tree. When describing Daniel's jealousy and rage, I downplay his violence. I want to protect him and fear that if I reveal everything, my friends will hate him and tell me to leave. Some days I inform Hannah that I'm getting Daniel to see that there are better ways of managing anger and sadness. Other days I say I feel like my head is about to explode.

"You can't let this be your life, or let his reality take over yours," she says.

While screaming at me one evening, Daniel punches himself in the face. The next day he shows up in Dwinelle with a split lip; his friends are concerned. When he tells them about his depression and his decision to start therapy, they become his support team, always ready to lend a sympathetic ear. Daniel warns me not to speak to them without him present, and when I do it's only to discuss what's best for him. We play basketball together on the court of a church near his apartment. Daniel gives us all nicknames; mine is Virginia Red. As we laugh and launch our flailing limbs at the basket, I stop worrying.

When we're sitting at our table in the history library, Daniel looks over my shoulder and sees a message from Hannah saying that she's afraid he's using therapy to manipulate me. "Because as long as he goes," she says, "it is like he is holding up his end of the bargain, no matter how shit of a partner he is." Daniel tells me that I violated his privacy by speaking to her and that she's a "privileged Ivy Leaguer" like me, a sheltered bitch who's prejudiced against the mentally ill and has no right to judge him. I disobey him by having lunch with Hannah and a former professor of ours who's in town. That evening, Daniel slams me against the wall in my apartment.

"You wanna tell me what you and your fellow Brown grad were talking about behind my back?"

"We weren't talking about you, I promise," I say. "Please let me go."

"What are you gonna do, call the police?" he says. "Go ahead, call them. You'll find out what real violence is."

He drops me and storms out. My hands shaking, I call his friend and roommate Evan. Telling him that Daniel is in a volatile state, I ask him to meet Daniel at home and make sure he stays there—for Daniel's own protection, I add. Someone is banging on the door. I open it and see Daniel standing in the hallway. I tell him that I'm on the phone with Evan.

"How dare you call Evan, don't you fucking tell him anything," he says, grabbing the phone from my hand and throwing it down the hall.

When we're lying in bed the next afternoon, Daniel suddenly starts yelling that I don't give a shit about him. He goes into the kitchen and picks up a cooking knife. As he walks toward me, he suddenly turns into the bathroom and closes the door. I call Evan, who comes home, knocks delicately, and suggests they take a walk around the block. When he emerges, Daniel tells Evan that he was having a depressive episode and I didn't care.

"Joy's so cold, she has ice in her veins," he says to Evan as they step outside.

As usual, the person who was incandescent with anger only a few moments before now looks like a wounded child.

"I've been better, but I'm getting by," I say whenever someone asks me how it's going.

I measure out my words in controlled doses. I might seem a little tense, but then again I'm supposed to be; I'm preparing for orals. In fact, I'm hardly studying at all. Whenever I get a few hours to myself in Doe, colors undulate across my vision until I close whatever book I have open. My heart sinks as my eyes pass over title after title that I won't have time to read. Midway through the semester, I ask my committee if we can push my exam back by a few days. I say I've been dealing with a difficult personal situation without specifying the cause.

At the end of April, Daniel takes his exam. The professors congratulate him on his outstanding performance. He proudly shows me an email from Anna saying how impressed his committee was by his "poise and eloquence." I hug him and tell him how happy I am for him. I know the hypnotic brilliance of his rhetoric; he's been practicing on me.

Daniel shows me a follow-up email from Anna. If he has time, Anna says, "help Joy stay sane before her exam."

Now Daniel has little with which to occupy himself, and the occasional moments I had to myself are gone. He always knows where I am, either around campus or at home, and likes to come looking for me. When I'm teaching section, he walks up to the door at the end of class and kisses me in front of my students. I never told him what room it was in.

On a quiet Saturday, we have lunch in the Dwinelle courtyard, where the midday sun illuminates the rose-colored walls. No one else is around.

"You betrayed me," Daniel says, as firmly and evenly as if he were delivering a keynote lecture. "You don't deserve any forgiveness for the way you neglected me. I can't be with someone like you—you revolt me. And look at you, sitting there like a fucking ice queen. You don't even care."

He stands up, rips the sunglasses off my face and snaps them in half, then throws them in a trash can. Next he grabs my reusable water bottle and starts bashing it against the concrete, carving long scratches down its sides.

"Do you care now?" he yells.

I run indoors. He follows me and punches the wall in the hallway by the grad student lounge. As the plaster shatters near my head I move faster, around the corner past the teaching assistant offices, toward the back stairwell and the exit. He grabs me and shoves me up against the side of the stairs. I break loose and run out the door in the direction of Telegraph. He calls me over and over. I finally pick up.

"I'm going to Hannah's to study," I tell him. "Please just leave me alone for a little while." I hang up and don't answer when he calls back.

He sends me a photo of us hugging.

When I don't respond right away, he shifts tactics.

"You really don't give a shit, do you?" he writes. "As long as there is something to do or someone telling you not to do something, you throw me to the wind."

Daniel finds me at Hannah's house and begs me to come out and talk to him. As we stand in the driveway, he hurls his phone against the asphalt.

"Look, there's no one I can contact for help," he says, pointing to his phone's shattered screen. "You have to come with me and make sure I'm okay."

I agree, dazed, and walk around the corner with him to his house, just like I did when he shoved me for the first time. If I stop resisting, his anger will eventually subside.

Hannah sends me a text telling me to come back to her place. She says that she and our friend Julia have called Alexander and told him that I'm in danger.

I reply that I'm with Daniel right now. "Please tell me later."

I silently urge Hannah not to say anything that will enrage Daniel if he sees it. When he walks into the kitchen, I delete my text message history with her. As soon as he comes back, I tell him that I'm afraid and need to leave. Before he has the chance to respond, I bolt out the door and down the stairs, back around the corner to Hannah's.

Daniel follows me again and tries to open Hannah's locked front door. From outside, he shouts at me to call his friend Bella to come get him.

I do, leaving out the details of what he did in Dwinelle. Bella says she'll take Daniel to her place to play video games and pet her cat.

In the morning, I wake up to a text message from him.

"How could you do this to me? After spending so much time telling you how I need your love and affection. After finally being calm after a day of horror. You tell me that you are afraid of me. Then leave me alone with no phone. Then have me be kicked out like an unwanted dog and have the door slammed shut in my face. Made me feel like a monster. Like my father. Until I yelled out and begged for someone to come for me. How could you do this to me? The pain is unbearable. There is no reason to live."

Just after I finish reading, I get a call from Mark, another grad student in the department. He lets me know that Daniel is cutting his wrists in Dwinelle and has asked Mark to tell me.

"Keep him there until I can figure out what to do," I say. "Don't let him leave." I know that as soon as Daniel realizes I'm not coming, he will come looking for me.

A few minutes later, I get another call from Mark, who tells me that Daniel tried to make a run for it. When Mark restrained him, Daniel started screaming that he was being attacked. Someone called the Berkeley police, who took Daniel to the psychiatric ward of a hospital near campus.

Alexander has ridden his bike to Dwinelle and asks to meet with me. In Alexander's office, we sit with a couple of Daniel's friends and try to figure out how to report to Berkeley's bureaucracy that he is in crisis. I say how worried I've been about him.

"Joy is an absolute saint," Bella says.

Alexander smiles in my direction.

This is who I want to be—the devoted confidante who does whatever Daniel needs and earns praise for my fortitude.

Daniel has been placed under a seventy-two-hour mandatory hold. He leaves me voicemails saying that he feels abandoned and needs me. That afternoon, only a few hours after he was taken in, I visit him with Bella. We bring him some books and a burrito, which he eats at a white tabletop. I look at his wrists and am surprised to see that they are marked with light scratches, not cuts.

"I love you, Birdie," he says, using one of his nicknames for me.

"I love you, too," I tell him. "Everything's gonna be okay."

The next morning, I get an email from something called the Path to Care Center, reaching out in response to the report that Alexander made to the university. I scan the email and see something about confidential support for survivors of gender-based violence. I don't understand why I've received it; my only interest is helping Daniel, and there's nothing here for him. I quickly close the message.

Hannah tells me that she and Alexander are talking about using the backyard cottage of another professor as a safe house.

"That's a great idea," I say. "Daniel likes her, and he would be safe there."

"No, it's not for him," Hannah says. "It's for you."

I don't understand. Daniel is the one who's suffering. Why would I need protection?

That afternoon I sit down in Doe to study for a few hours. I've just opened a book when I get a message from Bella. Daniel didn't seem to present any danger to himself or others, so the psych ward decided to let him go.

It's barely been twenty-four hours. I thought I had two more days. My heart starts to pound.

Relax, Bella writes: "I mean, like, he's not going to go looking for you."

A moment later I get a message from another one of Daniel's friends. He tells me that Daniel is on campus and trying to find me.

I call Alexander and say that Daniel is here and I don't know what to do. When I head down Doe's marble staircase and out the door, Daniel and Alexander are both walking toward me. I immediately relax: Daniel would never do anything to me in front of the man he considers a king. Alexander suggests that Daniel not contact me for a while, and that if there's anything he really feels he needs to say, he can send me an email. Daniel nods. Alexander leads me toward the parking lot, where his wife is waiting to drive me to the safe house.

Later that day, Daniel emails me that his night in the psych ward was his moment of clarity.

"I want you to know—I need you to know—that I love you deeply," he writes. The most difficult thing, he says, "isn't that you are not here with me, but that I can't be there for you when you're in need. I was that person for you for so long, and I promised to be that person till the day I die."

I'm touched and want to answer right away. Hannah says he's trying to manipulate me and urges me to sleep on it. I'm reluctant but agree.

The next morning, when I still haven't responded, I get a notification that Daniel has made a post in a Facebook group for current and former graduate students of our department with several hundred members. The post announces that he is struggling with depression and describes how alone he has felt through it all. "This weekend I hit rock bottom, and was locked in a psychiatric ward as a danger to myself," Daniel writes. He says how frightening the experience was, how much he missed everyone in the department, how he came to value them more than ever.

"I am deeply sorry if I caused any of you trouble," the post concludes. "I want to start building my life again, with an appreciation of what I have. I would like to have your support, if you want to give it."

There is nothing to suggest that Daniel has ever harmed anyone else. The number of likes and hearts keeps rising. Comment after comment commending his bravery says that everyone loves and accepts him unconditionally.

I recognize Daniel's tone in the email and the post. It's the one he switches on when he apologizes and says he's realized that the problem is only him. It has a thin, saccharine quality, like the icing on a supermarket cake. I realize that this performance, too, is intended for me, that he wants me to see how everyone embraces him as a victim and how I have no choice but to stay quiet and agree. The knowledge makes my head spin. I press it down until it disappears.

In my response to his email, I thank Daniel for his "kind and moving" words and praise how strong, brilliant, supportive, sexy, and funny he is. I say that our relationship has triggered his memories of painful experiences, and that this has made it "unsafe for you, and unsafe for me."

"I don't think you're a bad person," I emphasize. "I don't love you any less." I say how glad I am that he is seeing a therapist and suggest that he intensify his treatment: "What happened this weekend was a very scary reminder of the fact that it will take time for you to get better."

Daniel writes back quickly, without acknowledging anything I said. He writes that his day in the psych ward taught him invaluable lessons "about myself, about others, about the human spirit." He tells me that a number of graduate students are opening up to him about their own struggles with anxiety and depression. He says that he is going to dedicate himself to developing more awareness and infrastructure to support mental health in our department. I tell myself that he's not lying, that he really has changed and wants to help other people. Recognizing what he's done to me isn't important.

On the morning of my exam, as I sit in my advisor's dining room under the orange lampshade, I try to remember Miłosz's words about the questions that are more significant than mere force. I talk about the desire to believe in a system that claims to uplift the oppressed, how signs of apparent progress can outweigh coercion.

At the end of the exam, I step outside while the professors deliberate.

Congratulations, they tell me—I have passed with distinction.

6

DROP BY DROP

Though my reassuring message to Daniel is tinged with doubt, my suspicions, like those of other apostates, are slow to ripen. When the party activist Lev Kopelev heard Stalin's voice on the radio in 1941, promising a quick victory against Hitler after the Führer violated their mutual nonaggression pact by invading the Soviet Union, Kopelev immediately remembered all the lies that Stalin had told before. Nevertheless, Kopelev wrote in his memoir, "I believed him all over again, as did my comrades."

After Stalin's death, when his successor Nikita Khrushchev denounced the dictator's personality cult and some of his crimes, Kopelev began, "drop by drop," to relinquish the dogmatism that led him to participate in things he knew to be wrong. Kopelev reflected that although his generation's dream of speaking Esperanto in a world without borders had made them "accomplices in evil," it also provided "the vestiges of conscience" that allowed them, if they chose, to find a way out. Even so, Kopelev's disillusionment was gradual. He tried to ignore the Soviet crushing of demonstrations in East Berlin in 1953 and Hungary in 1956; he still wanted to believe that the ends justified the means.

Miłosz wrote that his decision to defect came less from reason than distaste: he compared obeying Stalinist mandates to the sensation of swallowing live frogs. In the early '50s, while still serving as a diplomat, Miłosz decided that he had to go back to Poland one more time to be sure that he wanted to leave. He needed, he wrote, for his "despair to come to a head."

―――――

At the beginning of May, Anna convinces Daniel to go home for a while and rest. He leaves on the day of my exam. Suddenly, I have time to myself. Over dinner with Hannah, Julia, and Rose, I say more about what's been going on. Later that evening, Rose texts me that she used to be in an abusive relationship and sends me a PDF of a book called *Why Does He Do That? Inside the Minds of Angry and Controlling Men*. I'm skeptical but open the file.

Author Lundy Bancroft begins by describing the counseling program for abusive men that he's been running since 1978. Due to the "tremendous denial, minimization, and distortion" with which such clients describe their actions, he says, the program's counselors always speak separately with the abused partner to get a more accurate picture of what's happening at home. "One of the prevalent features of life with an angry or controlling partner is that he frequently *tells you what you should think* and tries to get you to doubt and devalue your own perceptions and beliefs," he writes. I highlight this line and keep reading.

A primary obstacle to recognizing an abusive relationship, according to Bancroft, is that many people simply don't *seem* like abusers and maintain an appealing public image. Though their partners usually don't realize what's happening, the signs are near-universal:

> the escalating frequency of put-downs. Early generosity turning more and more to selfishness. Verbal explosions when he is irritated or when he doesn't get his way. Her grievances constantly turned around on her, so that everything is her own fault. His growing attitude that he knows what is good for her better than she does. And, in many relationships, a mounting sense of fear or intimidation.

One moment the abusive partner is terrifying, while the next he seems like a lost little boy. His partner gets caught up in trying to understand

and regulate his moods. Their relationship assumes a cycle, in which a honeymoon phase gives way to rising tension that culminates in an eruption, followed by apologies and declarations of love.

The PDF fills up with streaks as I mark almost every line.

"It's an exact description of so many things I have experienced," I text Hannah in disbelief. The sun lowers through the blinds as I stay in bed, unable to move until I finish.

In a chapter on different archetypes of abusive behavior, I encounter "The Victim," who emphasizes how cruel and unfair his life has been and how everyone has always slighted him. The Victim's partner worries about him, feels responsible for protecting him, and fears that he will hurt or kill himself if she leaves—fears that he feeds by framing himself as helpless and threatening self-harm.

My pulse accelerates. *That's Daniel.* I keep reading in search of signs that he might change.

According to Bancroft, therapy can help an abusive person process his emotions but often makes his behavior toward his partner even worse, as he gains more sophisticated ways to excuse his actions and make her feel responsible for taking care of him. Therapists unwittingly enable abuse by responding sympathetically to the client's version of reality and deepening their sense of justification, while perpetrators manipulate friends and family into serving as allies by presenting themselves as mistreated and creating cover stories for any compromising information that emerges. Though mental illness doesn't cause misogynist violence, Bancroft says, the two can interact; an abusive man with severe depression, for example, might be more indifferent to the potential consequences of his actions.

It hadn't occurred to me that Daniel's abuse was possible to separate from his mental health, or that he might have any control over how he treats me. Now, as I read Bancroft's words, I think about how Daniel always saves his violence for moments when we're alone. Still, I need to know whether there's any chance he might turn back into the man I thought he was on the night when we stood on my balcony and I asked him if he'd ever thought of being together. From the corner of my eye I can see the balcony's silhouette outside my window, only a couple of yards but a world of experience away.

Finally, I find Bancroft's answer. It's not encouraging.

Bancroft writes that abusive behavior is difficult to alter because it brings so many benefits: the victim becomes a "human garbage dump" who can be blamed for any problem and caters to their partner's every need. Leaving is difficult, and often dangerous. Abusive partners promise to change, start therapy, threaten suicide, and claim abandonment until they get their way. Most survivors try to end the relationship several times before they're able to make a final break.

I close my laptop and lie on my back. It turns out the bewildering hell I thought no one could understand is the stuff of an intro sociology textbook—a familiar set of tactics for acquiring dominance. I feel Daniel's power over me melting like greasepaint on the face of a prince.

A few minutes later, it all fades from my consciousness, and I start to worry about how Daniel is doing. As if he were reading my mind, I see a message from him, saying that he has a new phone and is waiting to hear from me. Hannah has been asking me to consider a restraining order, but the kaleidoscope has shifted again, and all I feel toward him is empathy.

The next day I have a phone call with Anna. She's been abroad on sabbatical this year and participated in our oral exams on Skype. She reached out to me over email after Daniel was put on a psychiatric hold. "It sounds as if Daniel is in acute trouble, but I can only imagine that you are feeling equally distressed," she wrote, adding that she didn't want to intrude on our privacy but was available to talk anytime. When we spoke on the phone, she urged me to take care of myself however necessary. This time, I've contacted her. Though I don't want to get into too many specifics, I do want her to know there's more to the story than she probably realizes and that I'm struggling to figure out what to do.

After we exchange a few pleasantries, I say that I've been reading about domestic violence and have realized that my relationship with Daniel follows a classic pattern.

"Yes," Anna says. "You're undoubtedly reading all sorts of things." I can tell immediately that since our last conversation she has spoken with Daniel. There is a distance in her voice that I recognize from my own. I tell Anna that a couple of my friends have been thinking about telling the History Department's chair that Daniel is creating an unsafe work environment. I emphasize that it's not my idea and I'm not sure what to think.

Anna replies that Daniel's reputation has already suffered enough. He has violated "the taboo of domestic violence" and is being judged for it, she says, but I must make my own decisions rather than being influenced by others.

"Hannah thinks I should get a restraining order," I blurt out.

"Hannah is very young," she says, in a motherly tone. "She sees everything in black and white."

"Yes," I say with relief. "She's just projecting her fears on me."

I'm grateful that Anna feels sorry for Daniel like I do and grasps the unique essence of our situation. Her words provide the permission I need to dismiss what I've been reading. Intellectuals don't have to believe in clichés like a "cycle of violence" or "domestic abuse"; we can dismiss them as social constructs that will follow others into obscurity and one day be unpacked at a seminar table. Daniel needs my love, support, and silence, and he'll get them. As soon as I hang up the phone, I text Hannah that I've decided not to file for a restraining order.

Anna suggests that I also go home and rest. Back in Virginia, I take a walk in the woods. As the path winds down a ridge, I'm enveloped in hickory, oak, and walnut trees, their leaves electric green in the middle of May. My heart races as my head fills with things that Daniel has said to me, words I've tried to bury deep in the soil of my memory so that they'll never resurface.

It's good to know you can't keep your mouth shut.

I saw you checking him out just now. You can't get enough dick, can you?

Lie to me again and see what happens.

As the trail curves back up, I look down on the forest canopy and think of the self-deprecating face that Daniel presents to the world, the vulnerable man who has already suffered enough.

I start shivering in the midday sun. It can't be the same person.

Hannah tells me that another woman in the graduate program, Amanda, has a story about Daniel that I might want to hear. I remember Daniel saying how hot she is and wonder if he tried to hit on her. That evening, I give Amanda an apologetic call and say I would be grateful if she could share what happened.

"Of course," she says. "It's no trouble at all."

Amanda tells me that one night the previous year, she and Daniel ended up at the same party. Though she didn't know him well, he cornered her and started complaining about some harsh feedback he'd gotten on a paper. She tried to politely comfort him and edge back toward the group. But then he abruptly shifted to berating her, telling her that her dissertation topic was stupid and that she had no business getting a PhD. When she left, in part to get away from him, Daniel did, too, and tried to walk home with her. Amanda was with someone else, and when their paths diverged, Daniel continued in another direction.

"I'm positive that if I'd been alone, he would have followed me," she says.

I remember the day Amanda is describing. That afternoon I took Daniel out for smoothies and reminded him that neither of us would ever let the other go down. As Amanda describes his swift transition from self-pity to hostility, I feel for the first time that someone else has caught a glimpse of Daniel's other face.

———

I get a recommendation for a therapist in my hometown who has experience treating victims of domestic violence. My pulse quickens when I walk into the room and see her digital clock: it's already 5:01. I apologize for my tardiness.

"You're only a minute late," she says.

The therapist has a thick southern accent and low tolerance for bullshit. I tell her about my faith that Daniel will change, how he had a difficult childhood and needs my support, how I still think there's a wonderful person waiting to come out and that I need to be patient and encourage his growth.

She points to the PC sitting on her desk across the room. "Can you turn this computer into a lamp by looking at it?" she says.

I shake my head.

"Even if you stare at it as hard as you can?"

I shake my head again.

"You can't change an adult man either."

She asks me why I would stay in a relationship with someone who puts his hands around my throat.

"I love him?" I reply.

"Well, butter my butt and call me a biscuit," she says sarcastically. "How romantic!"

When I describe Daniel's endless monologues about how I neglected him, she suggests that I read the manifesto of the Unabomber, Ted Kaczynski.

"He's another person with a deranged worldview who's convinced he's right," she says.

At the end of the hour, she hands me a stack of photocopies on codependency and tells me to start going to a domestic violence support group.

At our next session, I explain how, if I say that I was hurt by something he did, Daniel responds with a flood of accusations about why I am at fault, and how after he is violent to me, he immediately threatens to hurt himself. She tells me that this is called "flipping," and it's the core dynamic of abuse.

"The thing is," she says, "I'm not that worried that he's going to kill himself."

She pauses.

"Frankly, I think there's a much greater risk that he's going to kill you."

The therapist tells me that I remind her of a client of hers who was shot by her estranged husband; she testified at the man's trial. "This woman thought she could protect herself, but she couldn't. No one ever thinks it's going to happen to them."

She advises me to delete Daniel from my phone and stay as far away from him as possible.

"If you walk out that door and stay in contact with him," she says, "there's a chance that I'm never going to see you again."

I agree that yes, I will try. But as I head toward my car, my fingers are already reaching to check my messages. Because I've also been talking to Daniel, more and more often.

The first time I respond to one of his texts, he says he hopes I'll do it again.

"I get butterflies in my stomach whenever I see a message from you," he writes.

I do, too. Somehow, I feel closer to him than ever. We've been through so much together.

I try out my new therapy language and ask if we can take it slow. "Being able to establish boundaries is hard but important for me," I say.

Daniel says he understands.

We discuss the season finale of *Big Little Lies*, a show we've been watching together. I say that it felt strange to watch the scenes in which Nicole Kidman's character is being hit and choked by her husband.

Daniel says he knows.

"Yeah," he replies. "I would always look at your face during those scenes to see how you responded."

It's the closest he comes to a confession.

I try bringing up some of the things he's done to me in hopes that he'll acknowledge them. Though he says they're too upsetting to hear, or that he doesn't remember, he stays miraculously calm.

"I'm sorry if I've ever upset you, Joy," he says patiently. "But you have to understand that you've lived a very sheltered life."

I decide not to push the point—he keeps talking about how he's healing.

Daniel sends dirty texts about how he can't wait to get me in bed again. I flirt back.

By the end of the month, we're both in Berkeley.

———

When Daniel was in the psych ward, Hannah contacted my mother (with my permission) to give her a sense of what was going on. Now that I'm back in Berkeley, both she and my mom are scared that I'll start seeing him again. Most of our friends have gone away for the summer. I assure Hannah that I'll only meet Daniel in public places, but that he's changed and there's no need to worry. Hannah tells me that she can see me vacillating between more and less positive interpretations of his actions.

"[Your] proximity to him and his narrative and his version of everything that happened is fucking terrifying," she texts me.

During a phone appointment with the therapist in Virginia, I admit that I haven't been able to cut off contact. She says that this is normal, but suggests that I make a list of abusive behaviors I'm no longer willing to accept and send it to my friends to help hold myself accountable.

Daniel and I decide to see the new Tupac biopic. When he meets me outside the door of my apartment building, he's wearing a denim collared shirt, the one he knows I like, and holding a bouquet. In *Why Does He Do That?*, Bancroft says that flowers are a classic move during the apology phase. I force the unwanted thought away as Daniel brandishes them toward me and wraps me in a hug.

As we eat burgers by the movie theater, Daniel tells me about how supportive graduate students and faculty have been. He says that Alexander confided in him about his own feeling of alienation at Berkeley, that Anna told him about her psychological struggles and invited him over to her house for wine, that the professor whose guest house I stayed in wrapped him in a "motherly hug" when she saw him in Dwinelle, that a renowned literature scholar he took a class with is sending him regular check-in emails. He calls the last one his "guardian angel."

"I'm really happy that you're getting the support you need," I say.

In our highly therapized and medicated circles, mental health issues are easy to identify with, and almost everyone we know seems to be reaching out to Daniel to tell him they understand exactly how he feels. I haven't made an effort to counter his public persona by providing more detail, but then again no one has asked. I think of how Anna responded when I tried.

When we get back to my place, we have sex, and our relationship resumes. Almost immediately, there are signs I don't want to see.

Daniel beams when he describes the attention he's been receiving, but when I say that my friends have also been worried about me, his face darkens.

"That's ridiculous," he says.

He keeps pushing me to say what I was doing on the days when we were apart and what people were saying about him. I try to give away as little as possible. I don't reveal anything about the house where I stayed, my new reading material, or my counseling sessions. Even though I want to trust him, my intuition tells me to keep some things private. To mollify him, I share one tidbit: that Julia's boyfriend offered to walk her and Hannah back and forth to campus if they felt unsafe. Daniel pressures me to agree with him that he has never put anyone in danger and that Hannah refused to let him into her house because she's hysterical and overprivileged. I don't agree but make it sound like I do so that he'll drop it.

When his anger starts to mount, I stop the conversation and tell him I won't tolerate being yelled at anymore. He tells me that I'm being overly sensitive.

"It's normal for couples to argue," he says. "Our relationship will never work if I'm not allowed to say anything to you other than praise."

To prove how much he's changed, he offers to take me on a trip for my twenty-ninth birthday. I'm nervous but eventually say yes. I decide not to tell my friends or family so that they won't worry. I imagine myself proudly telling them afterward about how the whole thing went off without a hitch. Daniel and I fly to Texas.

In Houston, we visit NASA and eat steaming piles of brisket with slices of white bread. On my birthday we go to the Funeral Museum, where we look at Civil War–era embalming tools and mourning jewelry made of hair—objects that attempted to preserve traces of the departed as they had been on earth. In the gift shop Daniel buys me a black mug.

"The perfect gift for Lady Death," he says.

As I drive us to Austin in a rental car, Daniel pushes for more intel on what people have said about him. I keep trying to change the subject. He won't let it go.

When we get to a beer garden, Daniel grabs my phone. To my relief, he doesn't open my messages, but instead goes to photos. He starts flipping through them until he finds the kind of surprise that he's been looking for—a photo of me and Alexander after my oral exam, taken next to his dining table. We are smiling with Hannah, Julia, and Rose, who came to pick me up when it was over. Alexander has poured me a congratulatory glass of cognac, which I am raising toward the camera.

Daniel looks up from my phone.

"Why didn't you tell me that your exam was at Alexander's house?" he asks.

I tell him I didn't want to upset him, that we just thought it was safer to do it away from the department.

"Why would you need to be kept safe when I was the one who was in danger?" he says.

"I was in danger, too," I reply softly.

"What the fuck did you just say to me?"

His eyes flash, and the horizon tilts. We're back on the other planet. Daniel launches into a monologue about how he's barely ever touched me.

"You're just a pampered white bitch," he says.

He is holding a full pint of beer. As he yells, he raises the glass and dumps its contents onto my face. The liquid runs down my cheeks and hair and onto my lap.

"I saw that, asshole," a male voice calls out.

Daniel turns around to confront him. I seize the moment and run inside, pausing to hand our server money for our drinks. She gives me a look.

"Are you okay?" she says.

I smile and nod, yes, we're good, everything's fine. I run outside. I can't think. I decide to get a cab back to our motel, grab my backpack with my laptop, and go from there.

I feel a blow on my back and stagger forward. Daniel has thrown his arms around me and is trying to force me to the ground.

"You wanna call the cops?" Daniel is yelling. "Go ahead and try."

As I scream and try to break free, the people passing us on the street look away and keep walking. Eventually someone stops and pulls Daniel off me. Daniel shouts at him as I run down the block toward the Lyft that has almost arrived. Daniel catches up to me and hops inside, too. I try to visualize the spot on the floor where my bag is lying so that I can grab it immediately and run back out.

Daniel follows me into the motel room.

"You're not going anywhere," he says, shaking his head as he closes the door and bolts it behind him. As I look into his eyes, all the warning signs I've ignored snap into focus and I see it: I'm going to die now. Everything I have ever said or done or dreamed was a road to nowhere that ends here. I don't want to go.

I.

I beg him not to kill me because it would upset my parents. After a few minutes Daniel falls on the ground, weeping like he always does when the wave of violence breaks. I pull him into bed and wait beside him until the sun rises. A roach scuttles across the bathroom floor, trying to slip away unnoticed. Our flight to Berkeley is in a few hours. I just need to keep Daniel calm until then.

———

"You're not mad at me, are you baby?" Daniel says as we walk to our gate, his tone as sweet as the McFlurries we ate before returning the car. I put on a smile.

"Of course not," I say.

My only friend in Berkeley for the summer is Rose, who emailed me Bancroft's book on abuse. As soon as I'm alone in my apartment, she comes over and helps me pack a bag.

"What about my laundry?" I ask.

"We'll do it at my house," she says, picking up the floppy bin.

In my texts to Daniel, I make up excuses to explain why I need to be by myself for a little while. I try to make it sound as if this were just a brief stage before I forgive him, a familiar step on the road to reconciliation. After a day passes, his texts and calls start coming at a faster clip. I receive a message from his sister, whom I met once and hadn't given my number, offering to make peace between us. Daniel texts me that his mom wants to talk to me.

I finally pick up one of his calls. Daniel says that he just got a little upset because he'd had a drink, that he'll go to counseling for alcoholism, that it will never happen again.

"We'll have a beautiful life together," he says, his throat thick with tears. "I promise you. One hundred ten percent." He keeps repeating this impossible number.

Though I still feel sorry for him, I can't forget what I saw in his gaze. He's the insecure soldier, and I'm the goose with the exposed neck. He has so many ways to justify breaking it.

"Daniel is part of me," I say to Rose as we sit at her kitchen table. "Leaving him feels like chopping off my own limb."

"It's a limb that was sewn on," she replies gently. "You never needed it."

Rose rents a room in a big, shingled house with a garden in southside Berkeley. Sunlight streams through the window onto the blue kitchen cabinets. Her roommate's bulldog is sprawled out on the floor; bits of stale rolls from Cheese Board lie on the table. As I crush the crumbs between my fingers, Rose is telling me that choking is one of the abusive behaviors most highly correlated with homicide. Daniel can't know I'm leaving until I'm already gone.

Bukharin tried to overcome his divided consciousness by submitting to Stalin's will. But then again, he didn't have much choice; the script was already written, and the hangman was at the door. As I stare at the sink and will myself to leap into an uncertain freedom, I feel that I don't have the strength to leave for my own good. I'm too worried that Daniel needs me and too scared of facing whatever is left of myself. I want to stay in halls where faith and disillusionment, terror and salvation are abstractions to be weighed from a distance. I want to keep living the dream that we are outside time.

While sitting in Rose's kitchen, I remember a conversation I had over the phone with my mom a couple of weeks ago, not long after I'd arrived back in Berkeley. She told me that a friend of ours from church recently attended her niece's funeral. The niece had an abusive husband. One day he ran her over with his car, and that was that. Her life was over.

I decide to leave for her. "I" is not enough; I want a different kind of "we."

Part 2

7

TARGETED RISK

MAYBE THE SELTZER WAS A BAD IDEA ON TOP OF THE COLD BREW. I have to pee but they are about to call.

I am alive. Staying that way requires telling a story.

What story, whose?

There will be questions. I'd better have answers.

Get the story straight, iron out the details. The past is a sheet I can pull on for protection.

Coffee, seltzer, pee, call.

How much did you have to drink? Did you pee before or after the call? For how long? On what date? Did you tell anyone when you went to the bathroom? Is there any documentation you can provide for this alleged urination?

In my dreams Daniel chases me. I wake up and see that I am lying in my friend's attic in Providence, Rhode Island.

I am having an "acute stress reaction," the domestic violence counselor says. Intrusive thoughts, rapid pulse.

Historians like to talk about contingency—tears in the fabric of time when things might have been different.

I picture Daniel standing over my body. I am gone, and he is the only one left. He is crying—not for me, but for himself. I laugh. Spooky!

I laugh all the time. The counselor calls this "inappropriate affect."

I can't stop laughing because I chose a different thread. I am safe in the attic, and today I am going to talk to the Title IX office.

On the morning I depart Berkeley, Rose suggests I leave Daniel a letter telling him not to contact me for at least six months. I sit at her kitchen table, choosing words to cauterize the growing rupture in my heart. I write that I will never stop loving and caring about him, but since his violence toward me will never stop, it's better for both of us to be apart. After sealing the envelope, I block him on my phone.

As the plane ascends, euphoria fizzes in my chest. *I escaped you.*

During my layover I open a copy of *Men Explain Things to Me.* It had stood on display by the cash register at Moe's Books on Telegraph when I was hurrying to purchase a goodbye card for Daniel and feared that he might see me on this quick foray out of the house. On our trip to Texas, I'd brought along Roxane Gay's *Bad Feminist.*

"How redundant," Daniel said smugly when he saw the title.

Now I sit and read, uninterrupted, Rebecca Solnit's essay on the silencing of women, as intently as if it were a spell that could summon back my voice.

After landing in Boston, I take a train to Providence, and finally sink into bed at my friend Cassandra's house. She's already finished her PhD and carries herself with tenacity I'm desperate to channel.

Updates arrive from the other coast. Daniel's friend Bella texts me that she gave him the goodbye letter as I requested. I've already blocked him on email and am about to proceed to Facebook when I see a message from Hannah.

"Did you see his post?" she asks. "Sorry but you should know." She sends a screenshot from our community Facebook group.

"It is with a heavy heart that I post this. I am leaving the history program. I came to this decision on my own. I am like an extra, who had missed his cue to leave the stage. Well now I am exiting." Daniel will miss everyone terribly, he says, and hopes there's a chance they might miss him, too; he looks forward to reading all their books.

I know that Daniel is not really planning to leave the department; this declaration is for my benefit. But the supportive, unsuspecting responses are already coming in from our colleagues.

———

Though the domestic violence counselor from my hometown helped me see what I denied about Daniel, her domineering style doesn't let me think for myself. A few weeks ago, I started meeting with a therapist in Oakland whose vibe is less Appalachian straight shooter, more Bay Area yogi. Our sessions continue online after I leave.

When she asks me how I feel, I can only say how Daniel does. She suggests that care-taking composure is a habit with a history and excavates secrets I'm not ready to reveal.

"Your issues fit together like puzzle pieces," she says.

Now the shape that fits my edges is gone, along with my ability to pretend like everything is fine. I have no idea what to do next. This fall Daniel and I are both supposed to be in Eastern Europe, doing research in the same archives, away from all our support networks. A country separates us for now, but it might not for long.

Hannah urges me to reach out to Anna with more details—this time, in writing, so she can't cut off what I'm trying to say.

"If you do it for real in one whopper email, you will never have to do it again."

We both think it's a question of information. If Anna knows more, then she will understand that Daniel can't be trusted.

"Perhaps from the outside, without having seen it or lived it, this concern seems like a misunderstanding or an overreaction," my email concludes. "I understand. But I have felt the sheer terror of being woken up in the middle of the night by his hand around my neck, and the feeling that this is how my life ends."

Anna's response is polite but distant. She says she hopes I'm taking care of myself.

"Probably you are aware that your e-mail, listing [Daniel's] abusive behaviors, constitutes a legal document. In case you would like to take this forward, by having me send a copy to a person who is competent to initiate legal action, please let me know."

I realize why Anna stopped me from disclosing more before. Professors are supposed to report things like this to the university—a duty she was probably trying to evade. Now that we're no longer in the shared position of protecting Daniel, my words are a liability. I reply that I want to handle this "in as discreet and sensitive a way as possible" but am afraid of what he might do. A few days later, Anna says that she has met with Daniel, and that he has agreed not to travel to where I will be in the coming year.

"I think you can rely on this information," she says.

Daniel and I will be apart, and I won't have to bring this up anymore.

A few days later, I get a text from Bella, who says that Daniel has been telling her about his upcoming travels. I ask if he mentioned that he's been instructed not to go to the locations where I'll be based.

"No, I didn't know he had been told not to go there," she says. "He told me that [Anna] said he should/could go."

I feel the attic's pitched roof lowering down on my head like the lid of a coffin. Daniel will lie and promise and flatter until we are back in the same place together. Discretion is a rope that will lead me straight to him. I beg Bella, once again, not to believe what he says.

"Is it conscious manipulation or is it delusion?" Bella asks. "Because every time I speak to him I feel like I'm speaking to this vulnerable, hard-done-by victim, and then every time I speak to you, I think: I have no idea how serious this is."

━━━━━━

Back in the spring, I closed the email I received from the university about domestic violence support, but I didn't forget it. Now I reach out to the Path to Care Center and have a phone call with a confidential advocate, who explains my options. I could make a report to the Title IX office without requesting that anything be done about it, or the office could issue a "no contact directive" asking Daniel not to talk to me. Actions that carry weight require more effort. On a call with the head of the Title

IX office, I learn that due to my accusations' severity, Daniel could be put under an "interim suspension" that would bar him from following me overseas. To issue it, however, the office would have to launch an investigation. While it's impossible to predict how long the investigation would last, she says, they would aim to complete it within sixty days.

I ask if the investigation could proceed without me. The head of the office says no: their team has determined that this is a "targeted," not a community, risk. Since I am the only one in danger, an investigation can happen solely at my behest. Daniel would know that I betrayed him and become my direct adversary in the case. I ask if he would be able to keep his fellowship and health insurance while suspended. She says yes.

At the end of July, I tell her that I would like to move forward.

To decompress, a friend of Cassandra's takes me to a shooting range. She's a Zen Buddhist with Sanskrit inked down her arms. After loading her rifle in the trunk, she says that target practice is a form of meditation.

"Why should the right-wingers have all the guns?"

After a brief training, I stand with my legs in a pyramid and feel the click of finger on trigger. I like the revolver's heft as my weight rotates the barrel and releases, in a mechanical maneuver as neat and precise as the ticking of a clock. The semiautomatic handgun unnerves me with its recoil—a motion that, once initiated, generates momentum beyond my control.

———

I assume a new identity: "the Complainant." The nomenclature of the Title IX system—or as it's paradoxically called at Berkeley, the Office for the Prevention of Harassment and Discrimination (OPHD)—numbs discomfort with bureaucratese. Daniel is not the accused but the "Respondent"; he will not be found innocent or guilty but "responsible" or "not responsible." The Notice of Allegations parcels out the mess of experience into specific "incidents of concern" that are in potential violation of the UC Berkeley Code of Student Conduct and the University of California Policy on Sexual Violence and Sexual Harassment. This terminology places the rot of our relationship at an anodyne distance, as if it were an

UNIVERSITY OF CALIFORNIA, BERKELEY

BERKELEY · DAVIS · IRVINE · LOS ANGELES · MERCED · RIVERSIDE · SAN DIEGO · SAN FRANCISCO   SANTA BARBARA · SANTA CRUZ

CENTER FOR STUDENT CONDUCT
OFFICE FOR THE PREVENTION OF HARASSMENT AND DISCRIMINATION

THIS IS AN OFFICIAL UNIVERSITY COMMUNICATION
DELIVERY VIA EMAIL

August 03, 2017

Joy Neumeyer

SUBJECT: Notice of Allegations
CASE NUMBER: 00686-003-2017

Dear Joy,

I hope this email finds you well. You are receiving this letter because the Office for the Prevention of Harassment and Discrimination (OPHD) and the Center for Student Conduct have jointly issued a Notice of Allegations to ▮▮▮▮▮▮▮▮ and OPHD will be investigating the report you brought forward. Attached to this letter you will find a copy of the Notice of Allegations letter that was issued to ▮▮▮▮▮▮▮

I will continue to keep you informed during the investigative process. In the meantime, please review the important information below describing the investigation process and resources that are available to you. If you have any questions, please contact ▮▮▮▮▮▮▮▮▮▮▮

---

abscessed tooth that could be uprooted and set under the bright lights of the dentist's tray.

Complainant—a part I will play for who knows how long.

I am unable to spell it. Shouldn't there be a *t* after the first *n*? An *i* after the second *a*? My brain refuses to remember what letters come in which order; it covets its customary role of the one who determines what happened. But the director has posted the cast list, and that part has gone to someone else: the case resolution officer, or "CRO." As for the Complainant, well—nothing she says can be trusted. All her statements are rephrased as a passive proposition:

It is alleged.

When the investigation begins, I have a hazy understanding of what is about to happen. Only once it's over do I fully grasp all the steps. After interviewing both me and Daniel, the CRO will ask each of us to submit evidence and provide the names of anyone who might be able to corroborate our stories. Once the CRO has interviewed these witnesses, along with anyone else whom she decides to contact, she will ask us to review and comment on whatever they said, as well as on the evidence submitted by the opposing side. The CRO will then weigh all these words and, in a "timely, thorough, and impartial manner," write the official version of what happened with the power vested in her by the University of California. Her report will conclude whether the Respondent violated any university policies, but it won't determine the institution's response. For this, the case will go to the Center for Student Conduct, which will decide what (if any) "sanction" he will receive. Either of us can appeal the outcome.

Complaining entails loss: of a love that had run to poison, my belief in always turning the other cheek. Grief, according to Sigmund Freud, threatens to overwhelm the sufferer. Through stylized reenactment, the mourner gradually releases the love object and re-creates a coherent identity. As a visual Freud invoked the *fort/da* games played by his grandson, who threw objects away and back again to cope with separation from his parents. Failure to perform the work of mourning leads to melancholia, that sense of loss so vast and vague it latches onto the self.

Sometimes I look in the mirror and wish I could change my face, as if altering my exterior might mend the schism between the part of me that sympathized with Daniel and the part that saw what he was doing and wanted to save myself. If I can't have a new body, maybe a bureaucratic title will do. While the rituals of complaint offer some comfort, however, they inflict an equal amount of pain.

━━━━━

Once Daniel receives the Notice of Allegations, institutional mechanisms swing into motion. Under the interim suspension, he can do research in another country but not where I'll be studying. He is also not allowed on campus. To keep receiving his fellowship payments, he must submit housing and travel receipts that show he is complying. He is invited to participate in a hearing to determine whether the interim suspension will be upheld. It is.

All I had wanted was to be free from Daniel while I was abroad. Yet the process required to make that happen rips open new vulnerabilities. For the case to proceed, I will have to submit text exchanges with my friends—the very ones that Daniel was desperate to see. They will then be turned over to him to read. After seeing a single message from Hannah warning that he might use therapy to manipulate me, Daniel furiously quoted her words to me for weeks while following me, throwing my things, slamming me against walls. How will he respond when he sees her texts begging me to get a restraining order and calling him "fucking unhinged"?

Members of our department will be asked to reveal what they have seen or heard about Daniel—not the courageous battle with depression he presents on social media, but the way he acts when he thinks no one is looking. Like me, his friends were anxious whenever he was upset and would drop everything to reassure him. Beneath their empathy, down in the bedrock they would rather not expose, I suspect that they are afraid of him, too. I remember Daniel sitting in Dwinelle, silently tapping his highlighters as he monitored conversations and glances, filing everything away for future use in his internal ministry of justice. So far, I am the only one who has seen him erupt. I am not as confident as OPHD that the risk is targeted exclusively at me.

8

DUE PROCESS

O N A GRAY AFTERNOON IN APRIL 2016, A PHALANX OF GRAD STU-
dents stood outside Dwinelle holding posters with phrases like
"We Demand Student Safety."

Two women were suing the university after a professor who'd sexually
harassed them faced no consequences, and I'd joined the crowd of students and faculty who came out to show their support.

Over the past several months, a series of articles had exposed prominent men at the university as abusers. The *San Francisco Chronicle* published a story on Berkeley's "history of tolerating" sexual violence and
misconduct. Title IX documents leaked to the *Guardian* described professors and staff soliciting sex and a massage therapist sexually assaulting
a student.

"Man is it disturbing," Daniel texted me with a link to the article. It
was only a few months before we started dating.

An OPHD investigation had found Blake Wentworth, a professor
in the South and Southeast Asian Studies Department, "responsible"
for sexually harassing PhD student Kathleen Gutierrez. Among other
things, he had touched her inappropriately, told her how attracted he
was to her, and boasted to her about snorting drugs off a stripper's body.
Yet her colleague, Erin Bennett, was told by OPHD that Wentworth's
actions were not "sufficiently severe or pervasive" to rise above the level of

merely "unprofessional." As months passed and more students filed complaints, Wentworth kept working. He told the *Guardian* that the allegations against him were "baseless" and "fanciful."

As the two women stood in front of the building that held both of our departments, I couldn't help staring. What was it like to challenge your professors and air embarrassing personal details in the public eye? In an interview with the *Guardian*, Gutierrez said she struggled to get out of bed every day and battled "extreme fatigue, unexpected body aches, and debilitating anxiety." An accompanying photo showed her sitting next to Bennett with clasped hands and pursed lips.

Isn't that shirt a little low-cut? a nasty voice in my head observed.

I willed my inner misogynist to shut up and be an ally.

Lunchtime Tupperware clanking in my tote bag, I signed a petition that was circulating through the crowd on a clipboard. A reporter asked me for a comment. I said something about the abuse of power before walking off to eat my sandwich and address more immediate concerns— leading an American history section I was unqualified to teach.

━━━━

In 1969, after completing her doctorate in education at the University of Maryland, Bernice Sandler was denied a faculty appointment on the grounds that she "came on too strong" for a woman. Together with Women's Equity Action League, she filed complaints against hundreds of colleges and universities stating that they were in violation of a recent executive order that barred federal contractors from discriminating on the basis of sex. Sandler's activism led to the passage of Title IX, a measure inserted in the Education Amendments of 1972 that prohibits sex-based discrimination in any educational program receiving federal funds.

In theory, anyone who had experienced unequal treatment could now file a complaint with the Office for Civil Rights. In practice, their words usually vanished into a folder. While most early complaints addressed hiring practices and athletics, over the following decades, they increasingly came to focus on sexual violence and harassment. In the early '90s, a boom of media coverage addressed date rape on college campuses. When a woman at Brown told a dean that another student raped her, he was assigned to write an apology letter. In response, Brown students wrote the names of men they said were rapists in library bathroom stalls. Following protests at various institutions, the Campus Sexual Assault Victims' Bill of Rights (1992) ordered schools to develop better procedures.

When I was a freshman at Brown in fall 2006, people on my hall swapped drugs and exotic names of New England boarding schools they'd attended—Choate and cocaine, Groton and crushed Adderall—as I selected a sparkly top for my first college night out. I would go on to spend many of my evenings in the same library where (unbeknownst to me) women had once graffitied rape accusations. In the first weeks of school, however, social hierarchies were inchoate and everything seemed possible. After pregaming from red cups, we walked toward a row of brick buildings by the dining hall.

"No, not that one," one of the savvier members of the pack said, laughing tipsily as she pulled us in another direction. "That's the roofie frat."

We assumed that nothing could be done about it.

In 2010, the year I graduated, the Center for Public Integrity released a report about sexual assault on college campuses. Its authors found that Title IX investigations were difficult to obtain, poorly conducted, and usually went nowhere. Many accusers dropped out, while the accused stayed and graduated. Victims, it concluded, "face a depressing litany of barriers that often assure their silence."

The report found a receptive audience in Barack Obama's White House, which created a task force on campus sexual assault. In 2011, the Department of Education's Office for Civil Rights issued a Dear Colleague letter (an official statement providing policy guidance) that charged schools with hiring Title IX coordinators, creating clear investigation procedures, and trying to resolve cases within sixty days. It also instructed investigators to use the "preponderance of evidence" standard applied to most civil claims—determining, in other words, whether a certain behavior was more likely than not to have occurred, rather than trying to prove it "beyond a reasonable doubt" (as in criminal trials, which carry the possibility of jail time). Schools that failed to comply with these guidelines risked losing federal money.

The Dear Colleague letter was a set of expectations without enforcement: no school has ever seen its funding revoked for violating Title IX. After its publication, however, students began drawing attention to their institutions' failure to address sexual violence. After Columbia University declined to punish the man whom she said raped her, art student Emma Sulkowicz lugged her mattress around campus like a padded cross. UNC Chapel Hill students Andrea Pino and Annie Clark made a complaint against their institution with the Office for Civil Rights, which opened a case.

After Pino and Clark were profiled in the *New York Times*, they connected with other students who said they'd been assaulted and encouraged them to file complaints, prompting OCR to launch hundreds of investigations. The movement peaked with the release of *The Hunting Ground* (2015), a documentary about sexual predation and official lethargy on college campuses. Lady Gaga wrote the movie's theme song, "Til It Happens to You," and performed it at the 2016 Academy Awards, where she was joined onstage by dozens of abuse survivors. Among them was Sofie Karasek, a Berkeley student featured in *The Hunting Ground* who cofounded the national organization End Rape on Campus.

According to an article she wrote for the *Huffington Post*, Karasek was a freshman when she felt "sweaty fingers crawling on [her] skin" while sleeping in a room with ten other people on a Berkeley Democrats trip. Afterward, she learned that other women had been sexually assaulted by the same student. They went together to OPHD. After not hearing anything for seven months, Karasek sent a follow-up email, and was told that the situation had been addressed through an "early resolution process." Only after the accused student had graduated did she learn that he had been put on disciplinary probation and "engaged in counseling measures." None of his accusers had been given updates or the opportunity to present evidence.

In 2014, Karasek filed a federal complaint on behalf of more than two dozen current and former Berkeley students that accused the university of deliberate indifference to sexual violence.

"Once you know it's as bad as it is, you don't want to spend your time doing anything else," Karasek told Berkeley's student newspaper. "Your conscience doesn't let you."

Campus activists said that survivors should be believed, and the media seemed to agree. *The Hunting Ground* didn't include any interviews with people accused of assault, except for one man who had done jail time and was shown without a name or a face. In fall 2014, my first semester of graduate school, everyone was discussing "A Rape on Campus," the sensational *Rolling Stone* article about a woman named Jackie who said she'd been gang-raped at a University of Virginia frat house. I knew a few people who went to UVA, and what I'd heard about its good ole boy party culture left me with little doubt that what Jackie said was true. Reporter Sabrina Erdely was equally certain; she didn't speak to any of the men involved, nor to Jackie's friends.

As other journalists looked into the case, they discovered that at least one of the men didn't exist at all, and that Jackie's accounts to Erdely and a friend had been highly inconsistent. *Rolling Stone* retracted the article and lost a defamation lawsuit by Nicole Eramo, a dean whom Jackie said discouraged her from reporting her assault. Some aspects of what Jackie described were real: when OCR released its investigative report on UVA, it said that statements made by Dean Eramo had created a "hostile environment" for victims of sexual violence on campus. The rape, however, wasn't—at least not in Jackie's case. Jackie appears to have lifted key details of her account from a 2011 memoir by Liz Seccuro, who was raped at a UVA frat party in 1984. When Seccuro reported it to the dean of students, the latter suggested that she was lying about consensual sex; university police never followed up. Twenty years later, Seccuro received an apology letter from her rapist and decided to press charges with the Charlottesville police department. After pleading guilty to aggravated sexual battery, her rapist (whom the trial revealed was probably one of several men who assaulted her) served less than six months in jail.

As Daniel and I made our way through teaching and coursework, the bad press at Berkeley got worse. A former student sued philosopher

John Searle and the University of California Regents, saying that she was fired as his research assistant after she rejected his advances. A Buzz-Feed article revealed years of suppressed complaints against Searle. Now, the university finally opened an investigation. In the wake of public condemnation, the harassing Nobel Prize–winning astronomer Geoff Marcy resigned, while Blake Wentworth (who didn't have tenure) was fired. Berkeley law school dean Sujit Choudhry sued the university for racial discrimination when it revisited his sexual harassment of assistant Tyann Sorrell, for which he had initially received a 10 percent pay cut for one year. Choudhry negotiated a settlement that allowed him to stay on for another year without teaching, then quit. Searle eventually lost his emeritus status.

In a belated effort to prevent public embarrassment (and declining donations), Chancellor Dirks tasked an advisory committee with reviewing Berkeley's practices. The administration hired an additional Title IX investigator, created a confidential advocate position that later expanded into the Path to Care Center, and appointed a "special faculty advisor" charged with overseeing the university's supposedly new and improved response to sexual violence. It was too late for Dirks, who stepped down. On July 1, 2017, the day that I left Berkeley, Carol T. Christ became the university's first female chancellor.

At institutions like Berkeley, the cycle had played out again and again. Complaints would emerge and recede as task forces and trainings accumulated like algae on a sunken ship. After decades of scandals and lawsuits, something finally seemed to be changing. Yet professors like Marcy, Choudhry, and Searle were influential men felled by extensive press coverage. Most Title IX cases continued to slip under the radar, and while the media focused on sexual harassment and assault, I'd never seen anything about domestic violence.

<hr />

In the preface to *Requiem*, Anna Akhmatova's poem about Stalin's Terror, she describes standing in line with the other wives and mothers of those who have been taken away. Day after day, they wait on exhausted legs for news that will never come. A woman in the crowd asks if she can describe what is happening to them.

"I can," the poet replies.

"Then, something akin to a smile slipped across what once had been her face."

I think of Akhmatova, a person caught up in considerably more epic events, as I sit in the court restraining order office in Rhode Island. A woman sitting near me is talking about her daughter's violent husband. I look down at the blank affidavit in front of me. I have two pages in which to tell my story well enough for a judge to grant me protection.

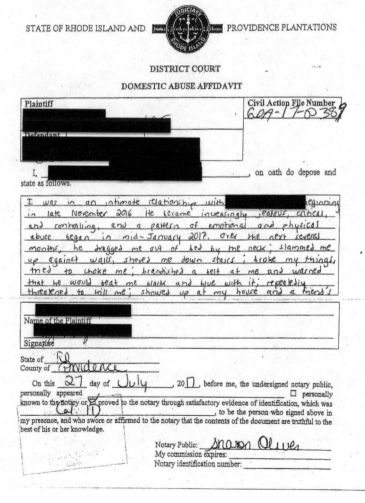

STATE OF RHODE ISLAND AND PROVIDENCE PLANTATIONS

DISTRICT COURT

DOMESTIC ABUSE AFFIDAVIT

Plaintiff

Civil Action File Number
6DA-17-0381

Defendant

I, _____, on oath do depose and state as follows:

I was in an intimate relationship with _____ beginning in late November 2016. He became increasingly jealous, critical, and controlling, and a pattern of emotional and physical abuse began in mid-January 2017. Over the next several months, he dragged me out of bed by the neck; slammed me up against walls, shoved me down stairs; broke my things, tried to choke me; brandished a belt at me and warned that he would beat me black and blue with it; repeatedly threatened to kill me; showed up at my house and a friend's

Name of the Plaintiff

Signature

State of RI
County of Providence

On this 27 day of July, 20 17, before me, the undersigned notary public, personally appeared _____ □ personally known to the notary or ☑ proved to the notary through satisfactory evidence of identification, which was _____ (CA ID), to be the person who signed above in my presence, and who swore or affirmed to the notary that the contents of the document are truthful to the best of his or her knowledge.

Notary Public: Sharon Oliver
My commission expires: _____
Notary identification number: _____

STATE OF RHODE ISLAND AND PROVIDENCE PLANTATIONS

. DISTRICT COURT

DOMESTIC ABUSE AFFIDAVIT

Plaintiff	Civil Action File Number
Defendant	

Continuation page if needed.

house and refused to leave while attempting to forcibly enter; searched for me on the campus of UC Berkeley (where we are both graduate students) and threatened until I left with him, threw alcohol in my face, threw, hid, and tried to break my phone; punched walls; restrained me with his whole body; threatened to kill himself and said it's my fault; locked me in a room and refused to let me out. These things have happened on campus, on the street. at my apartment. at his apartment. On more than one occasion I have been afraid for my life; on more than one occasion I have begged for it. After being physically aggressive, when I attempted to pull away, he would hurt or threaten to hurt himself. On April 30, he sent me a message saying that my abandonment had made him lose the will to live before slitting his wrists in the history department (our workplace) and asking a friend to call and tell me. After the initial apology, there has always been a sustained effort to minimize what happened and to convince me that I deserve to be treated poorly while physically assaulting me, he has repeatedly threatened me not to call the police. At the end of June, after another incident of physical abuse and intense pressure to forgive him, I fled California in fear for my life.

DC-57 (revised November 2014)

My head swims. I used to be a reporter; I'm doing a PhD. Words are what I know. Still, they barely come. Finally, I turn to my phone and open the email I sent to Anna, relying on the typed sentences to guide me.

After glancing at the affidavit, the judge approves a temporary restraining order (TRO) with a court date to decide whether it will be extended into a three-year one. A staff member in the History Department helps me figure out how to serve it to Daniel. The TRO exposes the state I'm staying in, but not my address, and I feel reasonably sure that Daniel wouldn't fly to an unfamiliar city across the country to track me down. He would wait until I came to him.

In the meantime, my Path to Care advocate puts me in touch with a detective at UC Berkeley's police department. The detective tells me that if I file a police report, it could help convince a judge to approve the long-term restraining order. The latter wouldn't be any use while I'm overseas but would at least be in effect when I go back to Berkeley.

Daniel talked a lot about the police. Back when we were friends, he told me about how the cops would cruise around his neighborhood and stop him and other boys when they were looking for a suspect. He said a childhood friend of his had been shot by the police. When we started dating, the cops stopped being a real presence from his past and became a menace that emerged only to intimidate me. Daniel would dare me to call them in the same tone that he told me to go fuck other men.

On my last night in Berkeley, as I bought time to prepare my departure by texting him that I just needed a little longer to be alone, Daniel sent me a photo of a squad car. He claimed he'd just seen a man hit someone with a baseball bat and made a report to the police.

"It's kind of weird to hear about you talking to the cops after the kind of stuff you were yelling at me on Sat," I replied. "But it sounds like it was stressful/scary."

"I don't like cops," he wrote back. "I found it stressful and emotionally wrought. But I was the only witness. I had to do what was right."

The cleavage between right and wrong always seemed to correspond with whatever made him look good.

After I arrive in Providence, Bella and another friend of Daniel's text me that Daniel has been making remarks around the department about how Hannah wants to "lock him up" for being a man of color who struggles with mental illness. I haven't even applied for the TRO yet, but he's already getting in front of the story.

Though I don't want Daniel to be arrested, I do want to create a paper trail in case he hurts me or anyone else again. My complaint to Title IX could vanish into the bowels of the bureaucracy; a police report would be harder to make disappear. I hear Daniel's voice in my head as I wait for the detective to call.

Go ahead and talk to the cops. Tell them how I couldn't possibly live up to the standards of privileged women like you and your friends.

While the people from the Title IX office speak in stiff euphemisms, the detective's tone is casual, in a good-cop way that makes me wary. As we talk, I stare at the red-and-white quilt on my bed in the attic, rearranging its permutations like a chessboard. At the end of a two-hour conversation, I ask what kinds of offenses I've just described. Even though I'm not interested in trying to press charges, and the report I'm filing is only to increase the odds of turning my temporary restraining order into a long-term one, I want to know.

"Felony assault, for starters," the detective replies.

As I head downstairs and stand over the sink washing dishes, I feel a strange sense of relief. All the lies and obfuscations—none of it matters anymore. What I experienced finally has a name, a tidy five-syllable label that I can repeat to myself while scrubbing out a glass.

When I receive a copy of the report, I encounter unfamiliar acronyms and numbers.

The text blocks strip away Daniel's excuses and expose his beliefs (*Bias motivation: anti-female*). I look up the penal codes listed, which address

INCIDENT REPORT

	Agency Name: University of California Berkeley		ORI #: CA0019700	Report Date/Time: 09/25/2017 07:39:52	OCA #: 17-01897	
LOCATION/TIME	Incident Start Date/Time: 01/24/2017 12:00:00	DOW: Tuesday	Report Type: INITIAL	Case Screening: ☐ CHP 180 ☐ Serialized Property ☐ Hate Crime ☐ Evidence Collected ☐ Gang Related ☐ PC 293 Sex Crime ☐ Domestic Viol.	Total Loss $0.00	
	Incident End Date/Time: 06/24/2017 12:00:00	Internal Incident Status: OUTSIDE AGENCY ASSIST				
	Incident Location: ████████████████			Secondary Location: Dwinelle Hall,UC Berkeley		
	Case Description: TMU RELATED	UCR Status:		Reporting Area: BEAT 1 CAMPUS		
				Operation Method:		

	Penal Code: 273.5 (A) PC	UCR Code: 04d.	F/M: F	Penal Code Description: INF CORP INJ ON SPOUSE/COHAB - HANDS/FISTS/FEET	Counts: 2	Comp/Att: ☑ ☐
OFFENSE	Structure OCCUPIED		TOD: Night	Bias Motivation: ANTI-FEMALE	Offense Location: RESIDENCE / HOME	
	Weapon Used:			Situation Code: SINGLE VICTIM / SINGLE OFFENDER	Premise: RESIDENCE (ANYWHERE ON	
	Penal Code: 422 PC	UCR Code: 09	F/M: F	Penal Code Description: Other Assaults	Counts: 2	Comp/Att: ☑ ☐
	Structure OCCUPIED		TOD: Night	Bias Motivation: ANTI-FEMALE	Offense Location: RESIDENCE / HOME	
	Weapon Used:			Situation Code: SINGLE VICTIM / SINGLE OFFENDER	Premise: RESIDENCE (ANYWHERE ON	

domestic violence, chargeable as either a misdemeanor or a felony, and threats to kill. However, the report's blunt wording does not endorse the contents of what I said, which unfolds over the following pages as a "narrative" taken down in the detective's notes. The narrative mentions non-existent witnesses and leaves out major events. I email corrections, which the detective tacks on as a "supplemental narrative." *Let it go*, I tell myself. *It's not like you're actually trying to prove anything.*

As I stand in the shower, hot water blasting over my estranged body, I address Daniel.

No one will know about this police report, I promise. *This is my act of mercy for you.*

A couple of weeks later, I show up in court for the restraining order hearing. In the proceedings before mine, landlords try to evict tenants behind on rent. Though the judge gives people another chance to pay rather than forcing them onto the street, the long-term outlook isn't any less bleak.

When it's my turn, the bailiff, who has a court-jester vibe at odds with the surroundings, jauntily calls out Daniel's name. As I'd hoped, Daniel is nowhere to be seen.

As the judge reads my affidavit, something creases his forehead—either concern for me or irritation I'm in the wrong state. Maybe both.

"Have you reported this to the police in California?"

I say yes. He approves the restraining order.

Back in the attic, I open my computer and see an email from the Title IX investigator. During our intake interview, she says, I mentioned that I might have some documents connected to the case, like texts and Facebook messages.

"Joy, could you forward those documents and any other relevant evidence to me?"

▬▬▬▬

For three years, Daniel and I trained to be historians together. We marked up each other's research papers, quizzed one another for exams, stored our books on adjacent shelves, exchanged notes and reading lists, sat side-by-side in working group meetings. Now we will compete to combine narrative and evidence into a superior version of our shared past.

After downloading message histories onto my computer, I start to scroll through the detritus of the past eight months. At first, my texts with Daniel seem hollow—empty shells stranded far from the sea. As I keep looking at the screen, they fill with fresh life, until I'm immersed in the waters I just escaped.

It's only material, I tell myself, trying to slow my breath. *Review the sources.*

I note down striking quotations and take screenshots of texts, Facebook posts, and phone logs (*April 29: 24 calls from Daniel in a row*). I highlight my assuaging words to him: "I want to show you that there are other ways of doing things, that you have the strength for them." I capture my messages to friends—"He was saying how he realized he just needs to get over jealousy etc."—and their incredulous responses ("'Just needs to get over jealousy' sounds not that hopeful").

My cheeks burn as I read Daniel's constant questions about the sex I had with other men.

"I want to know all of it, in detail," he wrote me, "so that I can take it all in like fuel, have my anger, frustration and sorrow light it up and I can explode into a million little pieces so that I may never be found again."

Yet Daniel was careful not to put anything too damning into writing, and so was I. Though some of my messages to friends said that Daniel insulted me or talked about how I "neglected/betrayed him," I provided few specifics, and framed whatever he had done as an expression of anguish that required my love and support.

February 6, 2:04 p.m. Text to Justine.

"I am thinking more and more about how he really needs mental health help (which he refuses). Something happened this weekend that confirmed that."

I didn't specify what that "something" was, and now I struggle to remember which events took place when.

February 9, 8:38 a.m. Text to Hannah.

"Any chance you're at home?"

"Yes." "What's up."

"Can I stop by."

"Yes come."

"It's ok, I deescalated."

"What's happening." "Are you safe?"

"We had an intense conversation, just wanted to know you were there."

I must have been afraid that morning, but I have no idea why.

After Daniel was violent to me on April 29, I texted Hannah that he damaged my things, but said nothing about how he harmed me. My censorship was precise; I even commented on it. When I talked to Alexander right after Daniel was taken to the psych ward, I told Hannah that "I really wanted not to demonize [Daniel] or make it about conflicts we've had, so I didn't really say anything about how he has treated me." Hannah reassured me that Alexander "knows [Daniel] has been abusive toward you."

After I started seeing the domestic violence counselor, my messages to Daniel began to refer to how I had been "hurt" and felt "fear," how I needed "boundaries" to ensure that "these moments" "will never be repeated." Daniel didn't admit to anything:

"After walking home early because I felt alone and alienated, I am treated to this. Thank you and goodnight."

Within days we were back together, and my attempts at self-assertion ceased.

———

In a seminar that Daniel and I took with Alexander, we read *Revolution on My Mind*, a book about Soviet diaries written under Stalin. Author Jochen Hellbeck, who also wrote the article about how Bukharin tried to justify his persecution, quoted enthusiastic entries by various people— a worker who aspired to be an intellectual, the wife of an esteemed engineer—who strove to bring revolutionary ideals to life. Another historian, perhaps more partial to Cold War thinking, might have read the same materials and concluded that Soviet citizens were brainwashed, or too afraid to admit their thoughts even to themselves. Hellbeck, however, framed their words as sincere efforts to align their souls with the spirit of history.

With the untested certainty of a third-semester grad student, I wrote a paper that critiqued his approach. "Hellbeck remarks that it is important not to quote diaries out of context, as vital content may be missing," I observed. "But in surrounding fragmented lines with a profusion of commentary, the book is reluctant to let readers form alternative interpretations." I argued that "such interpretations are not only possible, but necessary."

Though I didn't keep a diary during my relationship with Daniel, my phone became a similar stage for harmonizing dissonant impulses and purging the heresy in my head. To Daniel, I professed a devotion that in my messages to friends was tempered with panic and frustration. For all my audiences, however, I sought to present Daniel as sympathetically as possible. My mission to preserve our collective of two was antithetical to my current aim of assembling a case against him. My most eloquent opponent is my past self.

After a couple of weeks, I have fat files of screenshots but don't know how to make them cohere into an account. I worry whether they're enough to keep moving the case forward. The investigator is the historian here; all I can do is try to guide her hand. So, I surround fragmented lines with a profusion of commentary, starting with the first message I find that suggests there is something amiss.

December 16, 2016. Text from Daniel.

"It's 7. Did you run off with one of your white men? Knew this would happen."

"Haha we got to talking ☺. Heading to you from starry plough!"

Above this exchange, I explain what was happening at the time—"I was having a drink with [Hannah] and had agreed to come to his house around 7 pm"—and what it will come to mean later: "After Daniel and I began dating, he became fixated on imagining me with men I had gone out with in the past. Initially, this was presented as a problem that he was struggling with and would soon overcome. However, the narrative rapidly shifted to accusations that I was a whore."

I arrange all the shots in chronological order and accompany them with captions that identify context and key themes ("jealousy," "controlling behavior," "stalking," "threats"). I end on my recent text exchange with Bella in which she said that Daniel was still planning to follow me abroad.

I'm not sure who's more sincere—my past self, professing my love and admiration for Daniel while hiding how he harmed me, or my present one, trying to excise my affection and show only hurt.

———

My family has rented a beach house for August vacation. I sit next to a sluggish fan that blows hot air in my face. Boats drift past the window unnoticed as I stare at the texts on my computer screen. All I can think about is the case. My moments away from it are spent reading books like *The Gift of Fear*, on how to avoid danger through the magic of intuition (the same intuition that was so wrong about Daniel. Can it be fixed?). At dinner, I start crying over my corn on the cob. My brother's girlfriend politely looks away. She did not sign up for this.

Information keeps getting back to me from Berkeley that women graduate students I know are supporting Daniel. I can't blame them; they've seen his cries for help in our community Facebook group. It stings anyway. Hannah tells Carol, the PhD student who moderates the group, that Daniel is under investigation for domestic violence and asks her to ban him. Carol has a sweet, broad smile that exposes her gums. Daniel told me he likes her because she seems so inexperienced, unlike me.

"Innocent until proven guilty," Carol says.

Daniel stays in the group.

In Charlottesville, a man rams his car into a crowd of demonstrators, killing one person and injuring several more. They'd been protesting the Unite the Right rally, where men carrying swastikas and Confederate flags chanted "You will not replace us." My first impulse is to text Daniel about it, before I remember that we're not speaking anymore.

Though the evidence file has become my main assignment, in a few weeks I'm supposed to fly to Moscow to study the lives of people far removed from my own. To prepare for this project, I consult with Anna. When she returns my research outline with comments, she observes that a solar eclipse is underway.

"An auspicious sign for your dissertation about the end of times?"

My dissertation studies the generation of artists, singers, and writers who were born under Stalin and came of age during the thaw after his death. By the 1970s, as their youthful optimism faded and the political climate cooled, some of them produced morbid depictions of Soviet life before dying, one by one, until the country collapsed. I will read their diaries and letters to try to understand how life shaped art and art became a template for life. The archival materials I gather will "tilt everything a little bit," Anna says when we talk over the phone.

"You're going to present people we think we know well in a new light."

Death comes for all of us, she observes, but when individual losses are viewed in aggregate, they form constellations that reveal something bigger about a particular time and place. She suggests that my project is really about the death of the intelligentsia, the bespectacled class that considered itself the champion of the people, "since its essential feature—conscience—had been stripped away from it."

Although I've decided not to mention my Title IX case to Anna, I bring it up with Alexander. To make sure he understands that Daniel is dangerous, I email him a domestic violence safety checklist with a note that says Daniel meets nine of the eleven criteria for "elevated risk of serious injury or lethality" and that it's important we continue not to be in the same area.

"This is frightening to read," Alexander says. "Your decision makes perfect sense."

I feel embarrassed by my overexposure.

"I look forward to the day when all of this will hopefully be a distant memory!" I reply.

▬▬▬▬▬

Back in Cassandra's attic, I'm starting to pack my suitcase for Moscow when I see a headline on CNN: "Education Department withdraws Obama-era sexual assault guidance."

Trump's secretary of education Betsy DeVos, a major Republican donor and billionaire proponent of for-profit education, is realizing the Republican Party's 2016 campaign platform, which condemned the Obama administration's attempt to "micromanage the way colleges and universities deal with allegations of abuse." DeVos's pick to head the Education Department's Office for Civil Rights was Candice E. Jackson, a conservative lawyer and activist who tried to discredit the women accusing Trump of sexual assault as "fake victims." For months, DeVos and Jackson have been meeting with accused students, their parents, and men's rights organizations who claim that campuses are rife with bogus complaints.

This development has been brewing for several years. After the UVA rape story was debunked, it was touted by misogynist groups, as well as mainstream journalists and academics, who argued that the "campus rape epidemic" was imaginary and that flimsy stories were ruining the lives of innocent men. *Slate* reporter Emily Yoffe wrote that students accused of sexual violence now encounter a "Soviet-style show trial" in which their guilt is preordained by administrators who "default to calling for the accused's head." The American Association of University Professors published an article presenting Title IX as a threat to free speech and due process. Like all critics, they said that the "preponderance of evidence" standard is unfairly weighted in favor of accusers.

Media coverage of Title IX often repeats this claim. In the *New Yorker*, Harvard Law professor Jeannie Suk Gersen criticizes Title IX's "overreach" and lack of "fair process," especially for the accused, in an approving article about a book called *Unwanted Advances: Sexual Paranoia Comes to Campus*. According to its author Laura Kipnis, a film studies professor at Northwestern, Title IX is "officially sanctioned hysteria"—a hellscape of "overblown" allegations and "rigged" investigations comparable to the Salem witch trials and McCarthyism. The book grew out of two essays that Kipnis wrote for the *Chronicle of Higher Education*. After the publication of the first, which criticized the accusers in a case against Northwestern philosophy professor Peter Ludlow, two students filed complaints that Kipnis had violated Title IX's no-retaliation policy. Kipnis described the experience in a follow-up piece called "My Title IX Inquisition."

A masochistic desire to know what I'm up against compels me to download *Unwanted Advances*. According to Kipnis, thin-skinned female students are now "deploying Title IX to remedy sexual ambivalences or awkward sexual experiences, and to adjudicate relationship disputes post-breakup." In doing so, they exemplify a sinister new breed of feminism that casts women as damsels in distress. On the basis of emails that she received after her *Chronicle* essays came out, Kipnis concludes that respondents typically don't know who their accusers are (or even what they're being accused of) or get the chance to present any evidence or witnesses in their defense. Yet in the cases she examines at length, the accused are given ample opportunity to present their side and are found "not responsible" for some or all of the allegations against them. Kipnis herself was found not responsible, in a report that impressed her with its meticulousness; she remarks that the investigators had clearly "bent over backward to clear [her]." In Ludlow's case, the Title IX office made no finding on a graduate student's rape allegation. While the investigator concluded that Ludlow made "unwelcome advances" to a college freshman whom he had given alcohol, they were unable to determine whether he sexually assaulted her. Though in Kipnis's rendering, Ludlow was "burned at the stake," he actually resigned before the university reached any decision about his employment.

After leaving Northwestern, Ludlow sent Kipnis his case files. She interprets the evidence in the same way that I fear the CRO will read mine. Accusing the freshman of "A Selective Approach to Facts," Kipnis points to an enthusiastic email the student sent Ludlow and photos in which she looks "relaxed and happy," as if this meant that she agreed to whatever happened later. After introducing details from the student's sex life to depict her as promiscuous and mentioning a shoplifting conviction to imply that she was looking for money, Kipnis floats an armchair diagnosis of histrionic personality disorder. Kipnis subjects the "hysterical" grad student accuser to similar scrutiny, quoting loving texts this student sent Ludlow to suggest that any sex between them was consensual. As definitive confirmation, Kipnis quotes a female friend of Ludlow's, a fellow professor who was not present for the event in question but spoke in his defense at a hearing. Ludlow's friend rooted her certainty that he hadn't done anything wrong in her own experience of sexual violence: "If Peter had a predator bone in his body, I would know it."

Everyone wants to think they know what their friends and colleagues are capable of; this illusion of certainty makes the world seem safe. Yet an unfounded assumption is not a sign of enlightenment. While Kipnis writes that "exculpating evidence" (like affectionate messages, smiling photos, and skeptical statements by acquaintances) is unfairly ignored, the investigator in Ludlow's case was correct not to see such material as proof that nothing happened. Even so, they were unable to substantiate the accusers' central claims. For complainants like me, this outcome sends a clear signal: *give up.*

While I silently fume at my screen, views like Kipnis's are already in power. After Trump's election, the attitude that the system is deeply biased in favor of accusers became the official viewpoint of his administration. According to Jackson, Title IX cases have been destroying young men's lives for no reason. "90 percent" of complaints, she told the *New York Times*, "fall in the category of 'we were both drunk,' 'we broke up, and six months later I found myself under a Title IX investigation because she just decided that our last sleeping together was not quite right.'" In a speech at George Mason University, DeVos equated victims of sexual violence with "victims of a lack of due process," while focusing her concern on the latter. DeVos described an accused student who told her that he tried to take his own life after he was suspended and banned from campus without being informed of the allegations against him. "Whatever your accusers say you are is what people believe you are," he told DeVos.

Though the Dear Colleague letter called for information to be shared equally with complainants and respondents and for both sides to have the same opportunities to present evidence and witnesses, DeVos quoted a school administrator who said that Obama's Office for Civil Rights had "terrified" schools into implementing unjust procedures. The Trump administration, she has announced today, will be creating a new set of rules that ensure "due process." I have no idea what that means but am convinced of one thing: my case is more hopeless than ever.

9

THE FLOOD

O N A WARM SEPTEMBER AFTERNOON, I TAKE OFF FOR MOSCOW. MY seatmate on Aeroflot is an older Georgian woman who has been visiting her son in the US. She tells me that her father was in the Soviet secret police under Stalin. As we lower our tray tables and proceed through her life history, she says that when she was studying at Moscow State University in the '50s, she had a stalker. She informed the leader of the local Komsomol, the communist youth organization, who told the man to stay away from her. Evidently, he complied. As I describe my dissertation, I mention the name of a writer and director I plan to research.

"I never liked him," she says. "He beat his wives."

At the end of the flight, she writes her phone number down on a piece of paper and urges me to come over for cheese pies. Caught up in my research and the investigation, I leave the paper at the bottom of my backpack, where it eventually disappears.

I rent an apartment on the top floor of a high-rise, across the river from the Kremlin and around the corner from a candy factory. The smell of chocolate wafts over the dome of the pink-and-white Orthodox church next door. Though Stalin ordered most places of worship in the city to be destroyed, this one survived. The church's iron bells strike back and forth, up and down, in a rhythm that resounds like the drop of a gallows.

Every morning I walk across the water to the Russian State Library. By the entrance, a stooped Dostoyevsky statue sits under a wreath of pigeons. The building was erected as a palace of knowledge for the victorious proletariat, and most people still call it "Leninka," after the founding father for whom it was originally named. At the top of a grand marble staircase, librarians slip book requests into pneumatic tubes that suck them to other floors for retrieval. Under the glow of the library's chandeliers, I feel safe.

As I ruminate over whether my case will go anywhere, I start reconsidering my refusal to press charges. On the first night he shoved me, Daniel told me that he once pushed an ex-girlfriend and pinned her to the ground (and that she had ruined their relationship by holding it over his head). I don't know what else he did to her, and no record exists to warn whoever might be next. As the miles between us grow, I think more about what keeping Daniel's secrets might cost other women. I decide to contact the detective again.

When I'm done assembling my evidence file, the detective tells me to send it to him and says that he'll try taking it to the district attorney. I should hold off on showing it to the Title IX office: whatever I submit, Daniel will see.

"Information is advantage," the detective says. "The less he knows about what you have, the better."

A few weeks later, he emails me:

"The DA's concern when I spoke to him is that while [Daniel] clearly has an anger management problem, the DA did not feel that he could prove beyond a reasonable doubt that [Daniel] has been violent to you."

In cases of sexual and domestic abuse, there are rarely any eyewitnesses or material artifacts. Even bruises or broken bones can be dismissed as the result of an argument in which both sides share blame, or the consensual effects of rough sex. "He said, she said"—who's to say? Some of the students interviewed for the Center for Public Integrity report on Title IX said they took their cases to the police and were turned away. Most never try at all. Prosecutors want a slam dunk, and these victims are too far from the net. *Fort/da*: the grief is ours to throw back and forth.

According to the state of California, nothing happened to me at all, or at least nothing that would convince a jury. No one outside our inner circle will know what Daniel has done and could do again. The label of "felony assault" is a sign with nothing to signify. Title IX, with its lame administrative language and lower burden of proof, is my only shot at proving what took place and protecting others.

I send OPHD my evidence file.

━━━━━━━

The day before Daniel's first interview is supposed to happen, I receive an email from the investigator informing me that it has been canceled. The Respondent recently secured an "advisor," she says, who needs time to get acquainted with the case before attending the interview.

In the Title IX system, both complainants and respondents are allowed to have an "advisor," who counsels them on their case and is often an attorney, as well as a "support person," whose assistance is more emotional than procedural. I look up Daniel's advisor and discover that he's a criminal defense lawyer. Daniel is telling people we know that his legal fees are being covered by a literature professor at Berkeley, the one he called his "guardian angel." I feel foolish: I've already given multiple interviews and submitted evidence without any representation. Though the case has barely started, the stakes keep rising.

At Daniel's lawyer's request, OPHD issues an updated notice of allegations with specific dates and more extensive details for each "incident of concern," so that Daniel knows everything he is being accused of and can fully prepare his answers. Meanwhile, the CRO has already started reaching out to our friends and professors, inviting them to talk.

When Alexander is in Moscow for a few days, we meet for lunch, and mostly discuss Russian culture and politics. We concur that fears of Vladimir Putin's desire for world domination are misplaced. According to Alexander, Putin is not a zealot on some mystical crusade to unite the

Russian Orthodox world and rebuild an empire; he's a pragmatic head of state. I nod and agree.

Toward the end of our conversation, I mention the Title IX case.

"Surely they won't let him come back?" Alexander says. I tell him I don't know.

As we put on our coats and walk to the metro in the weak afternoon sun, I remember the moment when I ran down the steps of Doe Library and spotted Alexander standing next to Daniel, whom he'd intercepted before Daniel was able to come in and find me. Now, as Alexander and I hug goodbye, I flush with reverence for him. Though Alexander's comments about the situation have been characteristically taciturn, I feel certain that he's on my side. If I have the support of the great mind that Daniel and I admired, then what I'm doing must be right.

When Alexander's current and former students nominate him for a lifetime achievement award from our professional association, I draft my contribution to a collective support statement.

"When his students encounter difficult life events of all kinds, Alexander responds with sympathy and grace. No matter the situation, hour, or geographic location, he rises to the occasion with an exceedingly rare combination of unflappable calm, profound compassion, and practical support.

"Never impressing his own ideas on others, Alexander truly wants all of his students to be the best version of themselves."

—————

Shortly after I submit my evidence to OPHD, my personal reckoning coincides with a societal one. In October 2017, the *New York Times* publishes an exposé of producer Harvey Weinstein's history of sexual harassment and assault, and the hashtag #MeToo spreads on Twitter. Suddenly, the media is awash with complaints that feel like a belated outpouring of anger against Trump, who was elected despite his boasts about groping. Diverse stories share the common premise that violence is at the foundation of an order that denies power to women, who can be trusted as accurate narrators of nightmares no one else has seen. Like the Title IX

movement that preceded it, MeToo encourages accounts of sexual violence to be aired on social media and leaked to the press. "Let This Flood
of Women's Stories Never Cease," proclaims an article by Rebecca Solnit.
I eagerly read and share.

At the Russian state library, I pick up my reading material and head to
a table under a sculpture of a contemplative Lenin engrossed in a book.
An older man wearing thick glasses steps in my path.

"Excuse me, young lady," he says. "Would you like to accompany me
on a date? Perhaps to a club?"

It's 10 a.m.

Since leaving Daniel I've avoided contact with men. On the street
I try to gauge their concealed essence, the charge they leave behind in
the air. Whenever I'm alone with one—in a cab, an elevator, a building
entrance—my pulse spikes until I can get away. I shake my head at the
man in glasses and walk to another table across the room. He disappears.
But like so many people in these early weeks of MeToo, before brushing
it off and moving on, I think about all the other incursions on my body
and mind that began before I hit puberty, the energy I've put into determining whether someone is a threat and revisiting initial assessments
that turned out to be incorrect, the efforts to untangle whether I actually
wanted something or manufactured desire to match someone else's.

A friend sends me a link to a Google spreadsheet about abuse at universities. Institutions are named, while individuals remain anonymous.
We suspect that one unidentified professor at Berkeley, described as having disparaged a graduate student to his colleagues after she refused to
sleep with him at a conference, is someone we know. I contribute a couple
of lines about "domestic violence committed by a male graduate student
in my department."

For me and my friends in academia, MeToo hardens our sense that
personal misbehavior is related to intellectual output into a conviction
that no one should have to put up with it anymore. We text each other
images of Judith slaying Holofernes, a story excluded from the Bible in
which an Israelite beheads an Assyrian general while he's passed out
drunk. In the baroque artist Artemisia Gentileschi's rendition, widely

seen as the painter's revenge against her own rapist, Judith appears with an arched eyebrow, faintly repulsed by the mess as she plunges a sword into the tyrant's throat. My friends and I joke that we should print the image on T-shirts and wear them to this year's Slavic studies conference.

I receive an apology email from Bella, whom Daniel asked to accompany him to OPHD on the day he received the Notice of Allegations. When she confronted Daniel about what was written in the notice, he denied everything. Now she says she's decided to block him on social media and is sorry if she enabled him.

Under the sway of the moment, someone has finally turned the corner on Daniel. I wonder if anyone else will follow.

In the first weeks of the investigation, I check my email all the time. To reduce the adrenaline that pumps through my body and leaves me unable to work or sleep, I eventually direct OPHD's messages to a hidden folder that I open only in the morning. Every sixty days, I look expectantly for the required update on the investigation's status. Every sixty days, I close it in disappointment. The reasons vary, but the result stays the same:

Additional time is needed to investigate this case.

The temperature falls and the days grow shorter, until a narrow slit of light opens over Moscow before it descends back into gloom. At the end of the year, the investigator informs me that she is still reviewing "large volumes" of evidence submitted by both sides and interviewing witnesses. After my intake interview, I'd suggested that she speak with my close friends, who have already told me that she's reached out, as well as a couple of Daniel's, including Evan. Though Daniel's friends knew much less about our relationship as it was unfolding, I did share some details with them before and after leaving Berkeley and hope they might help corroborate what I told OPHD. I still don't know what names Daniel has submitted, or whom else the investigator has decided to contact.

In my next interview, the investigator says, I will be asked to respond to information that contradicts my statements. "An example would be,

Complainant said the car was red but two witnesses said the car was yellow." Both Daniel and I will be able to submit cross-examination questions for the other side, which the investigator will pose if she deems them relevant. This measure, she says, was "recently implemented to ensure due process." Though DeVos's Education Department has yet to issue its new guidelines, universities are preemptively adjusting their procedures to what they expect the Trump administration will require.

After Daniel hired a lawyer, I discovered that UC Berkeley has a contract with a domestic violence nonprofit in Oakland. One of their attorneys, Issa, has agreed to give me pro bono legal advice. Though "advisors" are not allowed to speak on our behalf, they can suggest what to say. Issa prepares cross-examination questions, grouped according to potential violations of university policy like "sexual harassment" and "relationship violence," that try to pin Daniel's words to what I've described.

Isn't it true you texted Complainant telling her that "we shouldn't be together anymore" due to her past relationships with other men? Were you writing her to end the relationship, and if so, why did you continue contacting her?

Before my interview, the investigator emails me a long list of messages I submitted that she plans to include in the report. Issa is worried that the messages highlight my willingness to talk to Daniel and my concern for him. She brainstorms the kind of undermining questions I might be asked so that I won't be taken by surprise.

If Respondent said he was done with the relationship, why did you continue?
If you felt uncomfortable with Respondent, why did you agree to have lunch?
If you were scared, why did you ask where he was and meet with him?

How easy it is to sow doubt around my story with my own words. How hard it is to prove that love can hold dread, like a worm in an apple core.

━━━━━

Resurgent feminism defeats patriarchy—or so runs the headline in my head when Weinstein is arrested. But Trump and his allies are still in power, while MeToo is summoning criticism that it is not as progressive as it appears. Roxane Gay, among other women of color, observes how credibility is unevenly distributed and that the wealthy white celebrities who became the faces of the movement obscure others from view. This reproach wants to extend support to more survivors. Another vein of commentary, however, joins the backlash against Title IX from the perspective of the accused. Instead of standing with Judith, it wants justice for Holofernes.

In an article calling MeToo a "moral panic" that equates accusation with guilt, *New Yorker* staff writer Masha Gessen conflates the movement with Title IX's preponderance of the evidence standard, which is supposedly "eliminating the presumption of innocence." As someone who's growing familiar with the system from the inside, I spot inaccuracies in the article: it states that the preponderance standard was an order by Obama's Justice Department, rather than a recommendation from the Department of Education's Office for Civil Rights, and that the previous standard was the criminal justice system's "beyond a reasonable doubt," when in fact "preponderance of evidence" was already used by most schools. While Title IX's critics fault its supporters for replacing informed assessment with superficial outrage, it seems to me that they do the same.

MeToo spreads to the White House when Trump aide Rob Porter and speechwriter David Sorensen are accused of domestic violence. During an FBI background check, both of Porter's ex-wives reported that he abused them. One of them said he shoved and pinned her down, punched her in the face, and choked her. Published photos show her with a black eye. Sorensen's ex-wife produces screenshots of berating messages and a photo of a burn from a cigarette that she says he put out on her hand. Porter condemns his former spouses' "vile claims" and says that the photos have a "reality behind them [that] is nowhere close to what is being described." Sorensen says that he has never hurt a woman and that he was the one being abused.

Though Trump remains untouchable, both Porter and Sorensen resign. The president defends them with a familiar refrain. "Peoples lives are being shattered and destroyed by a mere allegation," Trump tweets.

"Is there no such thing any longer as Due Process?"

Late in the evening Moscow time, I log on to a video chat. I am about to be confronted with what Daniel has been saying—his rendition of the past versus mine. The investigator reads from a list of questions while someone else takes notes. She speaks, as always, in monotone.

Respondent says that you initiated the relationship. Is this true?

I say that I did tell him I had feelings for him, and that a few days later, we slept together. Not long afterward he said he was glad it had happened.

Is it true that you flew to California over winter break because you wanted to see Respondent after he said he wanted to take a break?

Is it true that you visited Respondent in the psych ward?

I admit it all and try to explain.

The investigator recites Respondent's version of various incidents listed in the notice of allegations. He never dragged me out of bed by the neck, never tried to choke me, never slammed me against a wall, never threatened to kill me. I was never scared of him in Berkeley or Texas, nor had any reason to be. He was the one in pain. On a handful of occasions, he touched me in self-defense, or in reaction to my callousness.

Respondent told me that there was one instance when he did put his hands on your face and neck. It happened at Respondent's apartment in February 2017. Respondent remembered he was recounting his October 2016 suicide attempt while you two were laying down in bed. Respondent remembered telling you, "You didn't do anything to help me. No one cared. No one was there." You replied, "That isn't true." In response, Respondent reached over and grabbed your lower jaw.

I explain that, as far as I know, he never tried to kill himself in October; he told me later that he thought about it, and only mentioned it once we started dating when he wanted to make me feel guilty about dating other men. He didn't grab my jaw like that, I tell her—I have no idea what he's talking about. I remember him screaming at me and throwing my books on the ground when we discussed it.

Respondent denied pushing you down a flight of stairs. He says you were walking toward Dwinelle and arguing about why you didn't call him the night of his October 2016 suicide attempt. He told you repeatedly, "I was dying, I was dying."

"None of this is true. He was calling me a whore and said that I'm so disgusting no one should touch me. And he was not even talking about the October situation. It was a Saturday night. We were having dinner and he went on a rant. He said, 'I bet Saturday night was the night you went on all your dates.'" I describe how it continued to build from there as we walked back to campus and he repeatedly mentioned me sleeping with other men.

Respondent said you were walking and arguing; Respondent wanted to walk away but you continued to follow close behind him. You were following Respondent closely, and he turned and pushed you back and away from him. At the time of the push, you two were at the bottom of the stairs outside the building.

"None of that is true."

Respondent described the push as "More of a 'get away' kind of push back." Respondent said he didn't extend his arms.

"That's not true. He shoved me hard with his strength."

Respondent said you continued arguing as you walked up the stairs. You started to reconcile and talk it over once you reached the top of the stairs.

No, I say, we did not. He was very angry.

Respondent denied observing you from the bushes when you went inside.

"That's what he said he had been doing and he knew what I was doing inside the building so, I'm sure that is what he was doing."

Respondent denied telling you, "If you call the police you will know what real violence is." Respondent told me that he remembered saying that if you wanted to call the police, Respondent would call them for you.

"That's actually funny but that is absolutely not what he said."

Respondent said you were at a bar, you both were inebriated and started to argue. Respondent denied refusing to let you leave the hotel room. At the end of the night, you said that you wanted to sleep outside, and Respondent said, "No, why do you want to sleep outside? Stay in here."

"He's lying," I say, over and over, repeating what I said before, hoping that the details haven't shifted in my mind in the intervening months.

Only one question trips me up.

Respondent says you agreed with him that Hannah was overreacting in her belief that Respondent posed a threat to her.

It's the kind of thing I said to appease Daniel. I'm not sure how to explain that I would agree to anything in hopes of smothering his fury. Instead, I equivocate.

"I don't know, but I doubt I said Hannah was overreacting."

For the final round of questions, the investigator pulls out a color photocopy. I recognize my own handwriting, blown up several hundred percent. It's the goodbye letter I left Daniel.

Did you write Respondent this letter?

"Yes."

Respondent told me that he did not understand what you meant by this statement: "Next time I might not be so lucky. You might not be so lucky."

"I meant that he might seriously injure or kill me. And it was possible that he might injure himself, which he had threatened to do."

At the end of the interview, she thanks me for my time. Respondent and his attorney have not submitted any questions for me. The sooner my stories dry up, the better.

10

SWEET AS ALWAYS

WHILE THE INVESTIGATOR REVIEWS MY MESSAGES, I READ OTHER people's letters. In Moscow's libraries and archives, I resume the voyeuristic position of the historian, studying another time and place from a safe remove.

That's how I find Liza.

I encounter her for the first time while researching her husband, Oleg Dal, an actor who specialized in playing misanthropic men.

Oleg met Liza Apraksina in 1969, on the set of a *King Lear* adaptation. He was playing the Fool, and she was a film editor who cut the celluloid and assembled it into scenes. Actors wandered in and out of the editing room to watch the footage that had been shot that day. Oleg's jester was an ethereal, emaciated sage; the film's director said he looked like "a boy from Auschwitz." Liza was entranced by this man with high cheekbones and a haunted gaze. She was already being romanced by the writer Sergei Dovlatov, but when both men came to her family's apartment, it was Oleg whom she asked to stay the night.

Oleg and Liza came from different worlds. He was the son of a school-teacher and an engineer who hailed from Moscow's industrial outskirts, while she was born to the old literary intelligentsia in Leningrad. She grew up to work at Lenfilm, one of the Soviet Union's top studios.

Marx and Engels had seen the family as a site of exploitation and thought it should be destroyed together with private property. After the October Revolution, the Bolsheviks made men and women equal in law, and feminist Alexandra Kollontai called for the public raising of children and open relationships. But the prospect of female emancipation aroused anxiety among a political establishment that was still almost entirely composed of men. Under Stalin, the Soviet women's department was disbanded, and the "woman question" supposedly resolved.

By the 1960s, after Stalin's death, women had entered the workforce in record numbers, but stayed at the bottom of the ladder and continued to do most of the labor at home. The state did not tolerate any serious criticism of their inequality—purportedly a bourgeois Western problem. According to sociologists, exerting a proper feminine influence would keep irresponsible husbands in check and reinvigorate their flagging masculinity.

In her letters, Liza dubbed Oleg "your eminence" and extolled his growing fame: "Everywhere I hear: Dal, Dal!" He played her his favorite Coltrane records and told her that she relieved his sadness.

"I predict you will experience incredible torments with me," he wrote to her in a letter. "But love me! I need you. I need your shoulder; for I am a poor fellow [*bedolaga*] and a spineless madman."

Once they got engaged, Oleg insisted that Liza stop working, move to Moscow, and dedicate herself to taking care of him.

"By serving me," he said, "you'll be of more use to Soviet cinema than you are sitting at an editing table."

Liza complied. She accompanied him to movie sets, cooked his meals, knitted him sweaters, and stroked his ego. Oleg's career was struggling due to the unpredictable censorship that regulated the Soviet culture industry: several of his movies were filmed and completed, only to be found ideologically unsuitable and pulled from mass distribution. He still felt better than his peers—"I'm disappointed by actors and the theater in general," he wrote in his diary—and the population as a whole, whom he called "uncivilized cattle." Liza agreed that he was underappreciated. Oleg was a "diamond," she said, and her job was to be a "worthy setting" for his talent.

These details come from Liza's brief descriptions of their marriage, which appear as italicized notes in several edited volumes about Dal's life and work I find at Leninka. I skim through excerpts from their early love letters and make a note in my Word document: "correspondence with wife, not very interesting." It's an overcast December afternoon. My stomach is full of meatballs from the cafeteria downstairs, Lenin is reading the same page in perpetuity at the front of the room, and I'm getting drowsy. As I keep perusing, I come across a few paragraphs by Liza's mother, Olga Eikhenbaum. Liza was completely devoted to her husband, Olga says, but Oleg "turned into an animal" when he was drunk. On one occasion, for example, he "lightly strangled her."

I sit up and reread the sentence.

At the time, Liza was still living with her mother in Leningrad. When Oleg choked her, she managed to break free and run up to the attic of their apartment, where she hid until her mother came home. When Olga finally walked in, Oleg was sleeping peacefully. Liza told her mother that she had almost died.

"I thought that was it, he was going to kill me," she said.

Olga asked her why she had run to the attic. Liza replied that she had nowhere else to go.

Liza's mother never said anything to Oleg about the incident. She wrote that there was at least one other occasion when her daughter "saved herself by running"; this time, Liza left behind her wedding ring. Olga also mentions that a few years later they came close to divorcing but didn't. No further details were provided, here or in any other source.

Blood is rushing to my head, the soporific spell of the library broken. A few months ago, I ran away from a man who "lightly strangled" me. Now I'm sitting in Moscow, reading about a woman who did the same decades earlier. Unlike me, however, Liza kept going back. Her story seems like a strange mirror of my own, an alternative version of my life if I had played the role that Daniel had chosen for me. When we were together, I sometimes felt as if I were in the ocean, sinking to depths that no one would ever see or hear. After I leave, my thoughts keep returning to the people who stayed underwater.

I'm so sorry I left you, I think, *I'm so sorry.*

I tell myself that I need to know more about Oleg for my dissertation, but an invisible thread pulls me toward Liza. I learn that his personal archive is held in a theater museum. The museum was founded by a Moscow merchant in the late nineteenth century. Its wood-paneled rooms are filled with items that once transformed their wearers into someone else: an ostrich-feather fan held together by pieces of ivory; a flowing fur coat worn to dance the role of Anna Karenina; sketches of a blocky red-and-white costume for an unrealized production of *We*, Yevgeny Zamiatin's dystopian satire of groupthink. After wandering through the display, I present my documents to the museum's administration and walk up the back stairs to a small room on the second floor, where I fill out a paper order slip. A few minutes later, an archivist arrives with a trolley cart full of files.

For the next two weeks, I return every morning to this dimly lit room, wearing a scarf to stave off the cold. I read Oleg's notebooks and the drafts of his poems and short stories. The ill-tempered actor incarnated his characters. In an unpublished essay, he compared himself to "a person who is dying a strange, awkward, funny, and stupid death in a dirty wooden public toilet as he falls through the rotting floor onto a century-old pile of shit and drowns in it." His bile seeped into his work calendar: "Swine!!" "The same fuckery." "Idiots!" "Whores!" Oleg dreamed of living among the geniuses of centuries past ("Tolstoy and Chekhov, Shakespeare and Dostoyevsky . . .") and predicted that all too soon he would join them beyond the grave. I flip through the pages, looking for Liza.

I find her in a file box holding letters and postcards she sent to her mother. She wrote from film sets in Crimea, vacations in the Caucasus, and her new Moscow apartment. As my fingers turn the yellowed paper, my mind walks outside and turns onto the Garden Ring, the highway that encloses central Moscow. The B trolleybus, nicknamed the "bug," travels around the ring like the hand of a clockface. The sky brightens and darkens as the earth reverses its rotations around the sun until I no longer exist. Liza's story has taken over.

Moscow, summer 1977. Liza catches the B bus on her way home. White puffs waft through the air in the late afternoon sun—fluff from the poplar trees that Stalin planted around the city. Every June they unleash millions of seeds that float on the wind like summer snow. One of them lands in her brown hair, and she brushes it off as she steps aboard. She is carrying the collapsible string bag that she keeps with her in case of an impulse purchase. If sausage is in the shop today, it might be gone tomorrow. Today the bag is bulging with chanterelles, which have just begun to appear at the market.

Liza feels faint in the heat. She recently read that Chekhov, a medical doctor as well as a writer, advised consuming as little as possible to preserve one's health. To manage cravings, he suggested drinking a glass of milk, which is the only thing that she has had today. Oleg barely eats at all. She realized how thin he was the first time he showed up in the editing room, bones visible beneath his skin in a frame as light as poplar fluff. It is her duty to keep him from blowing away.

The doors close and a network of electrical wires propel her forward around the ring, past the triumphal arch that marks the entrance of Gorky Park. The canals of her childhood were winding and intimate; she can't get used to Moscow's superhuman scale. As the trolleybus heaves across the suspension bridge that straddles the banks of the Moscow River, she sees the golden domes of the Kremlin glinting on the river's edge. The bus hurtles on until she pulls the cord and it comes to a halt at Smolensk Boulevard.

Their apartment walls are covered with bookcases and photos of Oleg. Among them is a charcoal sketch of Liza's face, scribbled by an artist when she was a child. She tosses the chanterelles into a frying pan. As their orange bells collapse in the oil, she starts running through the familiar list of questions. What kind of mood will he be in tonight? Will he be drunk? Mean drunk or happy drunk? If he's mean, she reminds herself that she must not cry. Oleg hates whining. In fact, if he seems unhappy, it's best to give him an excuse to blow up at her. If he yells, if he throws something, that's good—the tension has released. Allowing it to build up is much worse. Anxiety creeps under the door and through the windows like mustard gas.

At last Oleg walks in, fresh off his flight from Prague, where he traveled with an official delegation from the Soviet film industry. He has brought back a bottle of slivovitz and is wearing a new pair of shoes. The Czechs live like gods, he says. Last night there was a farewell banquet, but to her surprise he doesn't seem hungover. The whites of his eyes are clear, his spirits are high, and he's not asking for a drink. The gas dissipates, and Liza starts to breathe. As they sip coffee with slivovitz, she dares to ask whether he might consider getting an esperal implant—a device that blocks the metabolization of alcohol, producing a severe and near-immediate hangover meant to discourage drinking. He says he will; she is overjoyed. After he lays down to sleep, she writes her mother a jubilant update: "He's nothing like he was then."

A few days later, she sends another letter: "It was bad—terrible depression, fear, etc."

Weeks later, one more: "Olezhechka," she writes, using an affectionate diminutive of his name, "is sweet as always." She signs off as a collective unit:

"Kisses, us."

Their relationship continued until March 3, 1981, when Oleg died in a Kyiv hotel room of a heart attack. Liza told a reporter that "it seems to me as if I was burned and buried too and only some fragment of me remains in this world. . . . It's what all lovers dream of, dying on the same day." She spent the next two decades preserving their apartment as a shrine. More and more photos of him appeared on the walls, until the drawing from her childhood was the only female face in a phantom army of Olegs. She corresponded with his fans and wrote to the Ministry of Culture demanding that more be done to promote his legacy. When Liza died in 2003 at age sixty-five, her remains were cremated and laid in the ground next to his. A short article about her in a Russian tabloid ended with a list of Oleg's best films.

The Greek nymph Echo, who is doomed to parrot the words of others, gazes at Narcissus as he beholds his reflection in the pool. When I read Liza's lines about Oleg, or my own texts with Daniel, I hear the echo of an echo. These men speak and speak, and demand we listen and repeat. Rather than allowing the sounds to fade away, I long to combine them and raise the volume until they form a resonant chord, so loud it drowns out the original source.

Some voices from the past are quieter than others. Enslaved people usually couldn't read or write and left hardly any official records behind. Almost everything that later generations know about them comes from the testimony of their enslavers, who created documents that justified their own grip on power. Scholars try to acknowledge and overcome the absences in the archive; as a college professor of mine liked to put it, they "read sources against the grain." Saidiya Hartman wrote a collective biography of "Venus," the countless enslaved women who appeared only in a legal indictment, the ledger of a slave ship, or the pages of a pornographic novel, and were often not even identified by name. "To read the archive," Hartman writes, "is to enter a mortuary; it permits one final viewing and allows for a last glimpse of persons about to disappear into the slave hold."

Liza was a literate woman with a prestigious pedigree. She was able to speak, but she edited herself, in accordance with cultural codes that fetishized male anguish and tasked women with pacifying it—not unlike how I thought it was my duty to nurse Daniel's wounds and downplay his effect on me. Liza strove to present herself as the happy wife of a genius and may not have seen what was happening to her as abuse. Yet I recognize the underlying tension in her words, her awareness that Oleg could flip at any moment, the constant monitoring that she thinks is care for him but is also an instinctual safeguard for herself.

While Oleg performed his torments, onscreen and off, Liza tended to his body and bore the brunt of his anger. When I envision a few hours of her life on the basis of written records she left behind, I supplement them with my knowledge of moments that leave no evidentiary trace. In her letters that are preserved in the archive, Liza never mentions an act of violence. As I read her looping cursive, my thoughts drift back to how I used to protect Daniel and the love I thought we shared. While writing messages about him, I chose my words with an eye toward the future when he would finally be different; I didn't want the sludge of winter to soil the coming spring. Liza, like me, was always eager to say that Oleg had changed and kept any counterindications vague. "Fear, etc": so much experience encoded in a two-word phrase. Maybe Oleg hurt Liza on that summer day in 1977, but he didn't need to. The fear is in the waiting.

I wonder if Liza ever suspected that the season we both yearned for would never arrive, that the way Oleg was "then" was more or less how he would always be. Even if I could somehow warn her, growing wings that would carry me into the past with the knowledge I've gained, she wouldn't be able to hear what I had to say. When I imagine approaching Liza in the attic where she hid from Oleg, she disintegrates into the dust on the file boxes in the trolley cart, the ashes buried in the shared cemetery plot under snow and ice. Time doesn't turn backward, and her story is inseparable from his.

███

In the same seminar where I encountered Benjamin's angel of history, we read Hayden White's conception of history as narrative. According to White, the past is chaos, a morass of disparate events on which historians impose order in the form of a literary plot. By deciding what details to leave in or out, play up or down, they mold raw materials into a familiar structure—romance, comedy, tragedy, satire—that reflects their moral and political impulses. Though Liza may have seen her story as a romance, I've selected quotations suggesting it was a tragedy and inserted it into a narrative about the Soviet Union's fatal hubris, which is colored by my own experience of disillusionment in Donald Trump's United States. Another narrator, perhaps unscarred by abuse, might focus on Liza's career in the film industry (while skipping over her despondent comments about Oleg) to show how Soviet society allowed women to have it all. This would be a comedy of emancipation promised and ultimately delivered.

In White's view, these accounts are equally arbitrary. There is no objective truth waiting to be uncovered; veracity is in the eye of the beholder, who chooses whatever story they are predisposed to find most powerful. It is a vision of history akin to Akira Kurosawa's film *Rashomon*, which presents a rape and murder from four contradictory perspectives—each of them persuasive and none superior to the rest.

"It's not philosophically rigorous," said the professor in our seminar, a skeptic. "But White is a figure you can't avoid."

Over the next several years, my training often reminded me of White's ideas. In classes and working groups, I learned that the historian's task was to be ecumenical. Was Stalinism a system of top-down oppression or a galvanizing mass movement? Tragedy or romance? There was no immutable answer—it all depended on who told the most compelling tale. We picked apart books based on the strength of their narratives, how well they spun facts into story. I wrote a research paper about late Soviet history, the one I told Daniel was for him, and called it a tragic farce.

Among historians of Europe, White's claim that all stories are created equal raised concerns that even industrialized mass murder could be dismissed as a matter of opinion. In a 1990 conference at the University of California, Los Angeles on the Holocaust and "the limits of representation," White faced off against his opponents on the nature of historical truth. Though the published volume of papers already feels like a relic—almost all its contributors were white men—their debates are no more settled today.

White's primary adversary was the Italian historian Carlo Ginzburg, who accused him of giving fuel to Holocaust deniers. Ginzburg described a 1348 massacre of Jews in Provence, the sole trace of which is a few lines that its lone survivor inscribed in a torah, to contend that "just one witness" is enough to know what happened in the past. Ginzburg's argument raised alarming questions. What if the only observer of the Holocaust had been Adolf Eichmann, the Nazi functionary who made the trains to the death camps run on time?

White backed down from the logical conclusion of his views on multiple truths. It is not the events of the Final Solution that can be questioned, he said, but merely the form of their narration. Martin Jay, an intellectual historian at Berkeley, responded that there is no event in human history that precedes our attempts to assign it with meaning, and that facts can be impossible to separate from the stories we tell about them. Although objective truth is inaccessible, historians can sort through narratives generated in different moments to reach a consensus about which version is most convincing.

Christopher Browning, a specialist in Nazi Germany, suggested that there is a continuum between fact and interpretation, and that the accumulated mass of facts should determine the historian's narrative. As an example, Browning recounted a massacre committed by a battalion of German reserve police officers in Nazi-occupied Poland and explained how he evaluated the credibility of various participants, who were interrogated about what happened over twenty years later. He compared the process of weighing testimonies, documents, and physical evidence to a civil legal procedure, with its "preponderance of evidence" standard. "Beyond a reasonable doubt," Browning concluded, can lie beyond the historian's reach.

After looking through all the published and unpublished materials I can find about Liza and Oleg, I'm confident enough that he was violent to her on the occasion her mother described, and probably others. To depict Liza as a paragon of fulfilled womanhood would be to miss a major aspect of her life and of the society that both nurtured and confined it. Yet no one is counting on my verdict in the nonexistent proceedings of Liza v. Oleg. Liza complained only to her mother, and neither party is around to contest the judgments I've imposed. I tried to figure out what happened to Liza merely to satisfy my curiosity, and maybe to distract myself from the uncertain outcome of my case. When I return Liza's letters, I'm still waiting to discover what sources will tilt the investigator's story about what happened to me.

11

OTHER VOICES

A S BUDS START TO DOT MOSCOW'S BRANCHES, I FLY TO WASHING-ton. My grandmother is dying. By the time I arrive, she is not eating or drinking anymore. She sits upright in her hospital bed, puffs of white hair encircling her head like a halo, blue eyes roaming the room in silent wonder at the world she is leaving behind. Every couple of hours I wet a tiny sponge and rub it around the inside of her mouth to keep it from getting dry. She opens her jaws trustingly as she gazes up at me.

On the morning of her funeral, I'm about to put on a jumpsuit in purple, her favorite color, when I check my email.

OPHD *PRIVATE* EVIDENCE REVIEW

There are approximately 1,481 pages of documents in Box. Most of the documents were submitted by Respondent. There are a total of 15 witnesses. Summaries of party and witness statements comprise approximately 102 of the 1,481 pages. You will have (2) two business days after your access to Box ends to submit comments.

After months of delays, OPHD has suddenly dumped all the case files in my inbox, with a short turnaround time to review them. Now I have access to all the materials in the case, and so does Daniel. The raw chaos of the past is on my screen.

As I click on the witness interviews, I see that they are not entirely unprocessed. Rather than providing verbatim transcripts, the investigator has edited them into overviews sprinkled with quotes. The write-ups of my statements seem accurate, so I move past them to the interviews with Daniel and the witnesses. Though the witnesses' names have been replaced with numbers, descriptions of what they teach or study at the beginning of each summary make them easy for me to identify. Yet I struggle to make sense of the mess before my eyes, in which facts I know to be true intertwine with assertions I'm certain are false until I can barely tell them apart.

I remember everything that happened better than anyone (don't I?). But I'm not the narrator anymore. As I read different versions of my relationship with Daniel, my head buzzes with a cacophonous hum. It sounds like the nighttime calls of cicadas and frogs in the thick summer air where I grew up, their invisible chorus rattling until the dark woods came alive.

——————

INTERVIEWS

RESPONDENT

Respondent never wanted to date me, he says, but I pressured him until he relented.

Complainant initiated the relationship and initially, Respondent resisted being in a relationship because he was having emotional problems.

Complainant knew that Respondent was having problems because Respondent would text her about problems; Complainant would be supportive. Eventually Respondent agreed to be in a romantic relationship with Complainant after she convinced him.

Respondent recalled that at the beginning of the spring 2017 semester, school as well as the relationship were going well for him. Respondent told me that he did have arguments with

Complainant because Respondent felt that Complainant did not care about him.

Respondent is a survivor of childhood trauma, which I triggered by failing to care for him. On the night that I said he shoved me down the steps at Dwinelle,

Respondent just remembers being very upset and doesn't remember what Complainant said. Respondent told me that his therapist told him his memory could be impacted. Respondent's therapist stated that when he feels like he is being attacked and experiences a sense of panic this could cause him not to remember events.

The emotional situation where Respondent feels a loved one isn't caring for him triggers previous memories of childhood trauma where his caretakers weren't protecting him. Respondent told me that this causes Respondent to go into "survival mode." Respondent would alternate between thinking about his past and present while reacting to what was currently happening to him.

Respondent did not have any issue with my dating history.

I said that it was alleged that Respondent was verbally abusive to Complainant and called her a "disgusting slut" on several occasions. Respondent explained that part of their relationship dynamic was that Respondent believed that Complainant did not care about him. However, this belief was not connected to sexual history.

I asked Respondent if he called Complainant a "whore" on multiple occasions. Respondent replied that again, he cannot remember the whole incident, but mainly their arguments centered on Complainant not caring about Respondent.

Though I see a few denials that didn't come up in the cross-examination session, like how he said he never shoved his ex-girlfriend or threw my books, I already heard most of his rebuttals. I move on from Respondent's interview to the statements of his friends, whom I've also come to think of as mine. They described his mental health struggles.

WITNESS 9 (RESPONDENT'S FRIEND)

In spring 2017, Witness 9 realized that Respondent was in crisis, but said that he could not recall the exact moment he realized this. It might have been Respondent's excessive drinking and his comments about depression and seeking therapy. Witness 10 would be present for these conversations too and she and Witness 9 would both discuss their mental health issues and encouraged Respondent to seek help.

Shortly after Respondent started treatment at Tang Center he would have more visible signs of anxiety and he would call Witness 9 when he started having panic attacks. Witness 9 would give Respondent breathing exercises to do.

Respondent's friends said they were worried about him hurting himself, as was I. They did not see any indication that I was afraid of him. To the contrary, said Witness 6, I sometimes forced myself on Respondent when he wanted me to leave.

WITNESS 6 (RESPONDENT'S FRIEND
AND FORMER ROOMMATE)

Respondent said he didn't see the point in living anymore. He felt like a failure and was not sure why he was attending UC Berkeley. As Witness 6 tried to comfort him, Respondent said, "Let me show you something." Respondent showed Witness 6 his broken belt. Respondent told Witness 6 that the night before he tried to hang himself. Respondent just wanted to see how it felt but, then he could not get out of it and had to free himself by breaking the belt. Witness 6 learned months later, after talking with Complainant, that Respondent did not tell the whole story and that actually Complainant cut him down.

Throughout the semester, Complainant would text or call Witness 6 regarding Respondent. When Complainant was not there with Respondent, she was worried that he might hurt himself. Witness 6 recalled rushing home to make sure that Respondent was all right. Complainant slept over at their place almost every night and Witness 6 thinks it was partly to keep an eye on Respondent.

Respondent and Complainant shared a sense of humor and they really liked each other a lot but, Witness 6 also remembers observing tension between the couple. For example, one day Complainant was standing outside their apartment. Complainant said I'm here to see Respondent. When they arrived upstairs, it was clear that Respondent did not want Complainant to be there. Complainant came in anyway because she wanted to see him. Respondent said "[Complainant] is going to leave now."

I thought that maybe his friends sensed what else was going on, even before I told them. But why would they? Almost everything they saw endorsed his self-presentation as a victim. According to the graduate student who witnessed it, Respondent kept mentioning me during his attempt at self-harm in Dwinelle Hall, but the only threat he posed was to himself.

WITNESS 3 (RESPONDENT'S FRIEND)
Witness 3 was in the shared office in Dwinelle Hall. Respondent came in later and showed Witness 3 an abrasion on his arm. It was a shallow, self-inflicted wound, but it had been bleeding. Respondent said, "I can't even do it."

Respondent asked Witness 3 to call Complainant. Witness 3 did so, and Complainant told Witness 3 that Respondent is a threat to her and to himself. Complainant asked Witness 3 to sit with Respondent until Respondent's roommate, Witness 6, could come to get him.

Witness 3 agreed and ended the call. He sat with Respondent and about 30 seconds later, Respondent asked Witness 3 to call Complainant again. Witness 3 replied that this wasn't a good idea and that they should wait for Witness 6. Respondent waited for Witness 3 to get momentarily distracted and then ran for the door. Witness 3 ran after Respondent and grabbed him. They struggled while Witness 3 tried to restrain Respondent.

Respondent asked Witness 3, "Is she coming, is [Complainant] coming?" Respondent continued to ask Witness 3 this question as he was being taken to the hospital. "Does she even care?" Respondent asked.

Respondent said he was being persecuted.

In the middle of the summer, Respondent contacted Witness 3. Respondent said, "They are trying to get me to go to jail." Witness 3 did not hear anything else about the situation again until August or September 2017. By that point, word had traveled and various narratives had spread around the department.

My vision starts churning with colors the way it used to. *Es schwindelt.* The white hotel bedspread beneath me glimmers like cut glass as I turn to testimony from our professors.

Witness 2, one of Respondent's professors, learned that he was dating me from another professor, Witness 7, on the day of Respondent's qualifying exam.

WITNESS 2 (PROFESSOR)

Witness 2 did not see Complainant and Respondent as a good pairing. Witness 2 recalled saying to Witness 7, "Respondent picked the most stable person he could find." Respondent was anxious about the exam and Witness 7 remarked that it seemed like Respondent was clinging to Complainant like a rock.

In the days after Respondent's exam, Witness 2 heard that he had been violent to me, again from Witness 7, but she assumed that whatever happened was minor.

I asked what Witness 2 meant when she said Witness 7 said "there had been violence." Witness 2 replied that she did not know what the violence consisted of. Witness 2 and Witness 7 are friends and she thinks he would have told her if he thought Respondent hit Complainant. They were both completely shocked by this. "I did not know that [Respondent] was taking medication. He seemed the last person who would do something like this. We were both trying to process this," Witness 2 said.

When Witness 2 met with Respondent, she asked him, "Why didn't you tell me that you were struggling?" Respondent replied he was embarrassed and thought he could handle it. "The relief of having the exams over was harder to handle than I thought," Respondent said. By this time Respondent had a different therapist and his medication was increased. Respondent told Witness 2 that he felt better.

Witness 2 wants to help Respondent keep recovering from his nervous breakdown.

"If there was anything I could do to support Respondent, I would," Witness 2 said.

I feel as if I'm eavesdropping. My instincts are telling me to stop listening and fall back into ignorance. Instead, I continue on to the testimony of a professor who advises two of Respondent's friends (Witnesses 9 and 10). This professor also heard that Respondent was going through a hard time and may have lightly touched me in a moment of distress.

WITNESS 5 (PROFESSOR)

Witnesses 9 and 10 alerted Witness 5 of the fact that a mutual friend was suffering from mental health issues.

Witness 10 also said Respondent did something violent towards his girlfriend who is also a student. Witness 5 can't remember a lot of details but, Witness 10 made it seem like the violent act was a manifestation of Respondent's distress. Witness 5 can't recall but, it also seemed like Witness 10 even qualified it by saying "it's not like a big thing." Witness 5 told me, "I think it was shoving."

Witness 5 explained to me that Respondent's violence toward his girlfriend did not unfold as something different, separate, and apart from the mental breakdown but rather as part of the mental breakdown. Witness 5 said he did not put it in a separate category.

My mom is asking me if I'm almost ready to go. I ignore her text as I see the testimony of the professors whom Daniel and I both work with—the people whose opinions I respect the most.

When a friend of mine called Witness 7 and told him that Respondent was putting me in danger, Witness 7 was taken aback.

WITNESS 7 (PROFESSOR)

Witness 7 recalled being surprised because his perception of Respondent was that he was quiet and shy. Respondent was extra polite, diffident, and so intelligent that it showed through his quiet demeanor. It was difficult to envision him as an aggressor.

Though Witness 7 was concerned for my safety and arranged for me to stay at Witness 2's guest house, he emphasized that whatever happened between me and Respondent was none of his business. He tried not to hear about it from me or my friends, including Witness 12.

"My basic approach to this was to not to talk to them about the substance of their problem," Witness 7 said. Neither Complainant nor Respondent told Witness 7 anything substantive. "[Complainant] told me a few words about how difficult the relationship had been for her," Witness 7 said.

Witness 7's original impression of the matter was that Respondent was volatile. "I did not think that there was physical violence until later," Witness 7 said. But this was after Complainant's departure. "I discouraged conversations about that," Witness 7 said.

At some point Witness 7 had lunch with Witness 12 to discuss her dissertation and research plan. By this time, Complainant had left California. During lunch, Witness 12 did not provide specifics but she did say, "It was worse than you think. You may not realize the degree of violence that had gone on." Witness 12 seemed to be implying physical violence. Witness 7 did not think it was his role as academic advisor to be privy to this private information. "I did not ask details and [Witness 12] did not volunteer," Witness 7 said.

Witness 7 continues to hold both me and Respondent in high esteem.

"I just feel terrible because I like both of them. I really have a great deal of respect for both of them as human beings and scholars. It's a terrible thing," Witness 7 said.

And here I was, so sure he was on my side.

My head spins even faster as I read the interview with Witness 8, who also says that she thinks highly of both of us. Though Witness 8 was on sabbatical in another country for the year, she heard rumors that Respondent had been violent to me. She can no longer recall certain details of her phone calls with me.

WITNESS 8 (PROFESSOR)

Witness 8 said she wanted Complainant to be making her own decisions and at that time she was getting a lot of input from other people. Simultaneously, she also felt that Complainant needed to be a safe distance from Respondent. Witness 8 said she does not remember having a conversation about a restraining order.

According to Witness 8, Respondent is the victim of a racially motivated smear campaign that has attacked him both online and on campus.

Witness 8 told me that she thinks everyone was worried about Respondent's professional reputation. However, Respondent came by the scandal honestly because he was abusive to Complainant and then engaged in self-harm on campus, Witness 8 said. The facts being what they are, Witness 8 still felt that the Facebook posts were not right. She is unsure about who made the posts. Witness 8 told me that she did not try to protect Respondent's reputation but, she did feel that Respondent was entitled to privacy.

By privacy, Witness 8 meant that someone's private records should not be open to public discussion. There is racism in the department and violence is also influenced by racism. For example, during the first week in May there were people following Respondent around campus to make sure he didn't hurt Complainant. There was a "lynch mob mentality" and it was already around Witness 9 and some of his friends. Some of which claimed to be Respondent's friends.

There was an uproar that happened that would not have happened had Respondent been white. Witness 8 said this was further demonstrated when some people came up to Respondent and said he shouldn't have passed his oral exam with distinction.

In May and June of 2017, Respondent sent messages that he intended to quit the program. Witness 8 and Respondent met to discuss this in July 2017. Respondent expressed insecurity about his ability to continue. Respondent felt targeted on Facebook and there were numerous posts. Respondent felt there was not a place for him in academia.

"No," I want to scream. No one can hear me. The chorus continues, louder and louder, and now the solo goes to Respondent's therapist, Witness 13.

Witness 13 reported that Respondent was aggressive to me when provoked by my failure to listen to him. But Respondent, he said, never took it too far.

WITNESS 13 (RESPONDENT'S THERAPIST)

I asked Witness 13 if Respondent discussed physical violence during the sessions. Witness 13 replied that initially, Respondent described talking with Complainant about difficult situations. He wanted her to listen and not offer reassurance or advice. If Respondent felt like Complainant wasn't listening to him, he would become frightened, upset, and then become enraged.

Respondent also reported touching Complainant. Respondent put his arm around Complainant's neck. Respondent told Witness 13 that he did not actually choke Complainant though. Witness 13 said the extreme things didn't happen often. Normally Respondent would try to hurt himself.

If Respondent felt like Complainant was being dismissive, through the course of conversation, Respondent would become distressed. Their conversations would usually be about Respondent's experience growing up, the history department, etc. He would also become upset if he felt like she was going to abandon him (and abandonment could also include not listening). Respondent put his hands around Complainant's neck. "It wasn't like he started to choke to her, he just stopped," Witness 13 said.

Witness 13 remembered Respondent talking about throwing objects, but not in Complainant's direction. "Nothing over the top" but things like that, Witness 13 said.

Respondent was severely neglected and abused as a child. Respondent has been diligent, thoughtful, and is working hard to correct some of this. He understands the behavior and is taking responsibility for the behavior and is trying to heal himself. Respondent is also worried that he will lose his insurance and thereby lose his ability to rehabilitate himself. Respondent needs long-term therapy.

"I hope that is being taken into account. I hope the punishment is not destructive and does not ruin his ability to complete his Ph.D.," Witness 13 said.

Any doubts about Respondent's harmlessness were surely put to rest by Witness 14 (Respondent's psychiatrist), who did not observe any signs that Respondent was aggressive. The only person he described hurting was himself.

WITNESS 14 (RESPONDENT'S PSYCHIATRIST)

Witness 14 told me, "Violence is not a symptom of the diagnosis I gave him."

Witness 14 did not think Complainant was in danger. In fact, in March 2017, Witness 14 specifically asked Respondent if he harmed anyone and he replied no.

As I look back through the interviews with Respondent's friends, I notice cracks in his version of reality. According to Witness 10 (who told the investigator she no longer considered him a friend), Respondent did not only talk about his mental health, but also about my sexual history.

WITNESS 10 (RESPONDENT'S FRIEND)

In February 2017, Witness 10 recalled that she and Respondent went for a drink. Respondent said he couldn't stop thinking about the other people that Complainant had been intimate with. Witness 10 replied that nobody wants to think about their partner's past relationships and those feelings are coming from Respondent's insecurity.

Witness 10 spoke to Witness 9 about it later and they both thought it was "weird" because it was almost like Respondent was saying that Complainant wasn't allowed to have previous relationships. Witness 9, who observed the couple's interactions more than Witness 10, would often tell Witness 10 that Respondent would become angry at Complainant and question her about her relationship history.

After I left Respondent, Witness 10 tried to confront him.

Respondent was attending therapy and said he was happy that he obtained mental health help. He never mentioned being physically abusive to Complainant. So, one day during a telephone conversation, Witness 10 asked Respondent in a circumspect way, if he thought it would be good idea to get help regarding his relationship with Complainant. Witness 10 asked Respondent to consider his conduct towards Complainant as abuse. Respondent went silent and said, "I can tell that you are mad at me. You don't have to see me or be my friend anymore," and then hung up.

Respondent didn't have many positive things to say about me.

Respondent would say Complainant is so cold and emotionless. Respondent would complain about Complainant's past partners. Respondent said that one of Complainant's past partners had "disgusting" political views. But now in hindsight, Witness 10 thinks Respondent meant it was disgusting that Complainant had previous partners.

I have to get ready. There's no time to go through all this now. Still, before closing my computer, I turn to the interviews with my friends. I need to hear voices that sound more like mine.

My friends' statements contain the story I expected, the one they helped me to see: that I'm a victim of domestic violence perpetrated by Respondent. Yet their perspective also contains some surprises. I wasn't covering up for him as well as I thought.

WITNESS 1 (COMPLAINANT'S FRIEND)
During the spring 2017 semester, Witness 1 noticed that Complainant changed her routine. They used to get coffee in Sproul plaza and then Complainant wanted to "hide." Complainant was "hiding" even before Witness 1 knew about Respondent's abusive behavior.

Witness 1 recalled that before she knew about the physical abuse, Complainant had been telling her for weeks about the emotional abuse. Specifically, Complainant stated that Respondent was controlling, angry, and would constantly mention Complainant's prior relationships.

Witness 1 told me that Respondent calling Complainant a "whore" was a constant occurrence. Complainant would be loving and forgiving towards Respondent but he would tell Complainant that she was a terrible person, neglectful, and sleeping around. Witness 1 said Respondent was not really "seeing" Complainant for who she was nor did he appreciate her.

By sharing observations I didn't realize they'd made, my friends created a very different image of Respondent.

WITNESS 12 (COMPLAINANT'S FRIEND)

Witness 12 has two friends who have been in abusive relationships and they shared the warning signs of an abusive relationship with her. Witness 12 noticed the warning signs in Complainant's behavior. For example, Complainant appeared tense and would go along with everything that Respondent wanted to do. Complainant was usually very composed, but Witness 12 could tell that Complainant was on edge and it was not just anxiety regarding her oral exam.

Complainant and Witness 12 would meet in Complainant's graduate instructor office to speak privately. Witness 12 remembers Complainant taking special pains to talk in a hushed voice and closing the blinds to her office. Witness 12 remembers generally that her conversations with Complainant were about Respondent constantly berating her and his jealousy of her past relationships.

He also said that because Complainant is a white woman who attended Brown University, she was responsible (privileged because of class and race) for the suffering that Respondent endured by coming from an underprivileged family. Witness 12 found it "mindboggling" that Complainant was accepting Respondent's rhetoric.

My friends remembered him making strange remarks.

WITNESS 15 (COMPLAINANT'S FRIEND)

Witness 15 surmised that something was going on but, she didn't know what. There was one interaction that Witness 15 thought was odd that occurred on January 31, 2017. Witness 15 went to Jack in the Box with the couple. Complainant was drinking a milkshake and Respondent made a comment about the way Complainant was drinking the milkshake was sexual. Witness 15 thought it was a weird comment. Complainant seemed uncomfortable. Respondent said it as if it was a joke but, he repeated it over and over.

Though I worried about Respondent, they said, I also began to disclose to them that he was violent. I recall these conversations but hardly recognize the version of myself that my friends encountered.

WITNESS 4 (COMPLAINANT'S FRIEND)

It was a predictable pattern: Respondent would be violent towards Complainant, call her names, and then disappear to make Complainant concerned about where he was, Witness 4 said. When Respondent would disappear, Complainant would talk to Witness 4 about his disappearance. People knew Respondent was depressed and overwhelmed so when he disappeared it was scary. Complainant was very concerned. Complainant would share that Respondent is hurting her and she is afraid of him.

Complainant would unsuccessfully try to suppress tears while she spoke to Witness 4. Witness 4 said Complainant's countenance changed. She looked scared. It was unnerving for Witness 4 to see the change in Complainant's demeanor.

As the semester progressed, my descriptions of abuse grew increasingly detailed.

I showed Witness 1 a series of text messages exchanged between Complainant and Witness 1 dated February 8, 2017. Witness 1 read the messages and I asked, "What did Complainant tell you the night before?" Witness 1 said that the text exchange happened the day after Complainant confided in Witnesses 1 and 12. Complainant shared that when they left the party, Respondent shoved Complainant to the ground and had really hurt and scared her. Complainant also shared with Witnesses 1 and 12 that while she was sleeping, she woke up to Respondent's hand around her neck.

During the [May 6] conversation, Complainant shared several instances of violence with her friends: Respondent choked Complainant several times; Respondent pulled Complainant out of bed by her throat while she was asleep; Respondent also pushed Complainant against the wall and held her there by her throat; Respondent threatened Complainant with a knife and belt; and Respondent broke Complainant's things.

Respondent seemed to not understand that what he did was wrong or that it was reasonable for Complainant to be upset.

Sometimes, by the end of the semester, I did not seem composed at all.

As they drove along the street, Complainant and Witness 15 saw Respondent walking by Witness 1's house. Complainant began shaking all over and she appeared terrified.

My friends felt pressured to be nice to Respondent like the other graduate students despite their knowledge of what he was doing to me.

Witness 12 was in the student lounge with another student. Respondent had just completed his orals and he walked into the student lounge. Someone asked Respondent how the exam went, and he replied that it went well. Witness 12's companions congratulated Respondent and gave him a hug. Respondent turned to Witness 12 and said "You don't want to give me a hug, do you?" Witness 12 felt put on the spot and reluctantly gave Respondent a hug.

Though I was terrified of Respondent, they said, I continued to worry mostly about him, even after he and I got back from Texas.

Witness 1 didn't know that Complainant went to Texas with Respondent until she called to report that Respondent had been violent towards her during the trip. Witness 1 said this was one of several times that Complainant felt like she might die. Complainant said she wished she had not been sympathetic to Respondent's efforts to make her feel guilty. Complainant would feel so guilty that it overrode her fear for her safety.

Lots of people in the department expressed support for Respondent in reaction to his social media posts, but they didn't seem to know what was happening behind the scenes.

Witness 4 thought it was strange that the person who was hurting her friend was getting so much sympathy. At the same time, Witness 4 also thought Respondent should receive some compassion too because he was hurting himself. Witness 4 does not think the history department knew about the violent aspect of Respondent's character. When Witness 4 left for Russia, few people had an inkling of the situation between Complainant and Respondent.

———

I shut my computer. As my shaking fingers pull up the zipper of my jumpsuit, I try to assume a stoic expression that conceals my shock. *See, you're always faking*, Daniel whispers. The master voice I've spent the past ten months trying to muffle is now as loud as it was when I left. As I walk out of my hotel room, I wonder whether the people I meet will sense the frenzy in my head, or if I will really know what thoughts are in theirs. Sometimes, I now realize, it's better not to.

12

THE REAL DANIEL

A T MY GRANDMOTHER'S FUNERAL, AS MY FAMILY FILES INTO THE
sanctuary, I can't hear the hymn. Though I'm here to remember
someone I've known and loved my entire life, my thoughts keep circling
back to the recent personal history I've been straining to forget. The
stained glass above the altar swirls, faces flicker in the pews, my body is
here but my mind is elsewhere.

*Not like a big thing nothing over the top a great deal of respect for both of
them difficult to envision as an aggressor the last person who would do something like this.*

That evening, after changing out of my church clothes, I start to click
on Daniel's evidence files. I see some things that are familiar, and many
others that are new.

Most of our text message history, hundreds of pages long. Discussions
of what to eat for lunch or which movie to see, gossip, sexts with photos
of my naked body (rendered as blank boxes with question marks). The
texts Daniel sent after I blocked him, which contain language similar to
the Facebook post he made when I didn't respond.

"You are the great love of my life. With you gone there is nothing left
for me here. The stage directions are clear: it is time for the poor man
dragging his burden of pain off the stage." "Goodbye to you. Goodbye

to Berkeley. Goodbye to the world that no longer has a place for me. I'll crawl back into the delirious night from which I came; there I will yell, howl, and no one will hear and no one will get hurt."

Loving messages and emails I sent him.

(no subject)

To: ▮▮▮▮ <▮▮▮▮▮▮gmail.com>   Tue, Feb 14, 2017 at 12:46 PM

The time we spend together is extremely intense and meaningful for me. You make me laugh and think and come more than anyone ever has. There are many things we see and understand and share in a way that is effortless. I know how incredibly rare that is, almost impossible- it's something I've never experienced before. Getting together has felt like when Dorothy gets to Oz and the film switches from black and white to color. Or to put it in terms closer to your heart, when the autocracy is toppled and the red dawn rises. That feeling that this, finally, is how the world should be.

But I also know that you aren't sure if you want me/this. You say you want something that doesn't have baggage. If that's how you feel, I think it's better for me to let go. I love you, and there is no one else I want to be with. But I would rather be alone than cause you pain or make you do something you don't want. It will not be easy to make the colors go back, but I will try. You should have the life you want. When I said I would do anything for you, I meant it.

■

A personal narrative Daniel has written that details his father's abuse of the family, and his mother in particular, and concludes with Daniel's transformation into an intellectual.

Photos of me smiling, eating stir-fried noodles, holding an X-Box controller, eating ice cream at a café.

Texts from Daniel to his friends. A stream of messages he sent to Bella after attacking me in Texas in which he apologized for being a burden, said certain people want to lock him up, told her how he loves her and she's the only one he can trust.

Emails that Daniel sent to our professors about his mistreatment immediately after I pulled away from him.

bConnected
powered by Google

<[redacted] berkeley.edu>

(no subject)
4 messages

[redacted] < [redacted] berkeley.edu>   Sat, Jul 1, 2017 at 8:06 PM
To: [redacted]   @berkeley.edu>

Dear [redacted]

This has been a very emotionally turbulent and painful period for me. I walked
out of the psych ward with a feeling that I had hit rock bottom, and that it was
time to seriously look at rebuilding my life. I had no idea that I was walking out
into a storm of a very different nature.

My emotional health began to deteriorate the more and more I heard about what
people were saying about me, about people advocating jail time for me,
restraining orders and painting me as some sort of monster. I was contrite and
remorseful, I know that i hadn't behaved well and needed to hold myself
responsible for my actions. But the accusations continued. Any time I wanted to
express sadness or alienation, as when I saw a picture of everyone having fun at
[redacted] house, I was quickly reprimanded and told I had no right to feel sad or
upset; I brought this on myself.

I broke down.

I am alone. I don't think I can be in Berkeley anymore. At least not at campus. I
know you and [redacted] said that time will heal the wounds, but if [redacted] who loves me,
isn't willing to see me beyond that paradigm, then how will others?

I'm sorry for putting this on you. its just that at this point I have no one to turn to,
outside of my therapist.

Thank you for listening to me.

Sincerely,

[redacted]

In an April 30 email he sent to Alexander while I was staying in the
safe house and hadn't responded yet to his message, Daniel said he had to
drop out of the program. While learning from professors like Alexander
has been "the greatest privilege of my life," Daniel wrote, his peers don't
accept him due to his background and, while he was suffering from mental health issues, "it became clear how people were not willing to go out
of their way to help me."

Alexander confessed his own familiarity with feelings of sadness
and exclusion and suggested they get together. After Daniel sent him a
thank-you email following their conversation, Alexander replied that "It is

my absolute pleasure talking to you. I must admit that I identify with what you are going through (with whatever limitations that identification may entail), but I hold you in high esteem and wish you well." Alexander said they should stay in touch even if Daniel decided to leave the PhD program.

"I hope I am not in trouble!" Daniel said after Alexander suggested they speak again the next day.

"The part we need to discuss is how to negotiate the pain that other graduate students still seem to be feeling acutely. In a community of young people, raw emotions really can lead to unwise words that can inflict further pain, which I want to help you avoid."

As the days and weeks passed, Alexander kept checking in with Daniel, expressing sympathy for the "terrible time" that he was going through and wishing him strength: "Please remember that you have friends, and that I am one of them." He told Daniel how lonely it is for people "like you and me" who are transplants to an environment different from the one they grew up in, how he has learned to cope with his feelings and how Daniel might, too.

Finally, I see that Daniel has submitted character references from graduate students and professors.

Dear ██████████,

I'm writing this letter in support of ███ ██████ as he faces investigation by the Office for the Prevention of Harassment and Discrimination at the University of California, Berkeley. I have known ███ since we entered UC Berkeley's Ph.D. program in History in August, 2014. Since then he has been a close friend and a valuable intellectual interlocutor. He was also my roommate during the 2016-2017 academic year, including for the duration of his romantic involvement with ██ ██████████ In this letter, I'll provide written testimony of my observations concerning the decline of ██████ mental health during this period.

Evan goes on to praise Daniel's personal qualities and detail his psychological struggles. At the end of April, he says, Daniel "punched a hole in the wall at the UC Berkeley History department, badly injuring his hand," without mentioning Daniel's violence toward me or even the fact that I was there (which Evan was not). My fear of Daniel was entirely "unfounded," Evan says, including on that day: "I don't think that [Daniel] forcibly kept Joy in our apartment that evening. As far as I know, she simply accepted his invitation to dinner."

Evan remarks on Daniel's "thoughtfulness, his brilliance, his gentle demeanor, his dedication to his studies, his relentless commitment to his views on political and social justice."

The letter concludes that "the real Daniel" is

the person I have admired since the start of graduate school—characterized, at his best, by thoughtfulness, serenity and intellectual generosity. He is not the person I witnessed his illness create.

For Evan, Daniel is still the man I was friends with until November 2016. What haunts me the most about his letter is that I could have written it myself. I prefer this version, too.

Ginzburg's principle that only one witness is enough, which was shared by MeToo's call to "believe women," can always be undercut by a counterexample like the *Rolling Stone* article "A Rape on Campus." According to an analysis by the *Columbia Journalism Review*, the reporter in that case sought out information that confirmed the story she wanted to believe while ignoring conflicting evidence. Throughout American history, single-witness accounts of sexual violence have fed racial fears and fantasies that provided a false pretext for extracting horrific vengeance. In 1955, white shopkeeper Carolyn Bryant said that Emmett Till, a Black fourteen-year-old visiting relatives in Mississippi, made lecherous comments and grabbed her while she was alone, after which her husband and brother-in-law abducted, tortured, and murdered him.

In our Title IX case at Berkeley, the investigator is a Black lawyer whose website says she has a background in critical race theory; what's at stake in her analysis is whether Daniel will continue his PhD at this university. Rather than relying on a single rumor, she has spent months reviewing documents and interviewing witnesses, comparing various statements against each other and the textual record, balancing narratives that were produced closer and farther in time from the events. Still, as the only direct observer of Daniel's violence, I don't know how much scaffolding is required for my story to stand up.

Daniel presented himself as a tragic hero whose fate was to be martyred by forces beyond his control. In interviews, he depicted his involvement as passive: I pursued him, provoked him, elicited memories of his past. By beginning his personal narrative in childhood and ending it with his first experiences at Berkeley, he could forever remain in the role of an innocent youth; his plotline didn't allow him to acknowledge that he was emulating his father. I'm surprised that Daniel asked the investigator to talk to his therapist, to whom he admitted certain things that he denied to everyone else. Yet his therapist was ready to place Daniel's actions in a narrative of trauma and recovery that kept him as the main character and minimized whatever he had done ("nothing over the top"). The therapist argued that the tragedy of Daniel's rejection could be turned into the comedy of reintegration, if only the university would allow him to continue his PhD.

During my relationship with Daniel, I accepted my role as a minor player in the drama of his life. I tried to endorse his self-portrayal as a victim who hadn't caused any harm (and was "better" now in any case), and his representation of me as a cosseted floozy who deserved whatever punishments he decided to mete out. I hoped that Daniel's demons could be banished by healing love, disaster averted and turned into a marriage plot. Creating a counternarrative had been a process full of revisions and reversals. Even after I'd settled on a final draft, my mind kept raising its customary objections in Daniel's defense. My past truth would never align with—or fully yield to—my current one. For some, however, the story stayed the same.

To most people in our community, Daniel appeared sad and gentle; only a few had witnessed his rage. Many of them, like me, were eager to frame themselves as his ally. His publicly broadcast struggles with depression, anxiety, and trauma were more relatable than my hidden experience of abuse. Daniel's mental health crisis was the story that made the most sense to his friends—though at least one of them came to question whether she knew him as well as she thought. For our professors,

Daniel was still the shy, attentive student he had been since he arrived at Berkeley and blossomed into a formidable scholar. As Daniel fed them details about his difficult childhood and supposed ill-treatment by his fellow graduate students, they distanced themselves from any violence he may have committed.

When speaking to the investigator, Alexander denied hearing anything about what Daniel had done to me ("I discouraged conversations about that." "I did not ask details." *Did not think it was his role as academic advisor to be privy to this private information*). Behind this detached pose was the hint of another stance, suggested by emails Alexander sent to Daniel that he assumed I'd never read: "I identify with what you are going through," "people like you and me." Meanwhile, Anna's desire to sympathize with Daniel apparently led her to invent a lynch mob. The cabal of students attacking Daniel on Facebook, following him around campus, telling him he didn't deserve high marks on his oral exam—none of the persecution that Anna described ever took place. Anna was thousands of miles away and didn't belong to the community Facebook group. So she must have repeated what Daniel told her and misconstrued whatever else she heard.

In his interviews, Daniel edited out his claim that I was a whore in favor of a story about my iciness and cruelty. Yet his obsession with my sexual history kept surfacing in written records and the recollections of our friends. According to my friends, who heard the most about his abuse as it occurred, I had submitted to "mindboggling" manipulation out of fear and guilt. The refractions of violence they witnessed—Daniel's criticism of my "sexual milkshake drinking," my trembling hands and tears as I hid from him, the details I whispered in panicked conversations—were enough to convince them that he hated women.

After leaving Daniel, I have often wondered what I would have done if he and I had stayed friends and I learned that he'd hurt his girlfriend. I'm almost positive that I would have submitted a good character reference on his behalf. We all have a natural tendency to deny the possibility that someone we like could have a dark side. It's tempting to adopt the narrative that confirms our views, even when it leads us to erase ourselves (like

Bukharin) or to justify the crimes of others, like the fellow travelers and latter-day Stalinists who have seen terror as a minor aberration along the way to a noble goal. As far as I know, Daniel's claim to be a survivor of abuse is true. So is my claim that he used it to justify abusing me. Yet multiple perspectives make for maddening irony; most of us prefer a clearer arc.

⸻

After the funeral in Washington, I'm still reading through Daniel's evidence files when I go to Berkeley to pack up my apartment. Though my grad school notebooks are still buried in a plastic box in the crawl space beneath Rose's house, I don't manage to retrieve them. I need to sell the bike under a tarp on the balcony where I told Daniel I had feelings for him, box up the velour sweatshirt with skulls on it that he gave me for Christmas, roll up the Goya poster across from the bed that we used to share.

While I'm in town, I join some graduate students from the department on an overnight road trip up the northern California coast. As my friend's car winds through a redwood forest, lines from interviews, texts, emails, and letters keep echoing in my head. *Stable composed cold emotionless shaking crying the great love of my life disgusting pampered whore fears unfounded felt like she might die simply accepted his invitation not like a big thing.*

As we walk to a rocky beach, I smile and talk to people whose words about me I have just read. When I feel eyes on me, or think I do, I hyperventilate and go sit on the porch. Though my close friends have stuck by me, I'm not sure if any of my other relationships in the department will survive. The investigation materials presented people I thought I knew in a different light, just like Anna said my dissertation research would. But I can't place them in a starry firmament that reveals a secret logic; I'm stuck down on the ground.

Reading letters in archives has always filled me with the thrill of the hunt. Now that I'm the one whose communications have been dragged out for consumption, I feel more kinship with the animal in the crosshairs. To endure the investigation, I have to maintain the psychic split that opened when I hacked my consciousness into two (*I am not me, the horse is not mine*). It's too humiliating to identify with the woman who tells Daniel she wants to feel him inside her in texts that bureaucrats and lawyers are currently reviewing on their computer screens—this Complainant who is either a compassionate victim (according to some) or a hard-hearted liar (according to others), but who we can all agree would have spared everyone a lot of trouble if she had just kept her mouth shut.

━━━━━

Once I finish reviewing all the interviews and evidence, I try to reclaim the narrative. I explain that Daniel was met with an outpouring of public support, that agreeing to go somewhere can be a "tool for de-escalation" rather than an indicator of safety, that people who were not present cannot say whether I had the right to be afraid or not. Issa sends a lethality risk assessment and a diagram of the cycle of violence to help put Daniel's behavior back in the context of abuse.

After submitting my comments, I return to Moscow, where summer poplar fluff is floating through the breeze. I'm still adjusting to the time change when I get an email from Anna. She's in town, inviting me out to dinner to discuss my dissertation. For four years, I've looked up to Anna and relied on her feedback and recommendation letters. Now the thought of it makes me sick. I reply that I recently had to read her statements to the Title IX office and don't feel like I can talk about my work with her. Anna writes back that she doesn't want to excuse Daniel's behavior and agrees that I shouldn't have to be in the same physical space with him. "Where we evidently disagree concerns his status as a graduate student, on which his medical insurance is contingent." It's safest, Anna says, if Daniel remains in the PhD program and continues his therapy and medication through the university health plan, while keeping away from me.

A year ago, I thought the same, but so much has changed since then. Letting Daniel stay would mean throwing away the case that I have spent the past year building, leaving the people who spoke out against him vulnerable, turning my back on the additional ones he might hurt. Like any other graduate student, Daniel can't stay on Berkeley's insurance forever. Maybe Anna is right that appeasing him is the soundest strategy, but I've seen the cycle play out too many times: Daniel promises to change and stays on good behavior until he gets what he wants, at which point all bets are off. I imagine Daniel looking for a girlfriend in unwitting new cohorts, teaching young women in the same halls where he hurt me, applying for professor jobs with glowing recommendation letters that tactfully avoid any mention of what he's done.

I write to Anna that I'm sorry the case has affected my relationship with her, but that treating depression and anxiety doesn't cure misogynist violence. Soon after, I fill out a form removing her from my dissertation committee. Seeing myself scrutinized in the case files has made me care less about what anyone thinks, which is clearly beyond my control. By the time I reemerged from the thicket of witness interviews, I'd shed my people-pleasing identity like a snakeskin. Whatever took its place is thicker and less pliable.

Alexander also takes a summer trip to Moscow. I hope that his more enigmatic position might leave room for a way forward. When we meet at a café in a calm, sunny courtyard, we speak Russian, the foreign language forming a diplomatic buffer between my measured words and my roiling stomach.

I tell Alexander I'm surprised that he withheld details about what he knew and expressed equal support for me and Daniel. After pointing out that the interview summary might have been incomplete, Alexander explains that he decided not to tell the Title IX office anything that he didn't witness firsthand. He observes that there were two stories, and he had no way of choosing one over the other or concluding what occurred.

Over his years as a professor, he says, he has learned to separate the personal from the professional. For him, all that matters is the intellectual work, and nothing else that someone does could change that: if one of his students were in prison, he would keep advising them. There's an awkward pause as I think about who could conceivably face jail time in this context and for what crime. He apologizes for this remark, and the conversation moves on.

We part on good terms, and I tell myself that everything is resolved. Afterward, however, I keep reflecting on what he said. Alexander seemed to think his attitude was in keeping with the historian's advice that he'd written on my research paper back in my first semester: avoid repeating "unconfirmed claims." In cases of sexual and domestic abuse, however, people called as witnesses might not have directly observed an act of violence, but by sharing what they did see or hear and when, their words can help an investigator determine whether an accuser's story is more likely than not to be true. Withholding information helps Daniel, not me.

Besides, the MeToo movement has revived second-wave feminism's argument that the personal is inextricable from the professional (and the political). Harvey Weinstein's job as a movie producer wasn't unrelated to the rapes he committed; he exploited his position to gain access to victims and keep them silent. If Alexander had decided to step back and function only as an academic advisor, then why had he written emails to Daniel that disclosed information about his own life and emphasized how he was Daniel's "friend" after he already had been told that Daniel had hurt me? At our courtyard lunch, Alexander mentioned that Daniel had sent him a narrative about his childhood and mental health struggles—presumably the same one that Daniel included in his evidence file. I wonder if Alexander is as good at abstaining from judgment as he thinks.

Either way, I push it to the back of my mind. I have dissertation chapters to write and new developments to address in the case. There's a second evidence review in which both Daniel and I see the comments and additional materials sent by the opposing side. Daniel said that he's recovered while continuing to deny or minimize most of what he's done. He submitted a mental health timeline that says his threats of self-harm were unconnected to me, as well as another letter from his therapist. Daniel and his attorney demand that I submit my entire text message history with him and my friends on the grounds that I am concealing exculpatory information—a request that reminds me of when he used to grab my phone. I refuse and ask myself if there will come a day when Daniel won't get any more of me than he's already taken.

As I scroll through thousands of pages of PDFs while writing these chapters, my head fills with voices again as if no time has passed. To quiet them, I attempt to see myself as a subject in a historical phenomenon called "gender-based violence." Objectivity feels like alchemy that can transform experience into parable. *If I just try a little harder*, I think as I strive to distill the sour rush of feelings, *I can be impartial*. I can morph from Judith, that tarnished symbol of a movement attacked from all sides, into Justitia, the goddess who holds balanced scales with covered eyes.

While looking through the witness statements and Daniel's evidence, I copy and paste, summarize, and condense, capturing what I think are the most important points while staying aware that each choice I make twists the conclusions that could be drawn from them. Another editor would have handled the sources differently, left other materials in or out, foregrounded alternative details. No matter how much I try to look past the particular in search of the universal, I'm left with my own perspective.

I remember the moment when, in one of Alexander's lectures, he described finding archival material which revealed that the dear friend of a woman he'd interviewed had denounced her. Alexander explained to the class why he kept his discovery a secret: "It's not the historian's role to play God." But there were no boundaries in the labyrinth of investigation. Here, I had to read and rebut the correspondence of living people for a power higher than myself. The betrayal in the archive entered the story of my life.

13

PREPONDERANCE
OF EVIDENCE

A T THE END OF OVER A YEAR OF INVESTIGATION, I RECEIVE A 167-
page report. I sit on the floor of a Moscow airport while preparing
to board a flight back to the US, shaking as I open the file.

After evaluating the witnesses' testimony against the evidence to
determine whether the events I've described are more likely than not to
have occurred, the report will conclude whether Daniel violated university policy. Even if he did, I remind myself, OPHD has no say over the
consequences; sanctions are handled by a different office.

The investigator begins by listing all the allegations, followed by an
initial conclusion. Using the "preponderance of the evidence" standard,
she has found that my allegations are "SUBSTANTIATED in part and
UNSUBSTANTIATED in part." I frantically scroll past the witness
statements, which are now footnoted with both sides' rebuttals from the
evidence reviews, until I reach the section that assesses the credibility of
each person interviewed.

I come first. The investigator says that I had direct knowledge of all the
events in question, described them consistently, and willingly addressed
information that I had not initially presented after it emerged in conversations with other people. Numerous witnesses and documentary evidence corroborated my allegations. I have been deemed credible.

In assessing Daniel's credibility, the investigator considered the fact that Daniel said his memory of the events in question was faulty due to post-traumatic stress from his childhood. While he did admit to "certain unflattering aspects of the alleged behavior," he denied many incidents that were corroborated by witness testimony and documents. His account also contained discrepancies. In his second interview, for example, he said he didn't touch me outside the bar in Texas. However, later in the investigation, when he responded to questions about the same event in writing, Daniel said he "hugged" me in such a way that a bystander felt it was necessary to intervene. "Regardless of the reason that it occurred," the investigator wrote, "I found Respondent's version of events was inconsistent with other evidence and sometimes inconsistent with his own prior statements." She concluded that Daniel was less credible than me.

She found most of the witnesses credible, including Daniel's therapist, who was brought in as his advocate but revealed information that Daniel denied. She was more skeptical about our professors. The investigator found that answers given by one of Daniel's professors regarding what she knew about violence were "evasive and implausible" and "inconsistent with other evidence," and that her actions suggested a bias in Daniel's favor. The assessment of Anna begins by noting that she submitted an unsolicited character reference on Daniel's behalf. It observes that she lacked any direct knowledge of the situation and appeared to be "attempting to protect Respondent." As a result, Anna was "less credible than other witnesses." Alexander did have firsthand knowledge of some events that were verified by evidence and witnesses. However, his "vague and implausible responses to questions about when and what was disclosed to him about Respondent's alleged physical violence toward Complainant suggested a motive to provide less than accurate or complete information." The report concludes that Alexander "lacked credibility."

My laptop almost falls off my knees. I feel a childish pop of glee, like the splat of a water balloon. It immediately evaporates as years of clever observations, constructive criticism, and mutual praise bubble up in my head. If Alexander's greasepaint has melted, if only in the context of this case, I don't know what to do with everything he's taught me.

I brush off this thought and move on to Part 2, "Factual Findings," which breaks down each incident into "undisputed facts" and "disputed facts." The analysis is empirical: it compares information from different sources, gives more weight to material produced closer in time to the event, and includes footnotes that acknowledge alternative interpretations and link to the evidence (appended as "exhibits"). Yet, to my surprise, it doesn't turn chronicle into narrative, which sets it apart from my training.

The omniscient voice favored by historians creates the illusion that their accounts describe events exactly as they unfolded. Readers pick up a finished garment without seeing the construction process. The Title IX investigator, who writes in the first person, shows all the seams as well as the discarded fabric on the floor. Rather than elevating some details and excluding others, she lays out all the available information, constantly making clear what she does and does not know. She hasn't arranged events in a hierarchy of importance: the report spends as many pages weighing whether Daniel once shook my arms when we went to get doughnuts as it does assessing whether he threatened to kill me. It's less elegant—but more honest—than the smoothly crafted stories that historians tell.

While the report determines that most of what I described was more likely than not to have occurred, certain findings are inconclusive. Under "Alleged Conduct #3," for example, I said that Daniel tried to strangle me while forcing my hand around his neck so that we could choke each other to death, leaving bruises on my wrist and jawline. There was one "undisputed fact": that Daniel bruised my wrists at some point during the semester. Daniel said this happened when I tried to walk away from an emotional conversation and he pulled me back. He also said it was possible that bruises appeared when he grabbed my jaw before punching himself.

In "determining what more likely than not occurred," the investigator gave weight to the fact that five different witnesses had been informed that Daniel put his hands around my neck or choked me. One of these witnesses was Daniel's therapist; others included my friends, with whom I discussed being choked in conversations that they referred back to in text messages (Witness 1: "Choking is not a cute mistake"). There were also references to choking or hands around my neck in the email I sent to Daniel after he got out of the psych ward, the email I sent to Anna right after I left Berkeley, and my handwritten TRO affidavit. Accordingly, the investigator said there was "significant evidence" that Daniel had choked me, which made his denials "highly unreliable." However, there were no witnesses or evidence to corroborate the rest of Alleged Conduct #3. Therefore, she found it more likely than not that Respondent tried to choke me, leaving bruises on my wrists and neck, but was unable to establish whether he tried to force my hands around his neck.

The report does not judge these events from the position of history or morality, but in terms of compliance with institutional policy. Since Daniel and I are both students and employees, we are subject to two overlapping codes. The report cites the rules against relationship violence and stalking in the university's Sexual Violence and Sexual Harassment Policy, as well as the prohibitions against physical abuse, harassment, and stalking under the Student Code of Conduct. In analyzing the former, it concludes that Daniel is "responsible" for relationship violence, which "requires bodily injury or fear of serious bodily injury." The investigator found that both occurred. The policy specifies that this must be done "intentionally, or recklessly." She determined that it was.

In reaching this conclusion, the investigator says she recognized that Daniel was struggling with mental health issues but was unconvinced by his assertion that he "didn't mean anything" by his repeated vows to hurt me. For example, when he told me that he would shove me down the stairs, he "expressly followed through on the exact conduct he had threatened previously." Daniel's psychological problems, she says, did not negate the "pattern of conduct" that he engaged in toward me over an extended period.

I can't believe it: she saw through him. I look up at the tired strangers clustered around my boarding gate as if they were teammates ready to lift me up on their shoulders.

The investigator also found Daniel responsible for sexual harassment, narrowly defined according to the Trump administration's anticipated standard as "conduct that is so severe and/or pervasive, and objectively offensive, and that so substantially impairs a person's access to University programs or activities that the person is effectively denied equal access to the University's resources and opportunities." However, my sense of validation is cut short when I read that Daniel has been found not responsible for stalking. Daniel's behavior was "concerning," the investigator concludes, but since we were in a relationship, it falls under the rubric of dating violence. Under the code of student conduct, Daniel has been found responsible for physical abuse and harassment—but once again, not for stalking.

The report concludes by saying that the investigator's findings will now be sent to the Center for Student Conduct, which will decide whether to uphold them and determine any possible sanctions. Daniel and I are both allowed to plead our case to the center's head. After arriving in the US, I Google him: like the investigator, he's a Black attorney with a background in race and social justice. In an online meeting a few days later, I tell him why I've come to believe that dismissal is the safest option and the only one that would end the silencing and denial around what Daniel did.

In September 2018, I receive an outcome letter. The Center for Student Conduct agrees with the Title IX office's findings and has decided to expel Daniel and bar him from campus. The letter expresses sympathy with Daniel's struggles and commends him for going to therapy, but says that his actions showed he was aware of the harm he was causing, that his mental health issues don't mitigate what he has done, and that therapy cannot guarantee he would not hurt me or anyone else at Berkeley again. Finally, it concludes, keeping Daniel around would be "inconsistent with the University's mission of eliminating gender-based violence and harassment from this campus."

I don't let myself feel relieved, however, because nothing is final. Now comes the appeal process.

A couple of weeks after I receive the outcome letter, Stanford professor Christine Blasey Ford testifies before Congress about her sexual assault at age fifteen by Supreme Court nominee Brett Kavanaugh. She remains steady under questioning while Kavanaugh yells and cries. Kavanaugh has received support letters from his female law clerks, state attorneys general, and students, alumni, and faculty from Yale, his alma mater. Some Republicans compare Kavanaugh—a white federal judge nominated to a lifetime position on the country's most powerful court—to Tom Robinson, the poor Black man who is wrongfully convicted of raping a white woman and fatally shot by a prison guard in *To Kill a Mockingbird*.

What Kavanaugh's supporters want is not more investigation, but less. They get it. The FBI declines to look any further into allegations made by Blasey Ford and other women; Kavanaugh joins the court. He sits on the bench alongside Clarence Thomas, who claimed to be the victim of a "high-tech lynching" when he was accused of sexual harassment by Anita Hill during his confirmation hearings in 1991. Hill—who, like Thomas, is Black—endured hostile questioning only to be ignored.

The MeToo tidal wave has already receded, leaving mangled claims of martyrdom in its wake.

———

As the appeal approaches, I'm reluctant to return to Berkeley when Daniel could still be welcomed back into the department at any time. After receiving a grant that gets me out of teaching, in September 2018 I move to New York, a city big enough to swallow me so that I can't be found.

Later that fall, Trump's Department of Education releases the draft of its new Title IX regulations. The *Nation* reveals that men's rights groups played a major role in writing them. Among other things, the proposed rules allow schools to adopt the unusually high "clear and convincing evidence" standard instead of the "preponderance of evidence"; free them from any obligation to investigate incidents that occur off-campus; and require them to include cross-examination at live hearings. Though Title IX's purpose is to protect a civil right—access to education—these procedures impose principles from criminal law on schools (which lack powers like the ability to issue subpoenas and authenticate evidence). DeVos and Jackson aren't improving Title IX; they're making it unenforceable.

The new rules will go into effect following a public comment period, after which the Education Department could theoretically change them. However, the University of California is already modifying its procedures to comply with the expected policies, which slows down the process in my case. Now, an email from Berkeley's Center for Student Conduct informs me, anyone filing an appeal has the opportunity for a "full evidentiary hearing," including live cross-examination of the Complainant, that rehashes every aspect of the investigation.

Title IX critics are fixated on live cross-examination as an essential defense against false allegations. By eliciting the accuser's fishy reactions to interrogation, the accused can supposedly prove she's lying. But there are so many behaviors that might render a victim unbelievable, like my laughter in the domestic violence counselor's office or the calm demeanor I've tried to assume everywhere else. Though the comment period is probably a pantomime of receptivity rather than an actual summons for feedback, I submit a letter that explains how grueling the process I've experienced already is and how the new regulations will make cases like mine even harder to pursue.

Meanwhile, Daniel remains on paid leave. Several more months pass before I receive the appeal brief that his side has submitted in advance of the hearing. Though his materials sometimes contain lawyerly boilerplate, I can tell that he has written at least some of this himself. Daniel was "hiding nothing," it says, whereas I have provided "a carefully-selected compendium" of evidence that creates a revisionist history of a happy relationship. My "apparent errors, deliberate omissions, and misrepresentations," as well as my refusal to provide my entire text message history, should discredit me.

"Ms. Neumeyer sought a relationship with [Daniel] knowing he was struggling with mental health. Ms. Neumeyer repeatedly declared her love for [Daniel] and sought him out for companionship, intellectual stimulation, and sexual satisfaction."

"Ms. Neumeyer omitted emails and text messages in which she expressed her understanding that [Daniel] was a very special and wonderful person whose abusive behaviors were part of a mental breakdown."

"Ms. Neumeyer's omission of text messages also left out things that were inconsistent with the narrative she was presenting to OPHD, including multiple instances of sexual fantasy and a few mentions of light drug use."

While noting the accommodations that Daniel received—extended deadlines for submitting responses, the ability to answer questions in writing, direct communication between his lawyer and the university (which is ostensibly banned)—the brief also claims that his due process rights have been violated because he wasn't presented with the opportunity to cross-examine all witnesses. It doesn't mention that his side didn't submit any questions when given the chance to do so before my cross-examination session, in which the CRO confronted me with Daniel's version of events.

Quoting from character references he received, the appeal brief says that Daniel has been "a beloved and successful student whom his colleagues and classmates described as 'gentle,' 'respectful' and 'kind.'" New support letters from faculty and graduate students support its characterization of Daniel as harmless.

"I never had the impression that [Daniel] was coercing or manipulating Joy into remaining in a relationship with him," writes a female PhD student in our department who is dating Evan. "I recall many times when [Daniel] expressed doubts about getting back together after a breakup, and communicated a desire to have space. On the other hand, it often appeared to be Joy who was taking the greater initiative in rekindling their relationship, and who approached [Daniel] with the proposition that they get back together."

"Never did I get the sense that [Daniel] used violence to manipulate Joy into staying with him, or anything to that effect."

A letter from the literature professor says that Daniel's appeal is a test of the university's "humanity." Kicking Daniel out of the PhD program would be "unnecessary and cruel," she says, and deprive him of his "lifeline out of the violent and abusive environment" of his childhood. The appeal contains additional pages that Daniel has written about his family history, with more disturbing details. I have no idea if they're true.

After fifty-five pages of downplaying and disavowal, the brief ends by stating that Daniel has taken full responsibility for what he has done. By supporting him, the university can prevent the past from repeating itself: "unlike his father," it says, Daniel "can be redeemed."

As I read page after page about how Daniel has suffered, including a new letter from his therapist about the investigation's devastating impact on his mental health, I consider including a letter from *my* therapist. With all the emphasis on Daniel's anguish, I worry that his actions are getting lost. But would trying to curry sympathy make me the same as him?

I decide to do it anyway. Though Daniel didn't manage to seize the narrative during the investigation and sanctioning phase, he could still do so now, when a fresh set of eyes and ears will assess the case all over again.

My therapist's letter explains how everything I've told her about my relationship with Daniel shows classic signs of intimate partner violence. She reveals that I have a diagnosis of post-traumatic stress disorder—a gift passed down from Daniel to me, linking us like a string of pearls.

The letter concludes:

"I have been treating Ms. Neumeyer regularly for the past two years and feel that I know her character well. I find her to be rational and credible and firmly believe everything she has told me."

Daniel's therapist, of course, would say the same.

14

THE HAMMER

O N THE MORNING OF THE APPEAL HEARING, I LOG ON TO A NEW video-chat program I've never heard of called Zoom. It's August 2019, two years since the case began, and I'm back in the beach rental, with the same rusty fan blowing the hair from my face.

"You look like Beyoncé!" my Path to Care advocate writes optimistically on Gchat.

Issa is attending in person at Sproul Hall, the neoclassical administrative building that was once occupied by the Free Speech Movement. She sits near Daniel and his attorney. I am appearing on camera. We have devised a system: I will mute the volume when Daniel is speaking so that I don't have to hear his voice, while Issa summarizes what he said over Gchat so that I can respond.

Since dawn I've been rereading the case files, trying to refresh my memory so that Daniel's questions don't trip me up. Near the beginning of the report, I scan over a list of materials that the investigator declined to consider.

| Character Reference | Witness 7 | This character reference has no bearing on whether Respondent engaged in the conduct at issue in this matter. |
| Character Reference | Witness 8 | This character reference has no bearing on whether Respondent engaged in the conduct at issue in this matter. |

The reminder that our professors submitted letters for Daniel jabs me in the stomach.

At the hearing, Daniel starts things off with an opening statement. "He's crying," Issa messages me. "He's talking about how now he's a member of the National Alliance for Mental Illness and attends their conferences." Daniel says our relationship was "loving and consensual" and that I knew he suffered from mental health issues before we got together.

When it's my turn, I read aloud from an impact statement that I submitted to the Center for Student Conduct. Issa drafted some of the final paragraph:

"I hope that the appeal hearing officer will hold Respondent accountable for his abhorrent behavior by ensuring that he never hurts me or another student, either on or off campus."

Abhorrent behavior—the words feel unnatural on my tongue.

Though my advocate has told me that crying is acceptable, even advantageous, the knowledge that Daniel is listening freezes my face. My voice breaks, but I can't summon tears. As usual, he's better at playing the victim.

Now comes the part I've been dreading most—cross-examination. All questions must be emailed to the Appeal Hearing Officer, who determines whether they are appropriate before posing them. Daniel's side submits questions for me: why didn't I tell the investigator in my initial complaint that I visited Daniel in the psych ward, why didn't I provide my entire text history, what did I mean in a particular email on a certain day. I object to their argument that Daniel's behavior toward me was an innocent symptom of distress:

"You can be a person who suffers from mental illness, as I believe he does, and you can also have extremely disturbing ideas about women's role in a relationship."

As the hours go by, my sweaty thighs cling to the bottom of my chair. Daniel has brought in his therapist, who testifies that when Daniel attacked me, he was in a "fugue state" in which he was "retraumatized" and not fully aware of what he was doing. If Daniel wanted to hurt me or anyone else, the therapist is sure that Daniel would have told him.

We submit questions for the therapist. Issa jots down his responses.

On what basis do you think that Respondent enters a "fugue state" and was in one while being violent to Complainant?

Daniel occasionally loses track of time, particularly if triggered.

Do you have any prior experience working with clients accused of domestic violence?

Currently Daniel is the only one. In his overall practice, they have been less than 1 percent.

Is Respondent aware of his impact on Complainant?

Not really. He is "intellectually self-absorbed."

A violet sky hovers over Manhattan on the evening when I receive the final outcome letter. I'm working on a dissertation chapter at Columbia's library, trying to retreat into the Soviet '70s and failing as I incessantly refresh my email. Finally, the subject line I've been waiting for arrives: "Appeal Hearing Officer Decision."

The officer has rejected Daniel's arguments. She did not find any procedural flaws or evidence of bias against him. Her letter points out that even Daniel's therapist admitted he had some degree of control over his actions, regardless of his psychological state. But the crucial factor in her decision to uphold the expulsion, she says, was the fact that "Respondent's own arguments for a lesser sanction minimized his responsibility and the harm he caused to Complainant." The appeal process is over, and the sanctions are now in effect.

The strategies that Daniel used to gain sympathy in our department cut against him with the bureaucracy. If he'd stopped trying to hide what he'd done, he might have been allowed to stay.

After two years and two months, the case is over. I want to emit an ecstatic scream so loud it shatters the library's windows into spikes that rain down on the books, their weight toppling until the facade carved with the names of great dead white men crumbles into the earth.

Instead, I smile silently as I zip up my backpack and walk to the subway. For once I don't want to be in any time or place other than here and now, under the purple smog that covers the stars.

In the evidence exhibits attached to the report, black boxes checker the photos of me that Daniel submitted. The university removed names and faces in deference to the privacy that had already been lost. As I look back at these pictures, they remind me of photographs of repressed Soviet officials, whose faces were clipped out by scissors or smeared with ink. Such images erased their subjects from history, as if they had never existed. The void left by their absence was the only indication that they had.

In a photo taken in Austin on June 24, 2017, Daniel and I stand before a mural on the side of a taco stand. The night before, I had looked into his eyes and seen a will to destroy. In the morning, I was trying as hard as I could to placate him until we made it back home. When we stopped to get breakfast, he wanted to take a selfie. I refused; he insisted.

During the investigation, Daniel produced the photo as proof that the trip had gone fine. Though the box over our faces obscures what's behind us, I have my own photo of what he chose as our backdrop.

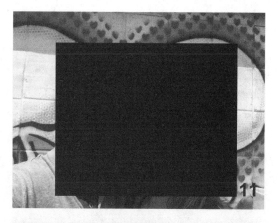

In the dramaturgy that Daniel laid out for us, I had to follow him to the precipice and wait for a push. The hero's salvation required my sacrifice.

If he had killed me that night, or on one of so many others like it, what would have been left to show what happened? In the report, the investigator was unable to corroborate certain incidents at all.

Alleged Conduct #5: *In or about mid-February 2017, it is alleged that while Complainant was cooking eggs in Respondent's apartment, he told Complainant that he wanted to hit Complainant's head with a hammer so that her "brains would come out like scrambled eggs."*
Undisputed facts: None.
Disputed facts: Respondent denied that this incident ever occurred. Respondent said the first time he heard about an alleged incident involving

a hammer and scrambled eggs was when he read the Notice of Allegations in August 2017. Respondent said Complainant previously mentioned other conduct to him but, she never specifically mentioned an allegation involving a hammer. Respondent also denies that there was ever a hammer in his apartment during spring 2017. Witness 6 (Respondent's roommate) corroborated that they did not own, borrow, or otherwise possess a hammer in the apartment during spring 2017. [Footnote: Witness 6's answers to emailed questions [are] attached to this report as Exhibit 22.]

After learning about Respondent's denial of the incident, Complainant maintained that it did occur. Complainant said, "It absolutely did happen." When I asked Complainant if she had ever confronted Respondent about this specific conduct, she stated that she raised the issue in a telephone conversation in late May or early June 2017. Complainant explained that the conversation occurred via telephone because Complainant was nervous to be around Respondent at the time. Complainant stated that: "I had a conversation with him about how he threatened to kill me." Complainant said she was loath to bring up specific incidents during this conversation because Respondent would become angry. Complainant indicated that when she spoke to Respondent about threatening to kill her she was specifically referring to Respondent shoving her down stairs, Respondent threatening to bash her head with hammer, and the mutual choking incident.

Factual Findings: The only corroborating evidence that the hammer incident occurred as alleged by Complainant were the statements of two witnesses (Witnesses 10 and 1), who Complainant did not tell about the incident until many months after she alleges it occurred. In late June 2017, Complainant told Witness 10 that Respondent had threat[en]ed to bash Complainant's head in with a hammer. Complainant told Witness 1 about this incident in July 2017. Witness 1 specifically recalled Complainant mentioning "scrambled eggs." No other witnesses indicated they had any knowledge regarding this incident, and there is no documentary evidence that corroborates Complainant's account.

The combination of there being no corroborating evidence from close in time to when the event is alleged to have occurred, and the fact that the witnesses were not told about the incident prior to late June 2017 when Complainant was moving toward permanently disengaging with Respondent, makes Complainant's account of this event less reliable than if she had shared her account with them sooner. I also considered the fact that Complainant did not mention the specifics of this incident in her TRO Affidavit.

I also considered the fact that Respondent's assertion that he had never heard of this incident until he read the Notice of Allegations was consistent with the evidence presented in this investigation. Furthermore, Witness 6's statement that there was not a hammer in their apartment, while not dispositive of whether Respondent made the statement (since having a hammer available is not a prerequisite to making the statement), was evidence that tended to weigh in favor of Respondent's account.

Ultimately, there was insufficient evidence to corroborate Complainant's account of this incident. Accordingly, I find that the preponderance of evidence does not support this allegation. I therefore find that the allegation that Respondent told Complainant that he wanted to hit Complainant's head with a hammer so that her "brains would come out like scrambled eggs" is unsubstantiated.

Daniel's tone was cool and detached. There was a hammer lying on the counter, which he looked at as he spoke. Did I imagine it later under the influence of his words? But it was there, I'm certain. At any rate, as the report observed, Daniel didn't need to have a hammer in order to say that he would bash my head in with it. The point was the aura of expectation that permeated the air around us. The fear was in the waiting.

Not dispositive. No documentation. Insufficient evidence to corroborate.

"We simply lack any organ for knowledge, for 'truth,'" Nietzsche wrote: "we 'know' (or believe or imagine) just as much as may be useful in the interest of the human herd." The concept of truth, he claimed, is a surrogate for God; better to dispense with metaphysics and find freedom in the present moment.

According to Ranke's positivist tradition, what distinguishes histor-ical research from fantasy is replicability. If done correctly, an inquiry can be reproduced by someone else and generate the same results. In our case, the Center for Student Conduct and the Appeal Hearing Officer reviewed the evidence and agreed with the investigator's conclusions. Then again, they were representing the same institution and had an inter-est in backing it up, not unlike how a historian might be motivated to endorse a book written by a colleague from the same graduate program.

Investigations of sexual and domestic violence dredge up displays of affection because most victims are abused by their friends or family mem-bers, teachers or priests—trusted associates who misuse their position in ways they might not realize or consider wrong. Though an incredulous reader of my case could easily find evidence to support the narrative that our relationship was "deeply loving," as Daniel and his attorney claimed, anecdotal examples don't add up to understanding. Browning, the his-torian of Nazi Germany, observed that while two scholars presented with the same materials might be able to agree on a basic set of facts, they would not reach identical conclusions about what those facts meant. Making sense out of muddle entails value judgments.

Depending on who narrates my relationship with Daniel and why, either of us could appear to be the victim. When we told our stories to university bureaucrats, we both claimed to have suffered. In the inves-tigation, our dueling perspectives canceled each other out, leaving only what was "more likely than not" to have occurred. Even then, however, the facts did not simply speak for themselves. Though the investigator avoided spinning a narrative, she used the lens of intimate partner vio-lence to reveal a whole that transcended any individual part. Combining research with interpretation allowed her to arrive at some semblance of truth. Yet much of the past, like the hammer, remains elusive. I'm the only witness, and one is not enough.

Part 3

15

MASTERING THE PAST

A FEW DAYS AFTER THE INVESTIGATION BEGAN, I SAT ON THE EDGE of a front porch, grass knifing through my toes. The August sky was suspended over motionless leaves, as still and silent as Daphne when she morphed into a tree to dodge Apollo's embrace. I'd stepped outside to talk on the phone to my advocate, who was warning me that regardless of the outcome, the Title IX process doesn't provide "closure."

"It's something you have to keep separate in your mind and try to find for yourself," she said.

Over the following two years and two months, I keep thinking that the story is over: when Anna tells Daniel not to do research in the same place as me, when I file a police report, when the university expels him. Yet all these endings depend on the mercurial rulings of outside judges. I need to erect a barricade so that Daniel can no longer lunge into my head. I want to transmute doubt into certainty, temper sand into steel.

I start trying on a train to Siberia. The investigation has been going on for almost a year, and I'm waiting for the latest update to tell me that "additional time is needed." In the meantime, I'm traveling to Russia's Altai region, with a stop in the industrial city of Yekaterinburg. A hundred years ago, in July 1918, Tsar Nicholas II and his family were shot and stabbed with bayonets in a basement there. The town was rechristened Sverdlovsk in honor of the man who oversaw the operation. After the Soviet collapse, the Russian Orthodox church canonized the last tsar, along with his wife and children, as holy martyrs. I lay on my bunk in a third-class train car as pilgrims chant the royal family's names until late in the night: "Nikolai, Alexandra, Alexei, Maria, Olga, Tatiana, Anastasia."

As dawn light creeps through the windows, Daniel's face materializes in front of mine. In this netherworld between Moscow and the Urals, consciousness and sleep, the past blurs with the present—Daniel is clutching my throat and telling me that liars get beaten, I'm Bukharin pleading with Stalin to forgive me. My therapist advised me to dispel such visions with a "self-calming technique" that entails tapping my arms while thinking of trusted friends. This time, I make instant coffee from the dribbling hot water urn at the front of the train car and pull out my laptop instead.

After arriving in Yekaterinburg, I keep writing, in the basement of a former housing development for secret policemen. Built in the 1930s, the complex was designed in the shape of a hammer and sickle that's discernible only from the air. Jaundiced paint peels off modernist angles that have been rediscovered by hipsters selling craft beer and sweatshirts with the city's discarded Soviet name. At a pub called The Sleeping Dog, I type the draft of what is turning into an essay on violence and truth.

My first attempts at putting our relationship into writing mentioned "some of the things that happened" and how Daniel twisted them, in a disturbing sort of listicle that I hoped would sound sober and to-the-point enough to convince my reader he was not what he seemed. The warm tone of the email I sent to Anna just after leaving Berkeley a year ago, which emphasized my ongoing "love and empathy" for Daniel, bleached out as I gained more distance from him. By the time I wrote the TRO affidavit, it was gone entirely. The Title IX process requires recalibrated phrasing. As I pursue my case, Issa encourages me to stress how "my ability to access campus resources was limited." It was, but the emotional fallout weighs more heavily on me than whatever opportunities I've missed on the university's grounds. As I bend my experience to fit the bureaucracy's frame, the investigation pushes the essence of what happened farther and farther away.

Now, with myself as the only audience, I want to form a more complete account of the past, outside of the institutional procedures that have further disfigured it, and recover the deeper truth hidden beneath the rubble of text messages and testimonies by "witnesses" who weren't actually there. On my computer screen, I'm able to distill my dynamic with Daniel into its most essential components. I can say that I loved him while skirting the passion that thickened the worse he treated me. I can write that he said he was cruelly neglected without going into the specifics of his childhood, or the diagnoses he offered as an excuse, or his claims that any criticism of his behavior was prejudice against his identity—all the points that he used to pressure me into silence.

Posing us like puppets in an abusive playhouse like any other allows me to put my experience together with my education and capture how it feels when personal and intellectual worlds collide. I compare our relationship to Bukharin and Stalin's, link the different stories that circulated about it to White's notion of history as narrative, revisit Ranke's commitment to empirical fact. The latter, which I'd once seen as naively old-fashioned, now sticks out like a fence post in the whirlwind of opinions.

I drain my beer and send the opening paragraphs to Hannah.

"There's a lot more," I tell her, "but it's hard to find a satisfying conclusion, in part because the 'story' isn't over."

The second evidence review just took place. I still have no idea who the investigator will believe or what conclusions she'll reach. All I'm left with are my disparate memories and desire to make sense of them. Though Hannah tells me to keep writing, I leave the essay unfinished and reboard the train.

A few weeks later, when I'm back in the US, I return to the abandoned Word document. The Title IX office has issued its report, and the case is now in the sanctioning phase. Though I don't know whether the report will be upheld, it allows me to write an ending with the lucidity I long to feel.

"For when faced with terror," I write, "we must couple ecumenicism with faith—in the ability to know, and the imperative to act."

While I fiddle with the draft, Title IX is back in the news. Avital Ronell, an NYU professor who used to teach in Berkeley's comparative literature department, has been put under investigation for sexually harassing a male graduate student. Ronell said that the student was simply insecure about his poor writing and that they shared "a penchant for florid and campy communications" with which he never seemed to have a problem. Ronell received a support letter signed by feminist luminaries including the pioneering historian of gender Joan Wallach Scott, postcolonial theorist Gayatri Chakravorty Spivak, and Berkeley's own Judith Butler, author of *Gender Trouble*.

These renowned specialists on gender and power suggested that Ronell's accuser had "malicious" motives and praised her personal and intellectual gifts—the same defenses that always crop up around people accused of abuse. While the letter writers noted that they did not have access to any of the materials in the Title IX investigation, they confidently agreed that "the allegations against her do not constitute actual evidence." As a queer, feminist woman, Ronell could only be a well-intentioned voice of the subaltern, not an authority figure who sometimes used her influence to malevolent ends—or so her peers believed. NYU's Title IX investigation found her responsible for sexual harassment, though not sexual assault or stalking; she was suspended for one year.

As the think pieces about Ronell multiply online, a couple of my friends encourage me to publish what I've written. After the peak of MeToo, "trauma essays" have been superseded by critical commentary, but they continue to appear. I consult with Issa, who as an attorney advises against it; since the appeal process is ongoing, anything I publish could jeopardize the outcome. Nevertheless, I decide to try. Most people who see results in Title IX cases seem to get them by going to the media, so I figure it might help more than hurt.

I submit the draft to the inboxes of a few publications. One politely declines; several don't reply; another accepts it, but then the editor ghosts me. After the last experience, I'm too burned out to try again and focus on finishing my dissertation. Once it's done, Hannah sends me a link to a new section at the *American Historical Review*, the flagship journal for our field. The section, History Unclassified, says it welcomes "unusual and surprising contributions," including "research experiences that raise new methodological questions." Though a first-person account of abuse probably isn't quite what they had in mind, suddenly I can't think of a more appropriate venue. Why not directly address the profession that both refined my brain and stabbed me in the back?

———

As I keep writing, I add more context about how both historians and researchers of domestic violence try to represent the invisible, and how MeToo trusts women to recount unseen horrors while raising old fears of their duplicity. Now that the case is over and I'm done with my PhD, I feel emboldened to hit harder, letting my repressed anger bubble into a sanctimonious froth. "For the scholars who wielded their power to protect the man who wanted to kill me," I write, "no amount of testimony could override the tale they found easiest to hear: the story of a martyred man." I also add a new note of ambiguity. Alexander, identified only as "a historian" sitting across from me in a courtyard, expresses the position I've been wrestling with since the first night Daniel shoved me and my world shifted on its axis.

I reference our conversation in Moscow: "There were two stories, he said with a shrug," I write, "and he had no ability to decide between them. 'How could I say what happened?'" Alexander had been referring to his refusal to discuss anything that he had not witnessed firsthand with the Title IX investigator, a decision that led him to avoid admitting what he'd heard from me and my friends. Once again, excising names and details allows me to make a bigger point—here, about the potential downsides of neutrality. I give the essay a title: "Darkness at Noon," after the novel I discussed with my students that acquired a secondary significance for my life.

When I submit the draft to History Unclassified, the section editor is very interested. So is AHR's editor in chief. However, he has concerns that the essay is unfair toward members of Berkeley's history department, though they remain anonymous. The scholars wielding their power make him especially uneasy, as does another line about professors and graduate students supplying my ex-boyfriend with character references. Though these letters were part of the Title IX process and the narratives it produced, it seems they are too incendiary to mention. The editor in chief suggests either publishing the essay under a pseudonym, with both my name and the institution's removed, or rewriting it in a way that does not implicate faculty in my department.

After sending the draft to all fifteen of the professors who compose AHR's editorial board, he reports that their opinions are "sharply divided." One anonymous reviewer said that the essay would renew a necessary conversation about historians' responsibility to engage with the issues of the day. Other board members, however, "adamantly oppose" publication. The editor in chief quotes a representative sampling which argues that the essay is excessively violent and possibly made-up.

"What if these claims are false and proven false by the University investigators?" the reader asks, even though the case has already been investigated. "How would that work out if we published it as fact?"

I want to laugh. Or scream. After everything I've been through to prove my credibility, this historian's instinctual response is to argue that I'm not telling the truth. No matter how many hoops they jump through, accusers can always be deemed unworthy of being heard. Even an official report is easily dismissed as unreliable or too risky to discuss—institutional waste to be buried in concrete so that its toxic fumes don't reach the ground. I tell the editors that I don't want to write myself out of a story that I fought to be able to tell and that the fact it took place at Berkeley, a university synonymous with progressive values, shows it can happen anywhere. Pointing out that the investigation has already concluded and been upheld under appeal, as I wrote, I say that the hostile reviewer's haste to suggest I'm lying (apparently without reading the entire essay) is part of the problem I'm trying to address.

The editor in chief fears that some board members will resign if he decides to publish. While he thinks it over, I send the editors the Title IX report so that they can check my account against the university's. After reading it, they identify a couple of things I could represent more equitably. The section editor, who is strongly in favor of publishing, says that although the professors involved should have reported what they knew to the Title IX office, as they are instructed to do, they did try to keep me safe in the moment (while also looking out for my boyfriend). She's right; the things they said during the investigation overrode my memory of the positive actions they'd taken. I add an acknowledgment of how faculty tried to help me by moving my exam to a different location and providing me with a safe place to stay.

The section editor notes that another board member asked: "Why does this person's version of events get to be privileged over any other?" She suggests preempting this line of attack by fleshing out the view of Daniel's supporters a bit more and recognizing inconsistencies in my portrayal of the relationship as it was unfolding versus after I left. As I revise, I delete a few of the more finger-pointing lines. The power-wielding scholars disappear, as does someone who "asserted that I could not have been under threat because he had not personally seen me being assaulted and thought I looked fine" (a reference to Evan's support letter).

This reworking reduces my story to what is least likely to rile the other participants. Though my memories chafe against the bridle of truth-by-consensus, I'm willing to wear it for the chance of being heard by the scholarly establishment whose opinion, despite everything, still matters to me. To show how domestic violence can surface unexpectedly in historians' archival work (in addition to our personal lives), I include a few lines about Liza, whom I describe anonymously as the wife of an actor I was researching. I write that my past self might have written off the revelation that he choked her and forgotten about it. Now, instead, I decided to include it in the dissertation chapter that mentioned Oleg while putting the details in a footnote, "a positioning I am still unsure about."

To draw out the historical implications of how detachment can facilitate the abuse of power, I add a reference to *The House on the Embankment*, a novel by Yuri Trifonov about Stalinist terror and its aftermath. In the story's key sequence, a graduate student in Moscow hesitates about whether to speak up on behalf of his denounced professor at a meeting. When an excuse arises not to attend, he's able to avoid deciding at all, and goes on to enjoy a successful academic career. The disgraced professor is transferred to a provincial teachers' college.

Finally, I write a new ending that refers back to White, who said that historians' narrative preferences are motivated by an illusory desire to impose moral clarity on the mess of life. Though another narrator could render my story differently, I write, "to believe that all tales are created equal is also a choice with consequences, as is the decision to cling to a version that doesn't fit." The competing voices in my case taught me the importance of acknowledging multiple truths and of being able to alight on one.

"If every story has a moral," the essay concludes, "this is mine."

This ending, however arbitrary, captures survivors' struggle to maintain their perspective and the necessity of doing so. Though a board member who reads the revised version thinks it still isn't appropriate for an academic journal, the editors accept it for publication.

When the essay appears online, I'm on a run. I glance down at my phone and see a message from a graduate student I've never spoken to, thanking me for what I wrote.

"I always took my experience of me trying to create a compelling narrative around my rape [. . .] as a sign that what happened to me wasn't real enough," she writes. "But hearing you explain it was really validating."

I stop running and start crying.

Her message is followed by others. A professor tells me that after he supported a Title IX case filed by women in his department, he received death threats, lost friends, and saw objects set on fire in his front yard. Abuse survivors describe how they also struggled to trust their perceptions, encountered disbelief from their community, or felt they could never articulate their experience convincingly. A male graduate student explains the narrative confusion he faced in trying to flee an abusive girlfriend. He says that a friend provided him with a safe place to stay when he left, but poked fun at the idea that he was in danger: "I think it shook his notion of how domestic relations are gendered. I laughed nervously, too, but it was true."

At least one person who reaches out to me is still in an abusive relationship. Her message contains the kind of obfuscation that I remember
all too well; she mentions "a small incident" that happened with her husband, only to quickly add that things are fine now. I write back with some
resources and tell her to reach out anytime. So far, she hasn't.

The incoming chair of Berkeley's history department posts the essay
on social media with an enthusiastic endorsement, which is immediately
reposted by the departmental account. The head of AHR tells me that
the forecasted wave of editorial board resignations didn't arrive; in fact,
there hasn't been any blowback at all. Our profession's public response
has taken shape, and it is positive.

This time, the outpouring of support is not for Daniel, but for me, in
recognition of what he tried to hide. I feel overexposed again, but on my
terms, in solidarity with other people who have been through it. The buzz
of insects in the bushes finally goes quiet, their rival melodies reduced to
a faraway hum. Dizzy with affirmation, I feel that now the story is mine,
and it's over.

And then, I receive an email from Alexander. Subject line: "Your
essay."

"In the interest of truth-seeking," it begins, "I would like to say a few
things."

━━━━━━

According to Alexander, no one ever questioned my account of what happened between me and Daniel. "As far as I knew, there was no competing
narrative. [Daniel] never approached me with one." He recognizes himself in the courtyard conversation, but views his stance as one of princi-
pled resistance to intimidation.

"I told you that I was in that [Title IX] office as a witness and that I
did, indeed, refuse, in the face of openly hostile questioning, to speculate
about things I had not seen or heard directly," he writes. "I was not going
to weave tales, no matter how hard they tried to get me to do so."

He is not a fan of Hayden White, and he believes in searching for
truth. But "there is more to truth—and to moral responsibility—than the

question of guilt or innocence." From what I can tell, Alexander means that it's possible to believe the victim while also trying to help the perpetrator. Alexander reminds me that he aims to treat all his students equally regardless of their character. He says he did his best in all respects and would behave exactly the same today. He concludes that I should have consulted with him and asked him "a few questions" before publishing.

"That is what a historian, or a friend, would have done."

Heart racing, I forward the email to Hannah. She reads it but has no idea what to say. Neither of us feels equipped to handle this. Alexander's opinion means everything to his advisees, who wouldn't dream of talking back to him. Though Alexander excels at withering criticism, he usually directs it against authors whose books he's reviewing, not his students. We are protected by his patronage—what Russians call a "roof" (*krysha*). What's happening now feels like an anxiety dream. The room around me falls away until it's just the two of us in a lecture hall. As I stand up and try to seize the podium, Alexander looks down at me in disgust, his habitual irony replaced by the wrath of a deity banishing an angel from heaven:

I'm the one whose word is law.

Alexander had always stressed his students' right to think for themselves and act as they choose—most strongly in that courtyard, where he said that no possible moral wrong his students could commit would lead him to stop advising them. Though the essay did polemicize anonymously with Alexander's relativism, which I shared but also came to question, it hadn't occurred to me that he would be angry about what I wrote. Even after everything I'd read, I'd somehow failed to foresee this predictable development: the patriarch swatting a challenge to his authority as if it were a fly that landed on his throne.

I'd previously emailed Alexander to tell him that Daniel had been found responsible and then expelled; Alexander thanked me for letting him know but didn't comment otherwise. Only Daniel and I received a copy of the report. Alexander doesn't seem to realize how both intimate violence and the Title IX process run on contradictory interpretations that distort the victim's sense of reality—or that Daniel submitted

Alexander's own deeply empathetic emails as evidence in his defense. It appears that rather than questioning his perceptions or trying to learn more, Alexander preferred to put me in my place.

We'll see about that, I seethe.

My initial shock has ceded to anger. I start typing an irate reply before remembering that I can't afford it. Alexander controls my professional future. I'm in the middle of applying for academic jobs; my employment depends on his recommendation letters. The power imbalance between us bounds our interactions. After waiting a couple of days, I try again, with a message that aims to be respectful while standing by what I wrote. Defending my point of view during the investigation has prepared me for this standoff better than I could have expected.

I express admiration for Alexander's teaching and scholarship, along with gratitude for his efforts to assist me at a frightening time. I tell him that the essay is not based solely on my impressions, but on the university's records. While I understand he thinks his remarks were taken out of context, I remember other moments from that discussion I'm not sure he does, like when I told him that Anna informed the Title IX office that Daniel was the victim of a lynch mob. I am aware that he separates his students' academic activities from their conduct and presume that he saw his decision to provide Daniel with a support letter in this light, even though "the boundary between the personal and the professional was already hopelessly blurred."

I finish with a backhanded compliment—that Alexander's training helped me write the essay.

"If not as a historian or friend, then maybe at least as a mentor, you can appreciate this."

At least I tried to be gracious, the prodigal Sunday school participant in me observes with sinful pride.

Though I'm not expecting a response, a couple of days later one arrives. Alexander offers some reciprocal praise before doubling down. He writes that he never said anything about not being able to decide between two different stories and that I made it up in order to tar him as an enabler. He also says that he didn't shrug. "You are free to question my sincerity," he says, "but you should not misrepresent my words and conduct."

Accordingly, the journal should retract this passage with a statement that it was based on an "erroneous recollection."

I know I didn't lie about what Alexander said, and he must know it, too: he identified himself as the speaker of those words without any context. Nevertheless, Alexander proceeds to explain to me the proper handling of abuse.

"Your essay and your letter suggest that the only punishment for a violent offender is complete ostracism. Your feelings are perfectly understandable, but can this position be maintained as a general, universally applicable principle? I do not think so."

The first reason, he says, is "professional." Alexander quotes from a letter that he says he provided to the Center for Student Conduct (at the request of Daniel's lawyer) about how he would continue to serve as Daniel's academic mentor. Alexander states that he stands by this principle "without apology or hesitation." The second reason is "broadly humanitarian":

"Believing the victim does not automatically lead to a total denial of the humanity of the perpetrator. Listening to a flawed individual does not imply condoning criminal actions or allowing oneself to be manipulated. Are there such things as reform and rehabilitation? Should your fellow students who taught at [San] Quentin be ashamed of themselves?"

Nobody asked him what he thought should become of Daniel, he says, but since this seems key to my criticism, he writes now that while banning Daniel from the university's grounds was necessary for my immediate protection (and Daniel's punishment), not allowing him to finish his PhD, and thereby "sending him back to the hard world he came from," might not have been the best way to secure the "safety of those close to him, his own safety, or his chance at some sort of redemption."

My head is spinning just like it did when I read the interviews, support letters, and appeal brief. Alexander sounds like Daniel's therapist and his lawyer. It seems to me like he's trying to regain the moral high ground by framing Daniel as an adolescent who needs more parenting from the university—and me as inhumane for suggesting otherwise. The essay didn't say that anyone who commits an act of violence should be totally ostracized or locked up for life and emphasized that I understood the people who stood by Daniel. Alexander's words remind me, yet again, of my own former desire to feel like Daniel's rescuer.

"There are some things that you just don't see, or maybe don't want to, about the dynamics of abuse and why certain responses to it are problematic," I tell him. "There are also some assumptions about my broader views on compassion and mercy that I don't endorse. Mercifully indeed, [Daniel] has never faced any criminal charges for the many acts of violence he has committed, much less been sent to San Quentin. He is an adult man with degrees from a great university who can do whatever he chooses (which I sincerely hope does not include misogynist violence against women), so long as it is not at the institution where he caused incredible damage." The notion that the wisest response to abuse is to quietly move the perpetrator to a different location within the same organization has been tested extensively by bishops in the Catholic Church. "This stance is highly compassionate towards people who commit abuse," I write, "but much less so towards those they harm."

Alexander replies that we're talking past each other and should stop. He affirms my courage and talent and adds that he would be happy to keep writing my recommendation letters. He goes on to make a couple of remarks about how I might revise my dissertation into a monograph, as I'm supposed to be doing now that I've finished my PhD. And with that, the status quo ante has been restored. He's the teacher at the lectern and I'm the student taking notes, allowed back into the fold after my insolent disruption.

Though I feel that his response proved my point about competing narratives, it also punctured my resolve. Even after hearing from so many strangers who identify with my experience and commend my "bravery," I doubt myself all over again. Why *should* my version of events be privileged? Does Daniel's pain excuse his actions? Does the pain he caused give me the right to say what should be done about them?

Alexander, at least as I and his other students knew him, always carved out thoughts in chiseled phrases with no excess fat. While we piled on words to impress him, his brevity attested to his superior erudition. The emails he just sent me are by far the longest messages I've ever received from him. While their tone is generally self-confident, their word count suggests that he feels threatened. It appears that Alexander isn't used to being challenged on unfamiliar territory. His formidable exterior cracked, revealing the imperfect mortal underneath. For me, Alexander has vacated the seat of authority. Though he helped shape my work, he doesn't hold any answers to the questions on my mind. By the end of our exchange, I've decided to shelve my dissertation and write a very different type of book.

16

PUBLIC PERIL

POTENTIAL DESTINIES EXTEND FROM EACH MOMENT LIKE THE RAYS of the sun; any attempt at "telling it like it was" is trailed by the afterglow of what wasn't. While the degree to which they defended him varied, Daniel's supporters shared an unspoken assumption that things would work out fine for me. I leapt forward into the future, because I was always going to, while Daniel was left behind in the amber of youth. Since my survival was inevitable, his exclusion was unmerited.

The German polymath Gottfried Wilhelm Leibniz determined that God imagines every conceivable outcome and chooses the most ideal. Voltaire's *Candide* satirized him as the complacent Pangloss, who declared that we inhabit "the best of all possible worlds" and therefore need not try to change it. Yet Leibniz introduced a speculative domain, on the edge of scholarship and sorcery, that would come to be called "counterfactual history." By separating events that are unavoidable from those that are subject to change, it tries to illuminate what lies ahead.

While reflecting on the experiences of readers who reached out to me and the factors that drive all our fates—the capricious marriage of the short-term and the *longue durée*—I keep thinking about something that Cassandra's friend with the Sanskrit tattoos told me after I left Berkeley. I'd arrived in Providence a couple of nights earlier. As we ate the steak she'd seared for dinner, I started to babble nervously about Daniel and my trepidation over what he might do.

A therapist who spent years as a social worker, she calmly put down her knife and fork and offered to listen to the voicemails Daniel left me in case there was anything I needed to know for safety planning.

I watched from outside the doorframe as she sat on her bed with my phone up to her ear. After a few minutes, she put it down.

"You need to be extremely careful," she said, and asked if I'd ever heard of the Tarasoff case.

On the southern border of Berkeley's campus, Bancroft Avenue rises toward International House, a looming tan structure topped by a red tile roof and a bulbed dome befitting an ancient caliphate. This eclectic architecture evokes I-House's stated mission of fostering "intercultural respect and understanding, lifelong friendships, and leadership skills for a more peaceful world." To us it was just another dorm that had rooms for graduate students, including Daniel, who lived there for his first two years in the PhD program. He occasionally invited me for dinner in the cafeteria, where we were joined by a protein-loading weight lifter who griped that the piles of spinach and beans he took from the salad bar were giving him gas. Daniel eventually moved to an apartment with Evan, a celebratory occasion for which I pulled up to the building's entrance in my Geo Prizm as they loaded boxes into the backseat.

In the fall of 1968, Tatiana ("Tanya") Tarasoff met Prosenjit Poddar at I-House's weekly folk dance. Tanya was the child of Russian immigrants from Harbin, China, a Manchurian city once inhabited by Russians who worked on the Trans-Siberian Railway. After spending years in Brazil, the Tarasoffs moved to the Bay Area when Tanya was thirteen. While studying at a junior college in Oakland, she took a class at Berkeley and was in the process of transferring there full time. Meanwhile, she kept living with her family off-campus. Prosenjit grew up in a village in West Bengal, India, as a member of the Dalit ("untouchable") caste.

A mechanical prodigy, he overcame enormous odds to win a seat at the Indian Institute of Technology, then a scholarship to Berkeley, where he was earning a graduate degree in naval engineering.

After meeting at I-House, Tanya and Prosenjit went on a few dates. On New Year's Eve, they kissed. Prosenjit thought it was a serious relationship; Tanya didn't. He made secret tape recordings of their conversations that he listened to over and over, looking for inconsistencies in her words and examples of how he felt she had mistreated him. He also started following her. He told a coworker at Berkeley's naval field station that he wanted to punish her for being interested in other men by planting a bomb on her block, at her house, or in her bedroom. A friend from back home who was also studying at Berkeley urged Prosenjit to try therapy. Prosenjit agreed and started seeing a psychiatrist and a psychologist at the university health center.

When Tanya went to São Paulo for the summer, Prosenjit's condition seemed to improve. When she returned in the fall, it got worse. He spent hours crying in the hull of a model ship he was building and started asking people how to buy a gun. He devised a plan: he would pay someone to proposition Tanya, at which point he would app˙ ˗ẇith the gun to "save" her and show her the error of her ways. After Prosenjit's therapist concluded that he posed a danger to Tanya, the therapist asked the university police department to put him on a mandatory psychiatric hold. When officers arrived to take Prosenjit in, however, they thought he seemed harmless and let him go. Prosenjit was polite and clean-cut—not like those dope-smoking hippies.

Prosenjit continued following Tanya around Berkeley. He'd recently moved into an apartment with Tanya's brother Alex, who had become a friend, around the corner from the Tarasoffs' house. In addition to studying on the same campus, Prosenjit and Tanya were now neighbors; she had nowhere to go. On the evening of October 27, 1969, Prosenjit rang the doorbell when Tanya was home alone. He was carrying a pellet gun and a butcher knife. After she came to the door, he shot and stabbed her repeatedly as she tried to run down the front steps. Tanya stumbled outside before collapsing on the front lawn. Prosenjit went into the house, where he called the police and told them that he had attacked his girlfriend.

The next morning, an article about the murder ran on the front page of the *San Francisco Chronicle*. It appeared to the side of that day's major story, about two Soviet cosmonauts who visited a local rodeo after returning from space. In photos, the beaming Russians pose in cowboy hats and wave to the crowds. They had flown back to earth while Tanya was running, falling, gone.

Berkeley Knifing

UC Coed Slain --Savage Attack At Her Home

A popular University of California coed was savagely murdered early last night by a man who stabbed her so many times police were not immediately able to count all the wounds.

Tanya's murder received a sensationalized round of local news coverage. In the media's depiction, she was a "tall, brown-haired coed," alluring and unobtainable, who had caused her own tragic death. Prosenjit, "a quiet man who minded his own business," was set off when she rejected him as a suitor. A classmate and coworker of Prosenjit's at the naval field station told the *Daily Cal* that he often talked about how "Miss Tarasoff had wronged him."

"I was so shocked when I heard about the murder," he said. "Poddar seemed very stable and quiet when I worked with him."

"He was very serious about her, but apparently the relationship was very casual to her," a source told the *Chronicle*. "He felt she had stood him up."

There was no mystery to the crime: Prosenjit confessed to killing Tanya, and several neighbors saw him do it. At stake was the narrative, over which Tanya no longer had any influence. Misinformation began to circulate about the events leading up to her death. Failing to mention the abandoned psychiatric hold, police told the *Chronicle* that Tanya and Prosenjit met less than a week ago and denied to the *Daily Cal* that they had received any previous tips about him.

At the trial, Prosenjit pled not guilty by reason of insanity. The defense said that he had been diagnosed with paranoid schizophrenia and could not have acted with premeditation or malice. A skeptical jury found him guilty of murder in the second degree, which carried a prison term of five years to life. In their appeal, his lawyers attributed the killing to a combination of culture shock and mental illness that was triggered by a provocative young woman. Tanya, they said, had been "tormenting" Prosenjit and prompted "severe physical and emotional changes" in him by expressing interest in other men.

The defense objected to the fact that the judge had not allowed a cross-cultural anthropologist to testify on Prosenjit's behalf, stating that jurors without a deep understanding of his childhood could not appreciate "the emotional stress that was engendered by the activities of the victim." They downplayed Prosenjit's repeated threats and stalking, saying that he was following her to try to clarify their relationship but that she refused to dignify him with a response. On the night of her murder, Prosenjit just wanted to talk, but Tanya started screaming for no apparent reason. Even in the act of killing, he was passive: "It is not entirely clear just what happened next, but in the course of events Miss Tarasoff received several pellet wounds, and multiple stab wounds from which she died." A psychiatrist for the defense suggested that Prosenjit was having a depersonalization episode and did not realize what he was doing.

The new judge lessened Prosenjit's sentence to voluntary manslaughter, which carried a maximum sentence of fifteen years. In February 1974, California's supreme court reversed his conviction on the grounds that the jury should have received better instructions on the definition of diminished mental capacity. In lieu of a retrial, the judge allowed him to leave the country. After four years in a medium-security medical facility, Prosenjit was free to go. In a court report quoted by the *Chronicle*, his probation officer said that he had made "maximum gains" through therapy.

"It appears he sees his offense as a learning experience about women," the probation officer observed. "He indicates that he learned a lesson and will even allow his father to choose a bride for him."

Tanya's death became history through legal precedent. Her parents sued the University of California for not informing them that Prosenjit had threatened to kill her. In 1974, the state supreme court found that a therapist has a "duty to warn" the potential victim if they think their client poses a serious risk of violence. According to the court, "the protective privilege ends where the public peril begins." A second ruling in 1976 changed this to a "duty to protect," which might include steps other than directly notifying the intended target. Some other states went on to adopt a similar principle. Many law and psychology students encounter "Tarasoff" in their training, where it is generally divorced from the context of gender-based violence and taught as a notice requirement law.

Cassandra's friend only told me the basic outline of the case to encourage me to take precautions. Later, when I seek out more details, I find scanned articles in newspaper databases and the briefs from the criminal trial appeal, which Berkeley's law school uploaded online for a class. I based my description above on these materials. Yet they reflect Prosenjit's version of events, not Tanya's. Though I wonder if she had any inkling of what he would do, Tanya remains a sphinx in a yearbook photo, an "innocent and wholesome" girl (in the words of a friend who spoke to the *Chronicle*) or a disdainful temptress, according to Prosenjit's side.

In search of Tanya's perspective, I try to track down the original trial transcripts to read witness testimony and evidence. I contact various state institutions, but no one has them. When I call the criminal records department for Alameda County, a friendly woman who answers the phone runs the names and numbers through their database. Though she can find references to the trial, the records themselves are missing. The most likely explanation, she says, is that the defendant had them sealed. According to *Bad Karma*, a book about the case published in

1986, Prosenjit went on to complete his graduate degree at an institute in Germany, where he lives with his wife and daughter.

At the time of the murder, *Bad Karma* author Deborah Blum was a sophomore at Berkeley. In the book's foreword, she writes that although she didn't know any of the people involved, she felt that what happened to Tanya could have happened to her. While researching the case, she came to identify with both Tanya and Prosenjit. The book is based on the now-closed criminal trial records and interviews that Blum conducted in the '70s and early '80s with their family, friends, and acquaintances, a number of whom have since died. Though *Bad Karma* is extensively sourced, the way it's written makes Tanya's viewpoint even harder to find.

Women have long practiced styles of history sidelined from the academy that allow greater room for invention, from spiritual biographies to true crime. (Herodotus, often seen as the first historian, is the founder of this tradition; he wrote in the first person and didn't distinguish between myth and fact.) *Bad Karma* fills the gaps in the evidence by making up scenes and dialogue and imagining its subjects' psychological states— precisely as I was instructed not to do in graduate school, where Alexander cautioned me to delete the embellished detail of a sculptor's pounding heart. The book describes bruises on Tanya's arms that she received from her father, but since it doesn't cite sources, I'm not sure if these hints of abuse are documented occurrences or creative license. When I reach out and ask, Blum tells me that she wouldn't have made up something like this, but since her research notes ended up in a long-lost box, she can't say for sure.

Fiction captures realms that evade academic historians, who are bound to the rock of empiricism (or at least its pursuit). In her 1995 book *Women on the Margins: Three Seventeenth-Century Lives*, Natalie Zemon Davis inserted made-up dialogues to overcome the absences in her sources, while making clear that they came from her head. The scholar Saidiya Hartman went on to call this kind of technique "critical fabulation." Such tactics have variously been lauded for rescuing underrecognized subjects from oblivion and chided for projecting on them. Either way, it feels safer to invent the words of people who died long ago than the missing viewpoints of those who are closer to us in time but separated by experience. Especially when applied to gender-based violence, fantasy can obscure as much as it elucidates. *Bad Karma*, which alternates between Tanya's and Prosenjit's perspectives, shows Tanya taking sadistic pleasure in toying with him shortly before her death: "while she felt a slight degree of guilt for sucking him back in again, that old feeling of revulsion was stronger, and it made her want to continue to punish him . . . at [the] sight of his hurt, imploring eyes, she suppressed a laugh."

I share Blum's craving to make the dead speak; I flirted with imagining Liza's thoughts and can envision Tanya's heart racing as she tried to escape Prosenjit. I'm also aware of how easy it would be, if circumstances were different, for someone to supply my voice in an equally unbecoming mode. This already happened during the investigation, when some of the witnesses reiterated Daniel's depiction of me as a "cold and emotionless" woman who provoked his distress. Blum doesn't really know what Tanya was feeling or thinking about Prosenjit on the evening of October 27, 1969, any more than Evan knew what I was going through on April 29, 2017, when Daniel attacked me in Dwinelle and followed me to Hannah's. Evan expressed certainty that I had no reason to be afraid that day; both he and his girlfriend portrayed me as the instigator, pressuring Daniel into being with me when he was the one trying to get away. If an author wrote about our relationship and I weren't around to present my side, she would base her characterization of me at least in part on such presumptions. No amount of research could resurrect Tanya's point of view, which was buried when Prosenjit took her life. By trying to re-create Tanya's consciousness, on the basis of words spoken by others, *Bad Karma* ends up leaving the same impression as the newspapers and the appeal brief—that she was a tease who got what was coming to her.

Some aspects of the Tarasoff case feel similar to mine: Prosenjit's obsession with Tanya's supposed promiscuity, observers' tendency to think that he was troubled but benign, the use of cultural and mental health explanations to portray Tanya as the aggressor and Prosenjit as the victim. There are also many differences, including Prosenjit's diagnosis of schizophrenia. Perhaps most importantly, rather than concealing his violence, Prosenjit told several people about his desire to kill Tanya. Sympathy for his plight, however well deserved, wasn't enough to prevent what he was about to do. Is there anything that could have?

According to *Bad Karma*, Tanya reached out to the university for help. When she called I-House and said she was having trouble with a former resident, she was put in touch with the foreign student advisor. The latter said that she was busy and could only meet next week, on October 28— the morning after Tanya's murder. Blum writes that a friend of Tanya's urged her to get out of town, and even offered her money to do so, but Tanya didn't want to give up her studies at her dream school. I imagine Tanya fissuring into two. One version of her collapses on the lawn and never gets up; the other moves back to Brazil, finishes her degree, falls in love—whatever she might have done with the life she never got to claim. The *Chronicle* article said that Tanya did translation work for professors; she spoke native Russian and Portuguese. If it were possible to pause and reroute the flow of time, maybe she would have become a linguist.

Making the second Tanya flesh and bone requires altering the elements that led to her demise. Different short-term decisions might have been enough. If the police had put Prosenjit under the mandatory psychiatric hold that his therapist requested, then maybe Tanya would have understood the threat she was under and tried to get away. Yet the crucial difference between our trajectories, to my mind, is the fact that Tanya didn't have access to any of the structures that helped me. In 1969, there was no law or framework that could have identified what she was experiencing or helped her leave. No one regarded her situation as intimate partner violence; this concept didn't even exist. Restraining orders, shelters, Title IX, laws against stalking and domestic abuse, resources on safety planning—none of it did. If a university administrator had gotten back to Tanya more quickly, they might have told Prosenjit to stay away from her, but even that would have been at their discretion. Schools had no rules or procedures for dealing with such things.

History doesn't unfold in a lab with replicable conditions; every occurrence, to some extent, is unique. All these options could have been available, and Prosenjit might have killed Tanya anyway. Today, measures like protective orders deter violence in some cases but far from all. Yet comparison can expose the mechanisms that help drive events in one direction or another. Even if the alternative outcomes of Tanya's case are unknowable, I'm certain that by the time Daniel and I were in graduate school, my escape and continued education were more assured.

▆▆▆▆▆▆

After filing our dissertations, my cohort comes up against a contracting system for which our advanced degrees left us unprepared. As we apply for the same handful of positions that attract hundreds of other perfectly qualified candidates, a handful of us win the academic lottery and get tenure-track jobs; some become adjuncts on short-term contracts that don't come with health insurance; and still more seek work with the government, or corporations that view a history PhD as an embarrassing gap in productivity. We commiserate over the vagaries of the market but deal with its corroding effects on our own.

I finish my dissertation in summer 2020 and attend an online graduation ceremony during the Covid-19 pandemic, when almost no one is hiring. The following year, when I have a postdoc, I'm invited to interview for a job that I want but don't get and am rejected for several others. Though Berkeley is looking for someone in my field, I don't apply. According to a friend of mine, Anna told him that if I don't feel comfortable going for the job, which she assumes is the case, then there's no reason why Daniel shouldn't still be at Berkeley. Clearly my essay didn't change her mind. Trying to win over professors I just called out, in a place where I would be easy for Daniel to find, seems ill-advised. After a couple months of vacillation, I decide to withdraw from the race and try to make a living as an independent writer.

In *The Captive Mind*, Miłosz wrote that breaking with communal pressures to strike out on one's own is "an act of faith" with no guarantees. I'm not certain whether defecting from a system that promises stability and belonging (in exchange for an unknown degree of compromise) is really the smartest move. After my essay came out, part of me fantasized that I would incorporate my personal misfortune into my research profile and be rewarded with prestigious grants, admiring graduate students, perhaps an endowed professorship in the history of gender-based violence. Yet I know that I couldn't keep writing about my experience if I were competing for the scant academic resources that still exist, and I'm not sure how much I want them anyway.

My conflict with Alexander reminded me of just how heavily the lowest members of the ranks rely on patronage in order to advance. The thought of spending years continuing to ask him for recommendation letters while trying to prove to senior colleagues that I'm a serious scholar who fills "lacunae in the historiography" and serves discreetly on university committees—not that melodramatic whiner who aired her department's dirty laundry in print—makes me faintly nauseous. Academia is both a boundless realm where people come to open their minds and a cloistered community where they are particularly susceptible to abuse. Title IX was created to try to counteract some of the dynamics that push them out. Though the process allowed me to finish my PhD, it couldn't undo the notion that intimate violence can be neatly cordoned off from intellectual work, which is supposedly all that counts—even though Daniel's behavior slowly extinguished my ability to think while he grew ever more confident in his command.

In the aftermath of the investigation, I also fissure into two. The version of me that's walking away from academia will never meet the one who didn't date Daniel (or make a complaint against him) and possibly went on to become a professor. I wonder what would have become of my double who donned the crown. I've had teachers who were careful not to misuse their power, and my friends with tenure-track jobs try to be as conscientious as possible. Yet my Title IX experience revealed a strain of hubris that can be infectious under prolonged exposure. Universities, like many institutions, task members with guarding their position through a delicate balance of beneficence and territorialism, humility and vanity. As students fall deeper into debt and schools eliminate tenure lines and entire departments, especially in the humanities, the select few who secure a place are often inclined to develop stronger myopia toward those below.

I fear that I would have grown so accustomed to my wisdom that I was blind to my folly, so oblivious to my influence over my students that I couldn't sense when it was hurting them (or would even take unconscious pleasure in the ease with which I lifted them up or cut them down). I picture myself sitting at a seminar table, posing subtly undermining questions that ensure the younger person before me doesn't learn to trust themselves. I remember how Daniel, in a flattering mood early on in our relationship, once said that I would be the perfect person to replace Alexander someday. He meant this as a compliment so lavish that it attested far more to the generosity of the giver than the merit of the recipient— the equivalent, in our cosmology, of saying "you could be God." Now I look back on it as a warning. Instead of gatekeeping a garden gone to seed, I'd rather find my own kind of damaged paradise.

After two years of weekly therapy and no dating, I fall in love again, with a man I met in Warsaw when I spent a few days doing dissertation research there in late 2018. A mutual friend put us in touch for a coffee that turned into an all-night conversation in a bar at the bottom of the Palace of Culture and Science, Stalin's neo-Gothic gift to Poland (a copy of Moscow prototypes) that celebrated the consolidation of Soviet rule over Eastern Europe. By the time the moon had mounted the palace's spire, I'd shed my usual self-protection and described the investigation and my attempt to write about it. He didn't question my judgment or rush to pronounce his. He wanted to know what I thought, and he really listened. We kept in touch after I left and eventually reconnected in New York. Though I jumped when he got near my neck and panicked at any sign of conflict, the calamity I was waiting for never arrived. Now that I've forsaken my efforts to join the tenure track, we move in together in Warsaw; Miłosz and I have traded places. But to understand the tides that divided my fate from Tanya's—and how other lives have emerged from the wreckage—I need to go back to California one more time.

17

NO MAJOR PROBLEM

A s I drive toward downtown Berkeley on a late afternoon in August 2022, the light gleams over the bay like it used to when I was hiding in the library, anxious about what evening would bring. Since the case stretched into the last year of my PhD, and I hurried to finish as quickly as possible, I never did move back here. My official reason for returning has already turned out to be superfluous: I'd planned to retrieve my boxes of notebooks, clothes, and kitchen supplies that were still growing mold under Rose's house, but her roommate recently mailed them.

Since the last time I was here, several of the professors I worked with retired. Berkeley's undergraduate population has turned over, and most of my friends from the PhD program have finished, dropped out, or moved away. One of them, who would sing and play guitar at our Russian history meetings until the last grad student was ready to call it a night, recently died of cancer.

Yet the moment I step into the eucalyptus grove on the western edge of campus and a cool pocket of air raises the hair on my arms, the expanding sliver of time that separates my Berkeley from this one melts. I could be walking to section, rushing to print my response paper for seminar, planning a comment on the reading so brilliant it will secure my place in the pantheon (or so banal it will eject me forever), eating ice cream sandwiches with Daniel on the grass as the runoff trickles down our fingers, carrying pizza boxes saggy with grease to working group (*pick up the pace, we're already late*).

As I walk up the slope toward Dwinelle, I see Daniel leaning against the concrete slab by the entrance—the spot where he always waits for me to get coffee, at the top of the steps that he shoved me down.

"Look who decided to grace us with her presence. Been having fun without me?"

I blink; the figure vanishes. Daniel isn't allowed here anymore, and I'm just a visitor.

In Doe Library, I slip my backpack into a quarter-operated locker and head toward the air-conditioning of the special collections division.

"What's the point of homecoming, anyway?" one of the students working the front desk asks the other as I sign a registration form.

Berkeley is a primary source now; I've come to read the university's records and find out what changed (or didn't) in the wake of Tanya's death. When I sit down at the long wooden tables in the reading room, the sepulchral peace that presides over every archive settles into me. As I start opening books and file folders, skimming articles and news clippings, my personal memories succumb to the pull of the deeper past.

I scan the *Daily Cal* headlines for October 28, 1969: "Pot Should Be Legal," "Frisbee Throwing Popular Here." Tanya died the night before, but the student paper hadn't covered it yet. Toward the back of the issue, a short notice announces that the women's liberation group is holding its first open house to clarify its "revolutionary vision." While Prosenjit was plotting to kill Tanya, Berkeley's campus was on fire. A group of graduate students and assistant professors burned their degrees on Sproul Plaza. As the paper crumbled into ash, they unleashed rage against the forces that had taken Tanya's life and would eventually reshape mine.

━━━━━━━

Berkeley's Free Speech Movement, which kicked off in 1964, was the first surge of campus dissent in the US and the founding moment of the New Left. In an acclaimed piece of oratory that he delivered on Sproul, philosophy major Mario Savio exhorted students to halt the machine of power.

The broader political movement that he helped spark aimed to fight injustice based on class and race but discounted gender.

"These radical men—self-righteous about the moral superiority of their politics, their opposition to an undeclared war in Southeast Asia, and to the oppression of people of color at home and abroad, quick to label a conservative professor or senator a fascist—thought nothing of forcing their will, not to mention their muscle, on the women they wanted to bed," Lisa Gerrard, who did her bachelor's degree at Berkeley and started her PhD there in 1969, later wrote. During her time on campus, she never considered reporting anyone; acquaintance rape, like "wife beating," was a shameful secret for which the victim bore the blame.

In the face of a male-dominated left, Free Speech alumna Jo Freeman created *Voice of the Women's Liberation Movement*, a newspaper that spurred the formation of feminist groups around the country. Activists at Berkeley staged "guerilla actions," like incinerating diplomas and invading male locker rooms, to publicize their demands: free childcare and parental leave for all students and employees, access to birth control and abortion, women's history and literature courses. Students who briefly occupied a local radio station adopted the names of past radicals including Rosa Luxemburg. Though Luxemburg had rejected feminism as a distraction from socialism, historical minutiae were irrelevant; the point was change now.

Feminists didn't seek to simply stop the gears of authority, but to turn them in favor of those who'd been silenced. As they shared their experiences, participants in consciousness-raising groups realized how acts of violence that they'd attributed to individual pathology were really tools of patriarchy. New terms, like "marital rape" and "battering," emerged for forms of abuse that were committed by intimate partners and relied on psychological coercion as much as physical strength. Activists organized crisis centers and shelters while state legislatures introduced restraining orders and laws against rape, stalking, and domestic violence.

For the first several years after its passage in 1972, Title IX was mostly applied to sports teams and hiring practices. The law had grown out of lobbying by activists who did not see themselves as subversives and worked within institutions to improve women's representation and pay. Over the course of the decade, however, Title IX was taken up by women's liberation, which declared that those institutions were rotten. Their ideas had yet to shake the bureaucracy in 1976, when the federal government required schools to submit reports about sex discrimination on their campuses. Berkeley's administration asked each department to do a self-evaluation. As I read through the folders, I'm surprised to see that they all say the same thing.

The comparative literature department reported that nothing "even conceivably discriminatory" was happening in its ranks. According to Berkeley's law school, "anything resembling a problem has been 'nipped in the bud.'" The philosophy department expressed outrage that it was being asked to comment at all, since "equality for women has been discussed and advocated for at least 2,500 years in the classical literature of western philosophy, from Plato's Republic down to the writing of Locke and Mill to the present." The real question, the department's chair wrote, was whether the government was discriminating against white men in favor of women and minorities.

At the time, the philosophy department had zero female faculty on the tenure track. Among the scholars it did employ was John Searle, the professor whose misbehavior would be exposed decades later in the movement against campus sexual assault. By fall 1977, women composed only 10.2 percent of all tenure-track professors, and 4.4 percent of full professors, at the University of California; of the 6.9 percent of full professors who were people of color, a mere 3 percent were women. Yet Berkeley departments unanimously declared that women at the university inhabited the best of all possible worlds.

Some voices lower down the hierarchy said otherwise, but their department chairs didn't listen. The women's graduate caucus in comparative literature submitted a letter outlining the kinds of sabotage women faced, like comments on their figures or invitations from professors to sit on their lap, that led some to drop out. The head of the department asserted in her report to the chancellor that female students "with more savoir-faire, or perhaps more self-confidence, regard such remarks as pleasantries rather than condescension." She concluded that the letter writers were distorting reality to suit their "feminist convictions."

If there were an issue, the chairs wrote, that would be very troubling indeed. When actual women they knew described one, however, it was all in their heads. Both male and female graduate students had difficulty finding the right advisor, the environmental design department said, but only the latter tried to cry bias. The head of the biochemistry department, which reported no "overt or subconscious" discrimination (and had no women tenure-track faculty), said that descriptions of unequal treatment by a staff member and two graduate students were fortunately refuted by other feedback that praised the department as a bastion of fairness.

As I flip through page after self-satisfied page, I'm reminded of Alexander's words: "there were no other narratives." "I stand by the principle without apology or hesitation." The university's archive testifies to how a lack of curiosity can drown disconcerting information even as it surfaces. The Title IX study's advisory committee reported to the chancellor that the study was too rushed to "permit the thorough weighing and analysis of evidence." These superficial results suited the administration's desire to maintain the current state of affairs by telling the government that there was "no major problem," in the words of multiple department chairs.

The files contain shimmers of submerged stories, like iridescent fish scales flashing through the current. In one folder, a handwritten note from the Center for South and Southeast Asia Studies describes a sexual advance that a lecturer made toward a student. Its anonymous author proposed that the university create a way to make a confidential complaint. Someone at the center wrote a note that they withheld this allegation from the department's report to the university and instead "discussed" it with the dean of the graduate division, with the implication that it was unrelated to sex discrimination.

In a letter that she wrote in blue ballpoint pen and slipped into her department's sunny self-review, a graduate student observed that people are reluctant to see the connection between rape and smaller forms of abuse.

"The sense of responsibility for human violence is so excruciatingly uncomfortable that there is nothing you won't do to forget it, avoid it, call it unjust," she wrote. "Yet I am quite sure that the violence and our responsibility for it does exist, in these days, in this place."

Some women were about to push the university to shoulder it.

━━━━━

A new label was emerging for the behavior that the grad students in comparative literature saw as detrimental and their department chair dismissed as innocuous—the interminable stream of propositions, "pleasantries," and touches which signaled to women that their minds mattered less than their bodies and their bodies were not their own. Carmita Wood, an administrative assistant at Cornell University, developed chronic health problems and quit her job after her boss, a nuclear physicist, repeatedly groped, humiliated, and tried to kiss her. When Cornell rejected her claim for unemployment benefits, she sought help from a group of feminist activists who coined the term "sexual harassment" in 1975.

The concept was picked up by Yale students including Pamela Price, who said that a professor requested sex in exchange for an A on a paper. She said no and got a C. In 1977, Price joined a lawsuit that, for the first time, framed sexual harassment as a violation of Title IX. Though the Yale women lost their case, schools began developing procedures to address sexual misconduct. Radical feminists' emphasis on gender-based violence as a building block of patriarchy was changing how institutions interpreted the law.

At Berkeley, women's liberation met Title IX in 1978, when several undergraduates and graduate students came forward about sexual harassment by Elbaki Hermassi, an assistant professor of sociology and development studies. The women said that Hermassi had kissed them, grabbed them, and solicited sex while signaling that he would only provide academic feedback if they complied. Hermassi, who was from Tunisia, said he was being scapegoated due to his national origins. When the university ignored them, the students formed Women Organized Against Sexual Harassment (WOASH) and filed a complaint with the Office for

Civil Rights. After a confidential investigation, Hermassi was suspended without pay for one quarter, in a year when he was already on sabbatical. As the group continued to protest, he resigned in 1980 rather than go up for tenure review.

For the students who spoke out against him, his departure was a mixed success. Hermassi was gone, but the university hadn't provided them with any recognition or developed a process to assist anyone else. At a 1979 meeting, the University of California's academic senate noted the institution's "virtual inaction" regarding Title IX. The senate suggested paying a coordinator whose attributes would include "creativity and willingness to develop the position (without models)."

Many women who came forward about sexual harassment, especially in low-paid staff positions, gave up jobs and relationships without getting much in return. Wood, the complainant in the Cornell case, lost her appeal, became an outcast in her community, and eventually moved across the country, while the professor who had harassed her kept his job and was elected to the National Academy of Sciences. Cornell's lengthy 2002 obituary in his honor said nothing about his role in a paradigm-shifting scandal. The group that assisted Wood quickly dissolved, due in part to conflict among its working- and middle-class members. Though the group had succeeded at drawing attention to sexual harassment, it also faced censure, like an article in *Harper's* magazine that accused them of portraying women as "helpless victims."

Bukharin had agonized over the relationship between the individual and the collective from a prison cell. Women's liberation activists encountered the tension between "I" and "we" in a new guise. Since they claimed that women's experiences were universal, radical feminists didn't know how to work with movements that focused on other identities—"Third World" (a term that tried to unite all people of color), queer, disabled, poor. Pamela Price, now a student at Berkeley law school, gave a speech at a WOASH demonstration that condemned the double discrimination she faced as a Black woman. Most of the group's members, however, were white and middle class. When WOASH reached out to Berkeley's Third World Women's Alliance and the Black Women's and Chicana caucuses, these organizations provided behind-the-scenes support but didn't want to be publicly associated.

A Sorbonne-educated intellectual from northern Africa, Hermassi could plausibly be cast as either the oppressor or the oppressed. He saw himself as a victim, and the media agreed. The *S.F. Bay Guardian* argued that his "hysterical" feminist accusers had "acted irresponsibly in their zeal for justice"; an editorial in the *Oakland Tribune* said he was the target of a "witch hunt." The zealous feminists debated whether Hermassi's association with the Third World outweighed his attachment to the patriarchy, and if the students he pressured for sex (one of whom was Black) were obligated to keep quiet and protect him. A graduate student who wrote a complaint noted that Hermassi was the only member of his department who specialized in "change and development in the Third World," forcing the women he hit on to either accept his advances or choose something else to study.

WOASH ultimately decided to proceed against Hermassi, but not to picket the shop of a Black man who was said to harass his employees. In a letter disagreeing with the decision, an undergraduate member argued that the discrimination women faced as a "sex class" was being downplayed in favor of other kinds. "Is racism in our interest?" a grad student replied in the margins. Like their counterparts at Cornell, the divided group disintegrated, long before the University of California created formal grievance procedures for sexual harassment in 1986.

I read about WOASH in a journal article coauthored by one of the group's former members, Linda M. Blum, who is now a sociology professor at Northeastern University. She was inspired to revisit the group's history after Sofie Karasek learned of its existence while preparing to file a federal complaint against Berkeley in 2014 and asked its onetime leaders to participate. The article argues that younger activists who denounce second-wave feminism's lack of intersectionality don't realize how some local organizers did try to bridge divides, however unsuccessfully. WOASH's disagreements over who should pay what price remind me of my own uncertainty over whether Daniel's needs trumped mine. The women's liberation movement had created new language to represent violence, tools to combat it, and vexed questions about how to use them.

In the late '60s, activists had seen feminism as part of the revolt against poverty and imperialism. By the end of the following decade, as the red wave of the '70s crashed against the Reagan era, their dreams of bread and roses faded. Politicians trying to prove they were tough on crime supported harsher penalties for violence while cutting funding for social services. Meanwhile, domestic abuse mostly stayed in the shadows—until it exploded in the public eye.

In January 1982, a man walked into a downtown office building in San Francisco holding a flower delivery box. Instead of a bouquet, it held a gun, which he used to shoot his estranged wife and the coworkers who came to her aid. Two of them died and eight others were wounded. In response, the *Daily Cal* ran its first-ever article on domestic violence at UC Berkeley. The student reporter determined that getting any sense of its scale in the community was "impossible."

"Reports of the crime are 'as scarce as hen's teeth,'" a campus police sergeant said.

At Doe I request a copy of *History at Berkeley*, my department's narrative about itself. After the university's founding in 1868, the History Department adopted Ranke's traditional focus on high politics and "great men." Renaissance historian Gene A. Brucker, who wrote one of the book's three essays, recalled how the generation hired in the 1950s pushed for the recruitment of bold young talent. The '70s and '80s saw greater diversity in faculty hirings and course offerings, though Brucker reassured readers that "not every historical topic studied at Berkeley involves issues of race, gender, and class."

The book, published in 1998, contains old photos of the annual softball game, professors with their wives, and Dwinelle in the '60s. Except for a couple of trees that were later felled, the entrance looks the same as it does now, down to the looping bike racks. Brucker quotes another member of the department, William Bouwsma, on how a professional community helps the historian to "resist the tendency of mankind to prefer confirmation in its collective self-esteem to the unflattering truth," and to overcome "the yearning to forget what is unlovely in the past even when this is essential to self-understanding." In its 1976 Title IX discrimination review, the History Department said that its focus on scholarship "does not allow us to entertain sentiments about sex." As I look at all the pleasant-looking men in glasses, I wonder what unlovely secrets they harbored beneath their smiles.

As part of Berkeley's celebration of "150 years of women" at the university in 2020, the department website posted an essay by Mary Elizabeth Berry, a professor of Japanese history hired in 1978 who went on to become the department's first female chair (2007–2012) and recently retired. Berry examined interviews that Berkeley's oral history center conducted with members of the department in the 1990s and 2000s to see what they said about women. Her essay gives a sense of what was missing from the department's official self-assessment: the new laws and campus activism that slowly led to an increase in female faculty, the tenacity they had to display when they were laughed at by students or called bitches behind their backs, the boozy camaraderie that got them through.

There are also hints of something darker. Natalie Zemon Davis, the author of *Women on the Margins*, was at Berkeley for most of the '70s. She recalled how the department's "brotherly spirit" protected a professor who pressured students and colleagues for sex. Instead of telling him to stop, Davis said, the professor's colleagues helped him by grading the exams of female students whose work he refused to look at because they'd turned him down (for what, exactly, she stopped short of specifying). Davis described the situation as "appalling." Another interviewee recounted a story from a colleague about the same professor entering her office one evening and trying to sexually assault her. She apparently defused the situation by telling him he was "confused" and offering him a cup of tea. Though these descriptions left the professor unnamed, Berry identifies him as a German historian named Wolfgang Sauer. As the professor Lawrence Levine put it in his oral interview, "Sauer did some stupid things with students . . . he had a problem." According to Google, one of Sauer's first publications was an essay called "The Mobilization of Violence," which he contributed to a volume on the Nazis' rise to power.

Davis said that at some point (probably around the time of the Hermassi scandal), Berkeley's administration made an announcement that students who had experienced sexual harassment should report it to university officials. Sauer circulated a letter that derided the policy and claimed that women were diversity hires whom he could no longer support. In her interview, Davis surmised that Sauer feared he would be publicly denounced and issued this memo as a preemptive strike. Then, during a departmental review of Lynn Hunt, a young historian of France, Levine recalled that Sauer showed up to vote. When Levine questioned whether it was appropriate for Sauer to attend, his colleagues were furious—not that Sauer was participating, but that Levine had challenged his right to do so. By supporting Sauer's right to weigh in on the prospects of someone whom he'd implied didn't deserve a job, they made it clear whose side they were ultimately on. In her oral interview, Hunt said she thought that Sauer got away with his behavior "because it was about a woman, and it was thought to be a psychiatric problem of some kind, a psychological problem, as opposed to a political problem." Her words make me think of how, four decades later, some of my peers and professors would defend Daniel by presenting whatever he'd done as the by-product of a depressed mind rather than a manifestation of belief.

After finishing at the library one afternoon, I walk up into the hills to talk to Beth Berry about her essay that revealed what being a woman at Berkeley in the '70s was really like, in hopes that she might tell me more. I arrive at her house flushed and sweaty; she is cool and authoritative, courteous but guarded. Sitting on a coach perpendicular to mine, under a wall hanging spotted with tigers, she says that her primary goal in writing was "to do no damage—not to malign the dead." This position seems somewhat at odds with talking about abuse. Beth also tells me that she "adores" the department.

"Do you really think your essay will work as a book?" she asks.

"Yes," I reply.

She doesn't say anything. I laugh to fill the silence and start overexplaining my ideas.

On the long walk back to south Berkeley, I feel like a grad student desperate for approval all over again. I reach into the bag of weed gummies I bought to ease my nerves. As the THC blankets my mind in a fuzzy haze, I think about what else Sauer might have done to the female students whose work he wouldn't grade because they wouldn't sleep with him (or whatever other favors he may have sought). Beth's generation entered academia as honorary men and faced a choice between proving that they could hang with the old boys' club or finding another line of work. Young female hires, who existed in much smaller numbers than PhD students, couldn't afford to tell truths that were too unflattering if they wanted to keep their jobs. In her interview, Hunt said that although she had many positive relationships in the department, the fatigue of being a "dutiful daughter" eventually contributed to her decision to leave.

The system that I encountered in 2017 was the result of a radical rebellion that ended with more bureaucracy—and, along the way, shed the broader vision of equality that feminists had initially promoted. It's the kind of trajectory that Trotsky, exiled from Stalin's Soviet Union, would have called "the revolution betrayed." For all the shortcomings of women's liberation, however, Title IX wouldn't have been applied to sexual and domestic violence without it. Cases like mine would continue to fester without any means of redress, and figures like Sauer would remain safe behind the shield of fraternal unity.

When my AHR essay came out, someone on social media sent me a link to an article about "institutional betrayal," a concept that gained currency among campus rape activists in the 2010s. It outlined the classic community response to revelations of abuse: denial, minimization, covering up for the perpetrator. Decades of activism have forged procedures that make such treachery a little less likely. For evidence of how they fail, however, I need not look any further than my department in my own day.

18

PATTERNS

THEIR CASE BEGAN NOT LONG AFTER MINE. WHILE I WAS IN Moscow, I heard the main allegations from Hannah—that a grad student had kissed a fellow student against her will, badgered another to sleep with him, slipped into a third woman's cab and pressured her into having sex when she was too drunk to consent. Hannah told me that after several women joined forces to make Title IX complaints against the student, whom I'll call Tony, other grad students in our department were giving him the cold shoulder. He denied the women's claims.

Though I'd barely spoken to Tony, I once heard him boasting in the grad student lounge about how easy it was for him to pick up girls in the country he studied. Daniel, who took classes with him, detested and envied the ease with which he seemed to move through the world. As vile as Tony's (alleged) behavior was, I felt a little envious that the women speaking up about him weren't alone, and that people in our circles—including some of the same women who were defending Daniel—automatically took their side. My experience, perhaps because it was abuse within a relationship that appeared a certain way to outsiders, was different. White, entitled, and relatively up-front about his objectification of women, Tony was what we expected misogynist villainy to look like in the Weinstein era.

However, the same actions that made Tony a social outcast in our department were dismissed by the bureaucracy. Just before I boarded the train to Siberia in the summer of 2018, one of the complainants against him published an editorial on Berkeleyside, a local news site, about the university's "problem with patterns." After nearly three months of preliminary assessment, OPHD had informed her that her claim was not "severe or pervasive" enough to count as sexual harassment. Accordingly, they had decided not to investigate and were handling her complaint through an "alternative resolution process" instead. Noting how three other women who came forward about Tony had been dismissed in similar terms, she argued that the university must come up with a way to address serial misconduct against multiple people and recognize "verbal coercion" as a tactic in sexual assault.

Though my cohort no longer tolerates behavior that past generations had seen as ineluctable, it still struggles to fix the border between the prohibited and the permissible. The failed case against Tony illustrates the difficulty of turning scattered, seemingly low-level incidents into a story legible to those with power. The most serious allegation against him—acquaintance rape in which both sides had been drinking—was difficult to prove even according to Title IX's standard of "more likely than not." The last I'd heard about Tony was that he'd moved back home. I'm curious how the women are doing.

I don't want to appoint myself to the position of investigator by determining what "really" happened in each instance they described; they were already denied that chance, and I'm no independent arbiter. I do want to know how it felt when the bureaucracy passed on their complaints and how they look back on the experience now. I'm not sure what I would have done if the Title IX office hadn't taken my case: Dropped out? Gotten back together with Daniel? Vanished possibilities linger in my mind like the last streaks of red at twilight.

When I walk to Dwinelle to have lunch with one of the women, whom I'll call Michelle, she's standing out front in a leopard print shirt and sunglasses. As we head toward a burrito place, she apologizes for being rattled: she just ran into Tony at Free Speech Movement, the campus café. He's returned from self-imposed exile.

The first time she met Tony, Michelle says, he told her that he'd flown over her hometown in his friend's helicopter. His comment immediately signaled that he comes from money. Michelle is a woman of color who doesn't. Tony was confident in seminar, chummy with their advisor in a way she didn't know how to be. She says that Tony forcibly kissed her at the end of her first semester, as she was leaving the annual Christmas party in Dwinelle. The next day, she says, she confronted him about it over text; he eventually apologized and asked her not to tell anyone. When she described what happened to a friend in the department, the latter shrugged it off, saying Tony was drunk. Her mom also advised her to keep quiet; she'd been sexually assaulted and knew the difficulty of trying to do anything about it. Michelle deleted the message thread and tried to move on.

When they served as teaching assistants for the same class, she says, Tony would talk about his sex life in their shared office. After a fall bar-becue to welcome incoming grad students, she found out that one of them said Tony got into her taxi after she'd been drinking and hounded her to sleep with him. The student told an administrator, who reported it to OPHD. Some of Michelle's friends were annoyed that she hadn't reported what happened to her. They thought it would help "build a nar-rative," a story of escalating predation that began with a kiss at a party and culminated in rape, with who knows what next. So Michelle made a complaint, too, with a request that it remain anonymous and that no action be taken.

Meanwhile, Tony kept working in Dwinelle. Several graduate students filed a union grievance arguing that his continued presence violated their employment contract, including its provisions on "health and safety," and requested that he be banned from campus pending the outcome of investigations. In a denial letter, the department said that it had provided accommodations for those who made complaints, such as reassigning them to different office spaces, but that any further measures would depend on OPHD's findings. In the meantime, it was organizing events with sexual violence and harassment training. The students replied that they were reconsidering their association with "a university that at every level tries to silence survivors."

It turned out not to matter that Michelle had deleted her text exchange with Tony. Since an OPHD administrator sent her an email saying that what she described "would not rise to the level of a policy violation" anyway, there was nothing to corroborate. Michelle was supposed to be preparing for her qualifying exam, but she was so distracted that she couldn't sleep and considered dropping out. To delay her exam date by a few months, she had to enroll with the disabled students program, which required her to report how many pages she was reading every day.

"I couldn't even string together a sentence on something I'd been studying for three years," she says as tears fall down her cheeks. She already felt like an outsider; the Tony debacle just seemed to confirm it.

These days, she spends as little time in the department as possible while she focuses on finishing her dissertation and applying for jobs. She's in a happy relationship with someone outside academia; they're moving in together and have a dog.

"I thought I had closure," she says. "But it's clear from this conversation and this day that I don't."

She smiles and pulls herself together: it's time to go teach.

——————

After talking to Michelle, I speak with Deborah Wood, the author of the Berkeleyside essay. According to her complaint, Tony kept pressuring her to leave a karaoke party with him, even though she was drunk and kept saying no, until friends pulled her away. Deborah said she didn't feel pressured to come forward; it was her idea to file the union grievance. Still, as the Title IX process unfolded, she grew anxious and depressed. This was the height of MeToo, when a new exposé about sexual violence was coming out every day, and she could think of little else.

Deborah forwards me the closing email she received from OPHD about the "alternative resolution" of her complaint. The CRO wrote that she had conducted an "in-person Targeted Education Meeting" with Tony, during which she told him to be "respectful" and "mindful of the impact versus the intent of his conduct." I read the email signature at the bottom; it's the same person who handled my case.

While listening to Michelle and Deborah and reading the documents they shared, I feel a prickle of guilt that the process worked out in my favor while dismissing them. As more women came forward about Tony, their collective frustration over the institution's tepid response kindled into a fire that blew back in their faces. My complaint had resulted in what they wanted—a temporary campus ban, an investigation, and ultimately, expulsion—while Tony was able to disappear for a while and come back. We all felt burned.

By the time the public comment period ended in early 2019, Trump's Department of Education had received over 124,000 responses to its proposed Title IX regulations. Though most comments, like mine, opposed the changes, in 2020 DeVos finalized them anyway. After President Biden was inaugurated in 2021, his administration announced that it planned to alter some of the Trump-era rules (for example, by making live cross-examination optional rather than mandatory and by extending Title IX protections to queer and transgender students, as the Obama administration had). Yet in the face of public pressure, universities like Berkeley had already introduced live cross-examination in cases like mine, even before it became a requirement. When I filed my complaint, I didn't realize that this would be part of the process. If I had, I'm not sure whether I would have moved forward.

For those who try, the burden of proof can be too heavy to carry. A 2020–2021 study by the organization Know Your IX found that 39 percent of survey respondents who reported sexual misconduct experienced "substantial disruptions" to their education. Twenty-seven percent took a leave of absence, 20 percent transferred to another school—while some did both—and almost 10 percent dropped out. The latter contingent includes Deborah, who took a medical leave of absence and never came back. She left the program for a variety of reasons, she says; this was one of them. After getting a certification in victim advocacy, she volunteered with the Rape, Abuse, and Incest National Network crisis line for several years. She's moved on to other work but might finish her PhD, someday. In an environment dedicated to growth, survivors who come forward face invisible obstacles that impede their progress. Whether they pursue a case against the wishes of people they trusted or get brushed off by administrators, their lives are upended.

It's simple to say, in hindsight, that someone with a decades-long track record of bad behavior should be kicked out of an institution. It's harder to know how to react when they're just getting started. For complainants, Title IX is appealing because it considers behavior that the criminal justice system usually doesn't, from rape and domestic violence to kisses and come-ons. Yet the process set up to address it often preserves the past under a touched-up facade of progressive language. The swelling bureaucracy can claim to have resolved a complaint with a training and to have fixed inequality by appointing another dean or task force that trumpets its commitment to "diversity, equity, and inclusion." The resources that universities pour into burnishing their image and discouraging litigation often seem designed to engineer the kind of situation in which Michelle and Deborah found themselves, with new red tape leading to a familiar result. In the end, all that Tony faced was an old-school shunning. When he returned to campus, he mingled with new cohorts who'd never heard the allegations against him. Only he knows whether social pressure changed him—just as only Daniel knows whether expulsion did.

———

Critics of Title IX (and MeToo) present a picture very different from what I've just described. While decrying MeToo's focus on storytelling, they tend to take its plot structures for granted and flip the script. The accused becomes the vulnerable victim; the accuser, the omnipotent villain. According to articles like "The New Puritans," a 2021 piece that Anne Applebaum wrote for the *Atlantic* which disparages Title IX as "mob justice," it is the accused who are covered in shame, crippled by self-doubt, and afraid they will never be heard. There are surely respondents who don't get the chance to adequately defend themselves, and a complaint (which can be made in bad faith) is always stressful for both sides. But the notion that campus morality police greet any accusation with the supreme penalty greatly exaggerates the ease of getting an investigation, much less a finding, and the severity of the consequences. My case lasted over two years, with extensive opportunities for Daniel to advance his story and try to refute mine, while Michelle and Deborah's complaints weren't investigated at all. According to the data, their experience is typical.

A number of universities, including Berkeley, now release annual reports on the Title IX complaints they handle. I prop open my laptop to read them at a café near campus that I used to go to with people from the department. The patio buzzes with grad students and professors decompressing after meetings and seminars. I see a face that looks like Daniel's: Is it him? The man smiles at someone and keeps walking. I exhale. As I scan the reports, I discover that most cases are like the ones against Tony: sexual misconduct that doesn't rise to a level that the institution deems worthy of consideration (or that the complainant doesn't wish to pursue) and never leads to any investigation or sanction.

In Berkeley's overview of 2017–2018—the year of my case, as well as the complaints against Tony—OPHD received 446 reports of sexual violence or harassment, most of which were made by third parties. Only 14 percent of the cases it closed that year included an investigation ("formal resolution"). The vast majority, 77 percent, were "administratively closed"—in other words, nothing happened (or, in OPHD's phrasing, "resources were provided" or "preventative measures" put into place). The remaining 9 percent were addressed through "alternative resolutions." In total, only twenty-five cases—5.6 percent of that year's complaints—resulted in an investigation that led to a finding with any form of sanction. The report notes that a Title IX investigation happens only if the alleged misconduct would rise to the level of a policy violation, there is enough evidence to proceed, and the parties do not agree on an alternative resolution—a bar sufficiently high to ensure that most cases never make it beyond the preliminary assessment phase.

Recalling how *Unwanted Advances* author Laura Kipnis compares the "rigged" Title IX process to the Salem witch trials, I pull up data from her institution, Northwestern. Northwestern's report for the 2017–2018 year, which began a few months after her book came out, shows that 10 percent of reports concerning students (twelve cases total) were investigated. Of these, a single case resulted in an expulsion. For faculty and staff, half of reports (twenty-nine cases total) were investigated, but here, too, only one case led to termination ("separation"). Several others resulted in administrative sanctions, a broad category that includes "restrictions, changes in compensation, or training requirements." If this is a witch hunt, it's one where the suspected heretics are generally allowed to keep casting spells or are let off with a polite request to convert. These statistics don't even include the untold numbers of people who experience harm but never file a complaint. Large universities like Berkeley and Northwestern have tens of thousands of students and employees. If only a handful of people per year face any repercussions for sexual violence and harassment, then Title IX critics' rhetoric about the constant, heinous persecution of respondents is about as convincing as Trump's claim to have been the victim of "the greatest witch hunt in American history."

Some critics, including Jeannie Suk Gersen, link their calls for more "due process" to concerns that the system could be racially biased against the accused. Schools don't track racial information in Title IX cases, limiting any discussion to the level of anecdote. Though critics tend to avoid discussing the background of victims, studies show that women of color and queer people of any gender identity are the most likely to experience violence and harassment at universities. While white activists received more press coverage, students at historically Black institutions including Spelman and Morehouse (two single-sex private colleges that are closely intertwined) had already been speaking out for years about their schools' inadequate handling of sexual abuse, as chronicled in the 2008 documentary *Broken Social Contracts*.

These survivors faced additional pressure to maintain "solidarity" by keeping silent—and felt even more let down when they weren't taken seriously. A Spelman student whose rape allegation was dismissed by administrators told a journalist that she'd expected to study in an environment where Black women were supported. "I felt like I was sold a fake dream," she said. When she was assaulted again, she decided not to report it. Wagatwe Wanjuki, one of the leaders of the Title IX movement in the 2010s, has observed that the call for ever-higher standards of proof requires a level of believability that survivors of color might never be able to meet.

After the *Guardian* article about the Wentworth case came out in 2016, I met Kat Gutierrez, one of the complainants, through a volunteer program. She was warm and perceptive, and I winced at the memory of my instinctive thought-bubble suggesting she'd asked for the attention when I first saw her photo. Like me, Kat was in the tricky position of getting a "responsible" finding from the Title IX office that some of her peers did not. The process of sanctioning a professor is much longer and more convoluted than it is for a student or staff member, requiring reinvestigation and review by multiple faculty panels before a final decision is made by the chancellor. Kat is sure that if the case hadn't received media attention, Wentworth would have gotten a slap on the wrist.

After Wentworth (who didn't have tenure) was fired, he sued Kat and two other accusers who spoke to the media for defamation. Though the case was eventually thrown out, they had to comply with a gag order for several years. When I call her to talk about it now, Kat, who is Filipina, stresses that the kind of harassment that she experienced is particularly common among women of color, who tend to feel the least comfortable on campus but might lack the social capital or resources to come forward. Before her case, Kat wasn't sure if she would stay in academia. After it, she decided that she should be "a mentor to people who want to study in peace," and to Southeast Asian students in particular. She's now a professor at UC Santa Cruz.

The Title IX system is a patchwork that varies from school to school and case to case. Though critics can always find an example in which the accused thinks they were treated unfairly, no individual's experience is representative of an entire institution, much less a national ailment. Any degree of questioning or censure likely feels unjust to the recipient. Both Tony and Daniel, like Wentworth, could say that their lives had been destroyed by flimsy accusations and produce materials that would seem to prove it. The narrative of Title IX's bias against the accused has been repeated so many times that its truth appears to be self-evident. But getting a real sense of how Title IX functions requires assembling facts into patterns, rather than retrofitting examples to suit a prefabricated plotline. The tragedy of widespread martyrdom by baseless accusations is a tale at odds with reality, told at the expense of the many people who try to come forward and are rebuffed—or don't bother because they fear the price.

As I read criticism of Title IX, I keep noticing that some of the system's fiercest opponents are women. Their depiction of accusers as coddled princesses reminds me quite a bit of Daniel's hyperbole, but much less so of any actual complainant I've met. As I consider where this hostility is coming from, I recall a couple of details from *Unwanted Advances*. Kipnis, a self-described left-wing feminist, calls on her readers to question the politically correct messaging that "it's the *perpetrators* who are the problem." To demonstrate how sexual assault is really the victim's fault, she recounts a story that a friend told her about how her sister was raped in college. Kipnis asked how it happened.

"'She got drunk, fell asleep on the couch in a frat house, and woke up with some guy on top of her,' my friend answered.

'I guess you couldn't see that coming,' I said.

We both laughed."

Later in the same chapter, Kipnis mentions that many years ago, a man tried to enter her bedroom window at night while she was sleeping. Frozen by fear, Kipnis found herself unable to scream; a male roommate who heard the noise that finally emerged from her mouth burst in and saved her. Afterward, she writes, she had "decades of nightmares" inspired by what she suspects was a thwarted rape. By mocking other women for failing to fend off their attackers, even while unconscious, Kipnis shifts her shame onto them, as if they were responsible for seizing the control that she could not. Blaming victims elides the discomfiting truth that power doesn't only come from the end of a gun. It's difficult to cry out when you can't move.

After all my meetings are over and I've returned the last of my books and files, I get a gyro and take it to the grass by the library. As I lick yogurt off my fingers, the Campanile chimes the same melodies it has for decades. In a demonstration I once watched, the player pressed wooden keys, which triggered a series of motions that struck the clappers on dozens of bells. At the beginning of finals week, the carillon always plays "Danny Deever," a ballad based on a Rudyard Kipling poem about a British soldier in India who was executed for murder.

For they're hangin' Danny Deever, you can hear the Dead March play,
The Regiment's in 'ollow square—they're hangin' him to-day

While taking in Berkeley's manicured landscape, I keep seeing the ghosts of those who were cast out of it: Tanya tying her hair in a ponytail as she finishes a translation, Prosenjit building mechanical models and watching her through the trees. Daniel looking up at me from under his long eyelashes.

I have a dream that Daniel and I are living together in a room in I-House. Daniel is sweet, shy, shit-talking, cooking sausage with peppers, asking me how to pronounce a word in French, feeding me an answer to an orals question ("tell them the course you'd teach about the twentieth century would be called The Age of Extremes")—all the best ways that I remember him as he used to be. I don't recall agreeing to move in with him, but it would be rude to back out now.

I decide not to tell my friends; they would only worry. *It was all a misunderstanding*, I think to myself. He'll be better this time—they'll see.

While the institution remains immutable, the figures on Berkeley's campus flicker and vanish, their stories overlapping and drifting apart before eventually fading away. I fought to keep my place on the magic mountain for a little while longer, only to find the altitude suffocating. Now, when the university beckons with its promise of escaping time, I don't want to stay. I need to go back to my current life in Warsaw, where the world I think I know has turned upside down once again.

19

WAR

A HAND ON MY ARM SHAKES ME FROM SLEEP. WHEN I RAISE MY EYE-
lids, I see the man I talked with all night under Stalin's spire, who
recently became my husband. I relax and roll away, not ready to get up.

"They've invaded," he whispers.

My eyes pop back open.

On the morning of February 24, 2022, when Russian bombs begin
falling on Kyiv, it's "fat Thursday" in Poland—a holiday before Lent when
everyone eats doughnuts stuffed with jam. The pastry sits uneasily in my
stomach as we walk to join a crowd of protesters outside Warsaw's Russian embassy. Most of them have tears in their eyes. Someone hurries out
of the embassy's front door carrying a box of files. "You fuck!" a man in
the crowd screams, raising his middle finger.

Like most people who study Russia, I hadn't predicted Putin's full-scale
invasion of Ukraine. In the preceding months, as the dictator amassed
troops at the border, it was more comfortable to assume he wouldn't go
so far. As I stand at the protest, I think back to the conversation I had
with Alexander in Moscow nearly five years ago: how certain he was that
Putin didn't pose much of an international threat and that any claims to
the contrary were exaggerated, how eager I was to agree. Now here I am,
living in Poland and questioning my perceptions—not of an individual,
but of a country.

For Poles, where centuries of partition and occupation have left an abiding fear of attack by their more powerful neighbors, Putin's war is an event readily assimilated to expectations. However, I and my American colleagues in Russian history had devoted ourselves to fighting stereotypes about the country's supposedly ingrained authoritarianism. Over years of flying there on research grants, we'd gained a deeper understanding of how it worked. Or so we thought. Now Putin is confirming the worst clichés about Russian barbarism, while we struggle to reconcile the place that we had patiently explained and defended to our fellow Anglophones with the atrocities we see on the news.

Individuals are not states; many Russians I know are opposed to the war. But they are unable to halt the actions of the one man who ultimately calls the shots. Though Putin, unlike Trump, is not known for committing violence with his own hands, he uses the levers of power to trample anyone who questions his desired version of the truth, in which Moscow has the right to dominate its former imperial subjects as well as any citizens who disobey. I'm still fascinated by countercurrents in Russia's history and culture, including the rebellious streak that once toppled the tsar and vowed to free the world. Yet I have to admit that my recent perceptions were wrong.

In the days after the invasion, as millions of people flee across Poland's border with Ukraine, my husband and I sign up to host refugees. One of them is Iulia, a woman around my age from the city of Kharkiv who escaped bombardment by walking through metro tunnels. Iulia arrives late in the evening, wearing a puffy yellow jacket. She asks if she can put her clothes in the washing machine as I make up a bed on the living-room sofa. For the next twenty-four hours, she lies on the couch with the curtains drawn. The following morning, as we drink tea in the kitchen, she says that she used to organize tours of Ukrainian dancers and circus performers in China. Now she has no idea where she is going or what she will do.

Iulia's life has been disrupted to a degree I can only imagine. Her city is being destroyed; the lives of everyone she knows are in jeopardy. All I can do is offer her fruit (the only thing she'll eat during Orthodox Lent) and directions around Warsaw. Still, there's something about her shock and disorientation that I recognize from experience: in a moment of danger, she made a choice to leave. After a few days, Iulia takes a job at an auto parts factory in southern Poland. On her days off, she rides the train, taking advantage of the free travel that Ukrainians are briefly granted around Europe to see Budapest, Vienna, Paris, Berlin.

When I return to Warsaw after my trip to Berkeley, seven months have passed since that winter morning of doughnuts and bombs across the border. The number of refugees arriving in Poland has fallen somewhat, but the conflict grinds on. Against the backdrop of war, campus violence seems trivial. Yet as I process everything I read and heard in California, I'm struck by how the questions surrounding Putin's invasion are related to those I faced when leaving Daniel—and how the same misdirection and denial that enable sexual and domestic violence can operate on a geopolitical scale.

In the wake of the 2022 invasion, some pundits began comparing Russia's attempt to dominate Ukraine to an abusive relationship. The parallels were obvious. Many Ukrainians wanted a closer partnership with Europe; Putin preferred to kill them rather than let them leave his orbit. His occupation of Crimea and parts of eastern Ukraine in 2014 had not been a one-off fluke, but part of an escalating pattern of violence. Even so, when I read think pieces that refer to Ukraine as a battered wife and to membership in the North Atlantic Treaty Organization as a restraining order, I flinch. Feminizing Ukraine as an abused woman places those who assist it (including the United States) in the dubious position of male saviors. Nevertheless, the war's violent masculinity is unmistakable. Putin has mockingly referred to Ukraine's leader Volodymyr Zelensky as a prostitute for receiving Western military aid. His claim that Russia is saving Ukraine from the rapacious West and its own base ("Nazi") instincts is the same kind of false gallantry that Daniel deployed to obscure his abuse.

However, there is another story circulating about Putin's war. While blue-and-yellow Ukrainian flags spread on social media, some commentators on both the right and the left speak up on Russia's behalf. These voices argue that Putin is engaged in a defensive conflict provoked by

NATO's presence in former countries of the Soviet bloc (which had chosen to join it). Ukraine was not in the alliance and was not about to be; it had even offered not to seek membership on the eve of the full-scale war, in a peace deal that Putin reportedly rejected. Yet a desire to criticize America's military empire leads these observers to mistake the Kremlin's narrative for truth. According to this standpoint, the perpetrator is the real victim, his violence is unfortunate but justified, and the solution is to give him what he wants. Meanwhile, Ukraine's allies, so united in the days after the first rockets exploded, gradually fall into arguments over how much help to keep giving and whether there's any path to peace that doesn't involve appeasement. Those in favor of withdrawing aid argue that Ukrainians are asking for too much, and that Russia's desire to maintain its "sphere of influence" must be accepted after all.

With gender-based violence, as in conflicts between states, the passage of time keeps altering approaches to victim, perpetrator, and the meaning of resolution.

When Sofie Karasek stood onstage at the 2016 Oscars while Lady Gaga sang the theme song to *The Hunting Ground*, the campus Title IX movement seemed to have been victorious—if not in eliminating sexual assault, then at least in forcing schools to take it more seriously. Before the ceremony, Sofie got a tattoo of a rose emerging from a flame, a symbol that some of the activists alongside her inked on themselves, too. The *Washington Post* ran a photo of her backstage with then vice president Joe Biden, who held her hands and pressed his forehead against hers in an awkward display of empathy. The paper wrote that getting universities to address sexual assault was Sofie's "life's mission."

At the time, she had recently graduated from Berkeley and was serving as the education director of End Rape on Campus, the nonprofit she cofounded. In addition to helping students file federal complaints with the Education Department's Office for Civil Rights, it lobbied for affirmative consent legislation which said that participation must be conscious and voluntary throughout a sexual encounter. These laws, which passed in

California and New York, tasked colleges with using the "yes means yes" standard in evaluating sexual assault. In practice, as institutions' annual reports and the failed case against Tony suggest, complainants in these types of cases still struggle for recognition.

Today, like most other campus activists, Sofie has moved on. After leaving End Rape on Campus in 2017, she became a consultant for other groups, including the Sunrise Movement to stop climate change. When I contact her from Warsaw to ask how she looks back at the Title IX movement now, she says she's proud it helped lay the groundwork for MeToo but feels deeply conflicted about its legacy.

"By the time MeToo happened, I had already started to shift my perspective around the role of punishment," Sofie tells me over the phone. "The movement was moving in a direction that inevitably wasn't gonna work."

In the wake of Black Lives Matter, she realized that feminism had grown too "carceral and privatized." She now supports a restorative justice approach to sexual violence, at universities and beyond, and tries to "have empathy for people who cause harm while not negating the person who has experienced the harm." To some extent, the organizations that Sofie's cohort created have shared her change of heart. When I search online, I see that Know Your IX, the other main group to come out of the movement, says it supports prison abolition and is against "punitive" measures on campus.

After talking to Sofie and reading revised mission statements, I feel whiplash. Over years of essays and interviews, tweets and documentaries, student activists had called out the lack of consequences for gender-based violence at their schools. "How many survivors does it take for a serial perpetrator to be punished?" Sofie had asked in an essay she wrote for the *Guardian* in 2014. Now, a number of the same people who made the outcome of my case possible say it's undesirable, while championing the kind of informal response they'd deplored as insufficient. The Title IX movement seems like a serpent eating its own tail. I imagine the fingers of Sauers and Searles rising up to resume their groping, Daniel and Tony exchanging a smirk as they walk into Dwinelle.

████████

After the initial cascade of women's stories in fall 2017, feminists faced the question of what to do about them. In the following years, the MeToo and Title IX movements fragmented into multiple truths about what counted as violence and whose feelings mattered more—that of accusers or the accused. As would-be allies turned on each other, varying responses to abuse blurred together until, in the eyes of some, all of them came to seem equally unwarranted.

Journalists, academics, and policymakers tend to describe Title IX hearings as "trials" with "charges" that lead to a "conviction." This linguistic slippage, which was modeled by men's rights groups and promoted by the Trump administration, is now part of a trend across the political spectrum that confuses Title IX with criminal justice. Kipnis writes that "carceral feminism"—a term coined by sociologist Elizabeth Bernstein to refer to state policing and imprisonment as a way of achieving gender equality—is "the guiding spirit in campus policy." In *The Feminist War on Crime*, Aya Gruber criticizes the Title IX and MeToo movements as a delusional outgrowth of second-wave feminism, which came to focus on atomized retribution instead of collective liberation. She rejects any form of penalty for sexual and domestic violence as "crime logic" that "legitimates incarceration and encourages policy makers to use criminal law as a tool of social engineering."

Many survivors of gender-based violence want nothing to do with the criminal legal system, which has already harmed their communities, will probably disregard them anyway, and may cause further damage in the process. The same laws used to punish abusive partners have served to criminalize self-defense among victims—especially when it's undertaken in queer couples (where police tend to arrest both parties) or by Black girls and women like Marissa Alexander, who fired a warning shot at her abusive husband. Even though no one was injured, Alexander was sentenced to twenty years in prison. She ultimately spent three years in prison and two under house arrest.

Rather than looking out for both sides, however, anti-carceral critics of Title IX can be disconcertingly quick to decry any potential repercussions for perpetrators while dismissing victims. Gruber, like Kipnis, argues that campus accusers chase clout by broadcasting an inflated "trauma narrative" that denies women's agency while ruining men's lives. This is the logic of abuse, which frames the victim's attempts to speak out or seek protection as a heartless overreaction. As I read Gruber's words, I hear Daniel's voice: *pampered white bitch, you just want to lock me up.*

I look up from my computer and scan my eyes across the row of illuminated shop windows below my Warsaw apartment—a bakery, a Vietnamese restaurant, a sex shop that no one ever seems to enter or leave—to ward off the memories swarming my head. I've sought out these texts to understand the feminist turn against Title IX, as well as to test my unsteady conviction that I did the right thing in coming forward. I argue with their absent authors more boldly than I talk back to the phantom Daniel who still inhabits my brain. The idea that every penalty is tantamount to imprisonment simply doesn't make sense, I tell them. Condemnation of Title IX as "crime logic" reminds me of economist Friedrich Hayek's famous 1944 work *The Road to Serfdom*, which argued that any form of government planning leads to the gulag. The difference is not only one of scale but of kind.

I find more cogent analysis in the writings of prison abolition activist Mariame Kaba, who began doing anti–sexual assault work on college campuses in the late '80s, when young women were writing names on bathroom stalls because they still had nowhere else to turn. Kaba distinguishes between punishment, which imposes torment, and consequences, which entail "losing some privileges." For Kaba, while depriving someone of the ability to ever work again is cruel and unusual, making him step down from a position in which he has caused damage is merely uncomfortable (and probably necessary).

Restorative justice techniques aim to achieve reconciliation through mediation, which can include the participation of supporters from both sides. Some institutions are experimenting with involving restorative justice centers in Title IX complaints. If used at the complainant's discretion, with consequences for those who fail to follow through on agreements, this approach could appeal to the great number of people who don't want to go through with an investigation, or are turned away because their case fails to meet the criteria. Yet there are already so many mechanisms that pressure victims to stay silent and put their abuser's reputation first, like the settlements used by Weinstein's team and the Catholic Church.

In the context of intimate partner violence, where apologies are just part of the cycle, treating all truths as equal can perpetuate abuse. If I had sat across a table from Daniel, our friends and professors encircling us as he said he was sorry, I would have stopped trying to separate my mind from his and probably have gone back to him. Even if such a process could have happened without my direct involvement, I still wouldn't have wanted to leave other people susceptible to whatever he might do next. Over the course of my case, I saw nothing to suggest that Daniel had actually owned up to his actions or was committed to not repeating them.

While some critics label it carceral, the Title IX system actually shares positive features with restorative justice. It provides a local, civil alternative to criminal law, which never takes up the vast majority of sexual and domestic violence cases anyway. Rather than imprisoning the accused, it is focused on accommodating victims' needs, like altering living arrangements or work schedules and providing confidential advocates who give psychological support. Title IX, for all its flaws, is better than the vacuum that preceded it, which sucked in people like Tanya and never let them out. Though my case cost me time and relationships I'll never get back, I don't regret it. I remember how, on the evening that Daniel lost his appeal, I took a selfie to capture the glow on my cheeks. In this brief, luminous moment, my face fully felt like it was mine again.

Still, I would hesitate to encourage anyone else to file a complaint. The process has grown so complicated and protracted that it often disserves the people who need it and exhausts those who run it. As my case dragged on over the years, I emailed various staff members at OPHD and the Center for Student Conduct only to get an automatic reply that they had left their jobs. The CRO—who, like many investigators, has a law degree—quit right after completing the report. According to her website, she now leads corporate diversity trainings. Though I'm curious about why she left, she doesn't respond when I reach out. I can't blame her; any comment she makes could expose her (or her former employer) to a lawsuit.

I take a break from reading and put on my shoes to go for a walk. The apartment we rent is in a building from the 1930s with a rickety elevator— one of the few structures in Warsaw that partially survived Nazi bombing during World War II. As Hitler's retreating forces reduced the Polish capital to ash, Stalin's Red Army stood on the other side of the river and watched. Stalin was content to take over a destroyed city, which would be all the more amenable to communist rule. Warsaw's urban landscape is a testament to bystander apathy, as well as to the ability to regenerate from ruins.

Still weighing the arguments that are marshaled on behalf of accusers and the accused, I enter a park that was once the estate of Polish kings. Peacocks strut on the grass, displaying their plumage to obliging tourists who take photos on their cell phones. I walk toward a palace—a onetime royal bathing pavilion, preserved by the Nazis as a barracks—that seems to float on water. Thanks to its position on an island, the building appears in double: upright, and as an inverted twin whose columns melt into wavy lines on the surface of the pond.

This warped symmetry reminds me of how those who commit abuse, whether in the home or at the head of state, usually rationalize it as a mirrored reaction to injustice—a dialectical force beyond their control. Frantz Fanon, who was born in the French colony of Martinique and glorified violence as a form of empowerment among the historically oppressed, also used this stance to justify beating his wife. While hitting her in front of other people, he would declare, "I avenge myself." In similarly dialectical fashion, Title IX and MeToo critics like Gruber and the philosopher Amia Srinivasan write that feminists must stop blaming gender-based violence on individuals and recognize it as a function of inequality. Yet framing abuse as a commensurate response to other forms of harm quickly fades into an excuse; anyone can claim the mantle of victimhood to do evil in the name of good.

The philosopher and sociologist Theodor Adorno tried to escape zero-sum struggle with the concept of "negative dialectics," or seeing multiple dimensions without reducing one to the other. For Adorno, there is no happy ending in which truth prevails over its opposite; the search for perfect mirrors is doomed to fail. Adorno's cohort of German-Jewish intellectuals was scarred by the crisis that drove them to flee abroad, in which a mass movement that twisted the truth beyond any possible recognition claimed to avenge Germany's hurt through the extermination of enemies like them. Adorno survived World War II in California, where expatriation brought further disenchantment as well as heightened perception. Rather than trying to synthesize conflicting stories, negative dialectics lets them dwell side by side. This idea might sound defeatist; the Hungarian Marxist György Lukács scorned Adorno's school of social theory as "the grand hotel abyss." I take it as a way of saying that there can be insight without tidy resolution, whether "formal" (in Title IX–speak) or otherwise.

Abuse survivors, still reeling from the distortions they have just escaped, are often told to be "nice" by forgiving and forgetting. In my experience, they do not typically lack compassion for those who hurt them, but struggle to keep some for themselves. Though victimhood doesn't bestow moral virtue, it can, like Adorno's state of enduring exile, bring a gift of sharpened vision: the capacity to perceive how a stellar friend can be a horrifying spouse, and how one person's regeneration comes at the expense of another's pain. When sundered from the urge to excuse, which tends to follow it as swiftly as the chain reaction that rings the carillon bells, this uneasy understanding reveals the wounds we all carry and our responsibility not to re-inflict them.

Daniel, focused exclusively on himself, never asked for my forgiveness. I never offered it. In place of reconciliation, I try to see his truth without letting it overshadow mine. Though Daniel's childhood shaped the adult he became, the trauma he carried did not cancel out the harm he caused and might go on to reenact. Maybe if he had stayed at Berkeley and gotten the redemptive arc that some people were eager to grant him, he wouldn't have hurt me or anyone else there again. However, I can only afford to consider counterfactuals long after the immediate threat has passed. Back then, I was trying to do whatever I could to keep myself from splitting irreversibly into two—the me who existed, and the specter who only could have.

Sofie is right to reserve empathy for both victims and perpetrators. After all, the categories tend to overlap. The challenge is seeing both sides without refusing to take a position—or reflexively defending the one that declared war while ignoring what it might cost the occupied.

20

LESSONS IN FORGETTING

I N THE CONCRETE BOX WHERE I CURRENTLY SIT, I FEEL LIKE A PERSON without a past. We recently moved to an apartment in a Warsaw housing block built in the 1970s. Socialism promised a break with tradition, and in terms of real estate, it delivered. In this prefabricated maze of identical windows and balconies, history vanishes like a mirage. When I see the old man who diligently leaves out a buffet of bread for the pigeons every morning, I feel as if we've both always been here, in an eternal present free from dust and bone. As much as I try to forget, however, I'm still living in the future that my relationship with Daniel and the investigation made—the experiences that link me to Liza and Tanya, to people I know and countless others I will never meet.

Over six years have passed since the afternoon when my advocate warned me that closure is something you have to find for yourself. Back then, as I tried to prove my case to the investigator and worried about what was to come, I had no ability to drift away from what happened or expectation of when it would relinquish its hold over me. Eventually, I started writing about it, in search of the sense of an ending that life does not readily provide. Yet as soon as I told my story in a form that felt final, a central player emerged to contend that I'd said it wrong. In this, too, I was far from alone.

The first time I saw the name "Amber Heard," I was staying at Rose's house in Berkeley in June 2017, hiding from Daniel and trying to work up the nerve to run away for good. In 2016, Heard filed for a temporary restraining order against her husband, the movie star Johnny Depp, which alleged that he had verbally and physically abused her; their divorce was finalized the following year. Rose sent me an article about the case to remind me that I wasn't the only one who had sympathized with an abusive partner before ultimately deciding to leave. The metal springs of her foldout mattress dug into my back as I read leaked messages in which Depp's assistant appeared to contact Heard on behalf of his boss:

"Think he's just texted you. He's incredibly apologetic and knows that he has done wrong. He wants to get better now. He's been very explicit about that this morning.

"Feel like we're at a critical juncture."

The texts matched my dynamic with Daniel so closely that it hurt to look at them. Shortly before I read the article, Daniel's sister had messaged me in an attempt to help us patch things up. I tried to see Heard as an inspiring example: if she got out, maybe I could, too.

As my Title IX case unfolded, Heard's saga continued. In summer 2018, around the same time that Alexander and I spoke in that Moscow courtyard, Depp sued the British tabloid the *Sun* for reporting that he had beaten her. Heard and the paper won, but only after an agonizing trial during which she received death threats from Depp's fans. The following summer, while I waited for the appeal hearing, Depp filed a defamation suit against Heard over an essay she wrote for the *Washington Post* in which she identified herself as "a public figure representing domestic abuse." Describing the "wrath" she'd faced after speaking out, Heard argued that survivors needed more support and criticized the Trump administration's plan to overhaul Title IX. Over the course of the defamation trial, Facebook and Instagram algorithms kept showing me videos mocking an apparently histrionic or deceitful Heard, which turned out to be part of a smear campaign funded by the conservative outlet the *Daily Wire*.

Then, in June 2022, after I had left academia and was writing this book in Warsaw, Depp won the defamation suit, and the court awarded him

$15 million in damages. I felt sick when I saw the headlines—yet another directive to me and anyone else who might come forward to keep quiet. I clicked on a YouTube video called "Amber Heard GETS WRECKED LIVE," a title that lay bare the pornographic schadenfreude surrounding her humiliation, and scrolled through hundreds of comments calling her a liar, telling men to stay away from her, saying she should be put in jail. In her *Post* op-ed, Heard had expressed optimism that female "rage and determination to end sexual violence are turning into a political force." Now, before encountering Heard's words, the reader sees the fruits of Depp's drive to convince the public that they're untrue: a disclaimer at the top of the page says that some of her statements have been found "false and defamatory." It reminds me of how Alexander wanted to attach a notice to my essay stating that it contained a false recollection.

A California attorney who specializes in suing universities on behalf of accused students has invoked the Depp-Heard case in media interviews to demonstrate how men's rights are violated by Title IX. He belongs to a cottage industry of lawyers who try to fatigue schools into dropping cases through techniques like submitting thousands of pages of "evidence" and demanding access to all the accuser's communications, like Daniel's attorney did. Since schools lack the powers of courts but are increasingly held to a criminal-justice standard, litigious respondents are well positioned to convince a judge that they've been wronged. Courts are not required to inform complainants about lawsuits filed by respondents; as a result, the former often don't get to present their side. Ironically, judges review these civil suits according to the "preponderance of evidence" standard. Complainants who sue a university, meanwhile, must prove that the institution showed "deliberate indifference," a high bar that requires a jury trial in federal court.

Some respondents also file defamation lawsuits against their accusers. They include Saifullah Khan, who was expelled from Yale in 2018 after a Title IX investigation found that he had raped a fellow student. Unlike in most Title IX cases, including mine, a criminal court also took up this allegation. At the trial, where prosecutors had to prove his guilt to a jury "beyond a reasonable doubt," Khan was acquitted. He later sued the complainant for comments she'd made during the Title IX process, in a case that's ongoing as I write. Even when these lawsuits ultimately fail, they can take years to play out and bankrupt the person on the receiving end.

Therapy, a setting in which each individual's version of their own past and present reigns supreme, might seem to be removed from combat. In the unusual circumstances of the Tarasoff case, Prosenjit's therapist recognized that his client posed a risk and tried to act on it, but the police ignored him. As the Title IX process becomes more invasive, however, the accused weaponize therapy to minimize their actions (like Daniel) or to discredit those who come forward, as in the investigation of Harvard anthropology professor John Comaroff. In the latter case, according to a lawsuit filed by three complainants, Harvard's Title IX office gained notes from the private therapy sessions of one of his accusers, without her consent, and showed them to Comaroff. His side then used the notes to present her as unstable.

Comaroff denied that he had done anything wrong. Though the Title IX office determined that he had engaged in verbal harassment, it found him "not responsible" for unwanted sexual contact. The university placed him on unpaid leave for one semester and temporarily barred him from teaching. Some of Harvard's most eminent scholars, including the historians Henry Louis Gates, Jr., and Jill Lepore, signed a letter defending Comaroff as an "excellent colleague, advisor and committed university citizen." A counter-letter written by other faculty members noted that their only knowledge of the case came from Comaroff's legal team. As unsavory details about Comaroff's behavior emerged in the media, most of the faculty who endorsed the original letter backpedaled and issued a new one, "We Retract."

Placing painful experience into a narrative, whether singular or collective, supposedly dulls its sting. For survivors, however, doing so opens them to further abuse. Those who publicly tell their stories are simultaneously overexposed and erased. Armchair critics drag out the detritus of their lives as proof that they're unreliable narrators, while any evidence they can produce is marked by self-censorship. Scattered premonitions and aftershocks of violence—like euphemistic phrases about being sorry and "getting better"—can fall into a perceptible image, if only the viewer knows how to look. Yet even the most "believable" victims (cis, white, thin, middle class, not engaged in sex work) are hastily discredited: she was drunk, she provoked him, she's exaggerating, she's nuts.

Bystanders who pen knee-jerk defenses of the accused are not particularly interested in the facts. Surely nothing happened, the thinking goes—and even if it did, who cares? Whether the victim flourishes or flails, it's because she would have anyway. Both rare, horrifying outcomes like Tanya's and more common, quietly aching ones like Michelle and Deborah's are declared unavoidable and cast aside. Her fate, whatever form it takes, is a foregone conclusion; only his matters and is possible to change. If she opens her mouth, she should be ready to "get wrecked."

———

Heard wrote her essay at a moment of tremendous faith in the power of female speech. After the flood of stories failed to solve the problems they described, anger flipped back against the words themselves. While scrolling through social media in summer 2023, I click on an article called "A Feminist Style." Author Caitlín Doherty, writing for the *New Left Review*, argues that feminists' once-radical aspirations have devolved into cultural by-products that valorize female speech (like *She Said*, the 2022 movie about the women who took down Weinstein) but are devoid of politics. Feminism has come to mean first-person narratives that fetishize womanhood as misery, with "participation credentialled on the basis of suffering." The movement must offer "verifiable truths about the current situation of women," Doherty warns, "or else it will be—only—a style."

Yet reports of the kinds of suffering that disproportionately affect women keep being dismissed as empty complaints. Decades after the Tarasoff case, domestic and sexual abuse often continue to be regarded as an issue of individual psychology or an unfortunate offshoot of social ills. Survivors grapple with invisible effects like traumatic brain injury, contributing to the perception that there's "no major problem" to address. Here's a verifiable truth: nearly half of all murdered women in the US are killed by their current or former male partners, with Black women the most likely to die of all groups. According to a 2021 study, around two-thirds of American mass shootings are rooted in domestic violence.

This constellation of losses reveals the misogyny that still underpins our politics—the belief in the male prerogative to rule that even the Bolsheviks couldn't dismantle because they were too scared of living in a world without it. Scholars Theresa K. Vescio and Nathaniel E. C. Schermerhorn found that approval of "hegemonic masculinity," or the idea that men have a right to dominate, was the strongest predictor of voter support for Trump in the 2016 and 2020 elections, surpassing other factors such as race, gender, education, and party affiliation. Trump, a competitor who refuses to leave the cockfight even when he loses, embodies the will to power; his boasts about assaulting women simply add to his appeal.

Writers like Koestler and Miłosz worried that the individual would be swept away by overwhelming currents, whether fascist or communist. In Trump's postmodern style of politics—which perpetrators of abuse might affirm or denounce in public but consistently enact in private—a single man's wishes are all that counts. I wonder if any of Trump's most devoted followers, the ones who have gone to prison for trying to seize the Capitol on his behalf, feel trapped like Bukharin (or I) once did. I wonder if they will manage to free their minds from a person who is ready to sacrifice their lives to his whims, which he dresses up as the will of history.

Lamentation won't solve the problem of violence against women. But neither will the dismissal of their stories as discursive self-indulgence rather than lived experience, or the perennial insistence that their pain is anecdotal and personal rather than rampant and political. Leftists shouldn't bend over backward to sound enlightened until we find ourselves mimicking the arguments of our opponents and mistaking them for contrarian wisdom. Even sympathetic critics of MeToo charge survivors with politely stepping out of the way lest they distract from some other, more worthy cause. I can't join this chorus. It would mean disowning the self I managed to save.

Everyone marshals "a carefully-selected compendium" of facts to support their allegiances; all history is revisionist. It is not only our task to tell a good story about the past, however, but to create the fullest and most accurate account possible. A narrative of MeToo that concludes with the downfall of a few media executives disregards how those most vulnerable to harassment are often too afraid of being fired or deported to complain. A narrative of women's liberation that condemns the harm caused by laws against sexual and domestic violence overlooks the people they've helped—and how feminists in many countries, including Russia, still fight to get them.

A few months before I arrived in Moscow to do research in 2017, Russia's parliament decriminalized some forms of family violence. In the following years, the number of domestic abuse calls made to police plummeted, while the percentage of women killed by partners and family members rose. Activists report that domestic violence rates have spiked even higher as soldiers returning from Ukraine bring violence back home. Russia doesn't have protective orders, leaving victims with little recourse. In the 2019 social media campaign #IDidn'tWantToDie, women painted bruises on their faces to call for a national domestic violence law.

Grassroots movements like Argentina's #NiUnaMenos have led similar struggles for basic recognition of gender-based violence, including protocols for schools and workplaces. In *The Right to Sex*, Srinivasan, a professor at Oxford, presents such crusades as a misguided Western import designed to "bring the world's women into the global capitalist economy, with the US at its helm." These women have purportedly been hoodwinked into trading the struggle against economic inequality for the demand not to be harassed or murdered, as if the two were incompatible. I can imagine listening to this interpretation in a classroom and nodding along in agreement. Things look different to those living and dying on the ground.

In studying the past, and especially that of another country, we tend to adopt what E. P. Thompson called "the enormous condescension of posterity" and assume we know better. Alexander tried to discourage this habit by getting students to relate to ambiguous subjects like Bukharin and ponder what they would have done in his stead. However, these risky exercises in self-identification were for undergraduates, not professionals. We graduate students learned to adopt the third person and try not to consider how the stories we told about others' lives intersected with our own. The Title IX case forced me to behold what's usually banished from our work. Once I started looking, I couldn't stop.

In the early stages of writing this book, I thought of Liza, and pulled up my dissertation to see what I wrote about her and Oleg. I searched in the chapter and couldn't find it. Though I was sure I wrote the sentences, I must have deleted them. My stomach dropped as I realized that the last erasure of violence was mine. After swallowing my embarrassment, I considered why I'd made this mistake. At the time, I was trying to create an intellectual product written in an authoritative voice; Liza ventured dangerously close to the personal debris I needed to excise. My dissertation doesn't include any hint of what was going on while I was creating it, save for a brief allusion in the acknowledgments. After scrubbing away the stains of my life, I was commended for exemplary hygiene: my dissertation received the department's prize for the best of the year.

This second, secret dissertation recovers the truth that I kept out the first time around, as well as the related stories that I removed. Here, I haven't corseted my memories to suit the gaze of an investigator, scholar, or judge. No one has been looking over my shoulder to check my words against a master account of what I've really been up to all these years. This version of events is mine, more likely or not. It's less like academic history than what Freud called "dreamwork," in which the sleeper wakes up and tries to develop the blurry negatives of night.

Nursing old wounds can feed narcissistic resentment: the Unite the Right rally's chant of "you will not replace us," Daniel's penchant for taking his hurt out on me. At its best, however, the refusal to move on provides an alternative path. The philosopher Sara Ahmed, who resigned from her position at Goldsmiths College after it failed to address students' complaints of sexual harassment, describes feminism as "memory work." Rather than clinging to her place on the ladder, Ahmed walked away, in honor of those who had been forced off it.

Many historians are skeptical of the word "memory." Since its boom in the 1980s, it has come to connote the soft-filtering of the past through the pastel shades of the personal—a soothing hug of self-help at odds with the cool, hard work of knowledge-gathering in which the professional academic is ostensibly engaged. I recognize this attitude in Alexander's assertion that since my opinion was colored by individual feeling, it lacked the universal validity of the judgments that he could form as an observer. But bystanders are not neutral, and victims' ugly emotions hold a truth that is all too frequently discounted. Since abuse doesn't fit with the stories communities tell about themselves, it is often overwritten accordingly.

My ending here could try to integrate Daniel's viewpoint with mine, revisit the decisions I made, and determine that his defenders were at least somewhat in the right. Though rendering life as narrative tends to defang it, I try to keep my memories sharp. For the real truth is this: I know why Anna says Daniel should have been allowed to stay, and why Kipnis rolls her eyes at accusers' claims. My first, unspoken instinct is to dismiss them, too. My mind wants to shrug off the burden of responsibility that the grad student with the blue pen identified in 1976. Abuse not only enlists victims in their own effacement, but can also blind them to others' agony.

After leaving Daniel, I switched my loyalties from the perpetrator of violence to other survivors, as my interests moved from the lives of prominent men to those in their shadow. My shift in sentiment retraced the steps of Marxist revisionists who tried to retrieve the individual's place within a collective cause—and multiple waves of feminists who, by sharing personal stories, created a movement larger than themselves. They did so only to learn that not all women were like them, and that the wider the circle of "we," the more people are left out.

At the end of *Darkness at Noon*, Rubashov realizes that he never found what he was looking for, the solution to the question of whose suffering mattered and how to fix it: "The Party had taken all he had to give and never supplied him with the answer." He concludes that he studied the wrong thing. As a young man, he had intended to focus on astronomy, which he abandoned for the earthly tenets of dialectical materialism. Now, before he falls to the ground, he reflects that there is no escape from the mysteries of the stars.

Once I rediscovered my "I" and kept on living, it felt most comfortable to slink back into the safety of the self. Yet the first person is not its own form of omniscience. It summons the true devil of solipsism: the dictator's tendency to self-deify and turn the world into a reflecting pool. Reading the words of people who survived the twentieth century's horrors and tried to regain hope—without ceding to new dogmas—has shown me how independent thinking need not be single-minded. I haven't renounced the tools I gained by becoming a historian or concluded that balancing different perspectives is futile; I still try to see the ocean beneath the waves. Studying the past appealed to me because it offered an encounter with places, languages, people, and conditions far removed from my own. Though historians seek points of similarity, they never stop reckoning with difference. Their conclusions are subject to reappraisal by the next generation (or their future selves, when they amend their work in light of new developments).

Though I keep studying sources in search of something like truth, I've seen the past change shape too many times to believe that historians re-create anything "as it actually was." Even the most carefully researched stories are haunted by all that was left out. Rather than rejecting narrative altogether, I try to be up-front about my motivations and open to reconsidering when the facts change. I'm also prone to acknowledge the current dilemmas that guide my hand. After meeting Iulia and other refugees in Warsaw, I wrote an essay about the history of relations between Poland and Ukraine that sought to understand how the two countries transformed from bitter enemies to supportive partners (and how this arrangement has continued to spurn would-be friends from outside Europe). The article dipped into the first person, darted back and forth between past and present, and didn't make any pretense of distance toward its subject or ambiguity about its political stance. Though an academic journal would have rejected such an approach, it met the approval of the editorial board inside my head.

Putting life to the test of books taught me how to observe from a distance. Putting books to the test of life taught me that the stakes are most visible at close range. Being a historian means turning my education against itself, pairing what my mentors taught me with knowledge that eludes their reach. As periods with labels like "MeToo" rise and fall, abuse survivors are left with shards of experience that don't fit into a sweeping story of retrenchment and rebellion, solidarity or betrayal. I learned how to say what happened, both to me and to others, in spite of—and thanks to—those who couldn't.

The distance of time doesn't always lead to superior insight. Its ability to knead the particular into the general can smother the pulse of a single life. My thoughts often return to the woman whose husband ran her over with his car shortly before I left Daniel. Like Tanya, she never got the chance to decide whether she wanted to speak out or determine what closure looks like. Hearing only one thing about her story—how it ended—helped steer mine in another direction. I want to hold more of her in my brain, grasp the fragments left behind by the whole.

On a visit to my hometown, I meet with her aunt Marty, my family's friend from church, to learn more about how she lived and died. We sit on a bench by the trails that loop through the woods, where I walked several years ago as I tried to comprehend what was going on between Daniel and me. Marty shows me her niece's photo and tells me her name:

Shannon.

Shannon met her husband when she was in high school and he was a youth leader at her family's church. Her mobile job allowed them to spend the final year of her life traveling across the country together, while he picked up work along the way. They posted selfies with scenic backdrops like the Grand Canyon. Marty heard details that didn't make it onto social media, like how Shannon's husband had a "temper" and smashed the windshield of her car. Marty had been in an abusive relationship herself and recognized the signs.

During an argument one evening, Shannon's husband rammed into her with his truck. She'd been standing next to it, outside the friends' house where they were staying after returning from their road trip. When he accelerated, the car's open door squished her into a fence post that snapped in half and transected her liver. He probably just meant to scare her, Marty says. Whatever his intentions, they didn't change the result. He pled guilty to vehicular homicide (defined as causing someone's death by driving in a way that is reckless, unsafe, or under the influence but is not necessarily on purpose); after three years and five months at a minimum-security prison, he's out. The cause of Shannon's death went unmentioned during her funeral.

Marty pulls up a video montage that was shown at the service. It displays photos of Shannon beaming through different ages. A baby with a Minnie Mouse doll turns into a kid holding a plastic stethoscope. A teenager in braces transforms into a young bride in a wedding dress, then a grown woman who blows out candles on a birthday cake and holds a sign that says "Sarcasm: just one more service I offer." While the slide-show depicts one history, there was a parallel version that did not appear on camera. With each image, the seconds count down to the end of the video and Shannon's life. Marty and I start to cry.

Suddenly, a loud crack ricochets through the trees. We look behind us in time to see a heavy branch tumble to the ground.

"People get killed that way, you know," Marty says.

Someone was killed that way a few years ago, in a backyard around the corner. When a tree fell during a child's birthday party, a man pushed his daughter out of the way, taking its weight onto himself.

While walking home, I stop on a bridge over a ravine and think about Shannon's last minutes. Marty said it took over an hour for her to bleed out from internal injuries; she was still talking on the way to the hospital. I wonder what was going through her head—if she was stunned, if she was lonely, if she could think at all. The best I can do is refrain from filling eternal silence with hollow words. In the moment her breath became air, Shannon, like Tanya, lost any control over her story. I only know Shannon's life as a tragedy, which is surely not how she would have wanted to see it. Though I don't want to reduce her to the circumstances of her death, I also can't leave her alone in the place that no one else sees or hears, the void that I escaped but won't let go.

Later that evening, when I try to find more details about Shannon online, my search produces local media coverage of her murder. The facts of Shannon's death didn't lend themselves to the melodramatic plotline of a jilted lover that filled the articles about Tanya's. The sparse reportage here was focused on how what happened conflicted with outsiders' impressions. A neighbor told a TV news crew that the couple looked happy.

"Facebook pictures say the same," the anchor said, as the screen showed a Christmas portrait of the spouses grinning with their dogs.

Their relationship, like mine with Daniel, seemed normal enough—until the story that was absent from the photos took over and left one final, terrible piece of documentation behind. When I get in touch with Shannon's mother, she tells me that after her son-in-law had already made a plea deal, she found out that the police had recovered an audio recording of her daughter's death. If she'd known about it earlier, Shannon's mom says, she would have pushed for the case to go to trial.

In the recording, which a forensic technician transcribed from her phone, Shannon begs her intoxicated husband to get out of the car. He calls her a "fucking bitch," shifts his truck into reverse, and guns the engine. As Shannon is crushed into the fence post, she screams. He yells at her to get up. Though the audio at this point grows muffled, Shannon's mom shows me police interviews in which bystanders recalled what happened next.

"I can't breathe," Shannon said repeatedly.

"Good," her husband replied, and called her a "bitch" again.

According to witnesses, he didn't try to help her. After one of the friends they were staying with called 911, he kept telling the first aid crew to go away; the friend had to physically restrain him in order for paramedics to perform treatment. Taken together, these facts strongly suggest that Shannon's death was no accident. Through her final moments, the person responsible made choices with consequences. Even so, an onlooker could easily miss the full picture: Shannon's obituary only said that she "died unexpectedly." She was twenty-four years old.

After Shannon's death, a friend of theirs from church formed a Facebook support group for her husband that gained over 150 members. The group's banner photo was a shot of the couple smiling. Comments described him as a "big teddy bear" and "a good man who made a mistake but meant no harm." As I look at the screenshots, I think back to the sympathy campaign that Daniel led for himself in our community Facebook group. I can only imagine what might have appeared there if he'd made a similar "mistake." Shannon's mom tells me she wishes the "fan club" praising her daughter's husband could hear the recording, so they would understand what kind of person he is when they're not around. But I know something that I suspect she realizes too: scales will never fall from the eyes of someone who doesn't want to see.

The key to working through trauma, I've read, is developing a sense of differentiated time: that was then, this is now. Famous men who philosophize about history favor vertiginous symbols, like Hegel's owl and Benjamin's angel, whose view from above transcends the fractured gaze of those underneath. This image reminds me of the time when I went to the viewing platform at the top of the Campanile during my first week in graduate school. My eyes wandered from Dwinelle all the way to the Golden Gate Bridge—a radiant panorama of steel, plants, and sea that's only visible in pieces on the ground. For the rest of my time in Berkeley, I felt too busy to return.

In looking back at what happened, there is no lofty peak of objectivity or elevator to the last floor. My mind lingers down below, not only to mourn or celebrate what came to pass, but to keep company with the doubles of the fallen who got up: the Tanya who became a translator, the Shannon who kept traveling and had the kids her obituary said she wanted. As the future turns into the past, we don't want to believe that we're the ones hitting the asphalt—or pressing the gas pedal—until it's too late. Yet all fates, however welded by structure and circumstance, can be altered by a conscious act.

Over and over again, we choose to identify with those who commit abuse over the people they hurt. When the "victim" fails to complete the metamorphosis to "survivor," the person who takes her life is still the one who suffers in the popular imagination. Her death was supposedly a fluke—an unstoppable and unpredictable misfortune, like scattered showers on a sunny afternoon. The truth is purged from written records and the public eye. This distortion of the past has implications now. Abuse sometimes takes lives suddenly, and more often corrodes them over the course of years. Neither outcome is predetermined.

Though history doesn't contain iron laws or ready-made parables, like gold waiting to be sifted from silt, we can still learn from the succession of lives that compose it. Time creates patterns, which we make sense of through stories. Their subjective, unfinished nature allows us to propose how elements could have mixed differently and try to change the fusions to come. This is the value of crafting narratives—the substance beneath the style. The visions we salvage from (or project on) the past catalyze new possibilities for us.

To study history, as Benjamin wrote, is not to learn what "really" took place: "It means to seize memory as it flashes brightly in a moment of danger." Thanks to women who didn't forget about Shannon—Marty, who told my mother, and my mother, who told me—the story of her death acquired another layer of meaning. Their account of the past, however incomplete, propelled me forward into the future she lost. I've written this story of what happened to me, in hopes that the truth I have to tell will live on in someone else.

EPILOGUE
A LONG TIME AGO

WHEN I WALK AROUND WARSAW AND SEE THE FACES OF PEOPLE who got away, I remember my last evening in Berkeley, when the same invisible thread that pulled me to read Liza's letters and meet with Marty tugged me to Tanya's house. Though Tanya's parents were long dead, her older brother Alex was still around. I tried calling a few times; no one picked up the phone.

The address was on Tacoma Avenue, where the flatlands curve into the hills. The single-story dwellings there, which used to be owned by working-class families like the Tarasoffs, now sell for millions of dollars. I passed front yards filled with lemon trees until I reached a house painted dusty pink. A man was washing his car in the driveway, near the spot where Tanya died almost fifty-four years ago. It was Alex.

I explained that I was writing a book about violence against women, in Berkeley and elsewhere, and wanted to say something about Tanya. Alex reacted politely to a random lady showing up at his door and asked what I wanted to know. I posed a couple of questions about what happened.

"I don't think about it much anymore," he said. "It was a long time ago."

I asked if anything could have prevented Tanya's murder.

"No, because it was so unexpected." Prosenjit didn't seem violent. "I thought he was more of a Gandhi type."

We exchanged a few words in Russian, which Alex grew up speaking at home, and he changed the subject to the war in Ukraine. He said he

259

was ashamed to be Russian these days and asked whether I thought the sanctions against Putin would work. It was after dusk by the time we said good night. As I followed the road up to the house where I was renting a room, the fog started to descend, clouding the light that radiated from the streetlamps.

According to the appeal documents I read, Prosenjit informed Alex that he had thoughts about killing Tanya and asked him how to buy a gun; Alex, sure that Prosenjit wouldn't really do it, told him to find another girlfriend. Now, back in Warsaw, I think about how hindsight blurs contingent events until they come to appear inevitable.

As the gray night sky shrouds Stalin's palace for the masses, the fog seems to have followed me here. It falls, thicker and thicker, until years and borders collapse like a civilization on a cliff that crumbles into the sea. I see a woman falling backward, shells exploding over an apartment building, a man saying he was provoked, a body lying on the ground in front of a home that should have been safe. Suddenly a voice cuts through the haze: *no no no no, you will not hurt her like you hurt me.* The car reverses, the bombs freeze in midair, she is standing again, she is free.

ACKNOWLEDGMENTS

Thanks to my brilliant friends from Berkeley, whose wisdom comes from life as much as books. Jason, we miss you.

To my professors at Berkeley for everything they taught me, by design or by accident.

To all the other great teachers I've had, especially Jettie Marie Waller, Cheri Armstrong, and Patty Worsham (at E. C. Glass High School) and Seth Rockman (at Brown University). I won't thank Ethan Pollock because now I'm lucky enough to call him my friend.

To the friends I made while the case was ongoing who helped me get through it, especially Gabby Cornish and Katie David.

To Kate Brown for making this possible, Lauren Sharp for making it happen, and Anu Roy-Chaudhury for her unparalleled eye and enthusiasm throughout. To all three of you for getting this project immediately and having faith that I could pull it off. Also for being so classy and cool.

To the people who reached out to me with their stories and everyone I spoke with for the book, including Beth Berry, Deborah Blum, Kellie Brennan, Nicole Britton-Snyder, Kat Gutierrez, Carla Hesse, Maha Ibrahim, Sharon Inkelas, Martin Jay, Sofie Karasek, Nancy Lemon, Stephanie Penrod, Karen Peterson, Erin Scott, Alex Tarasoff, James Vernon, Deborah Wood, and Marty Wright. Extra thanks to Maria Brandt for helping me read the Bancroft files that came too late and to Evan Penn for Bay Area moral support.

To Bathsheba Demuth, Maha Ibrahim, Kerwin Klein, and Vivian Lu for generously reading the draft and seeing what I couldn't.

To Kevin O'Flynn, my first editor (at the *Moscow Times*), whose ace bullshit detection and effortless creativity I will never match.

To Irina Teodorescu for saying, "But you must write about it!"

To my family for teaching me to be curious and always supporting my decisions, especially when they make no apparent sense.

Dzięki również mojej rodzinie w Polsce za ciepłe przywitanie.

Tadeuszowi i Czesiowi—mojemu stadku.

WORKS CITED

Note on Sources

This book is based primarily on my recollections of events that may or may not have left any evidentiary trace. All written quotations (from text messages, emails, case files, and so on) are taken from the original source. Capitalization and punctuation of text messages have occasionally been modified for readability. Spoken quotations from my personal and professional relationships are re-created from memory. In Part 3, quotations from interviews I conducted come from the notes I took during these conversations. Below is a list of books, articles, and archival collections that I drew on while writing or refer to directly in the text, listed in the order in which their information appears.

Part 1

Prologue: A Magic Mountain

Thomas Mann, *The Magic Mountain*, trans. H. T. Lowe-Porter (New York: Knopf, 1953, 1982).

Johann Wolfgang Von Goethe, *Faust*, trans. Bayard Taylor (Project Gutenberg, 2005).

Karim Doumar, "Fence Around Chancellor's Residence Completed at 2½ Times Original Budget," *Daily Californian*, May 26, 2016, https://dailycal.org/2016/05/26/fence -around-chancellors-residence-completed-2-5-times-original-budget.

Julia Carrie Wong, "UC Berkeley Denies Chancellor Built an 'Escape Hatch' to Flee Student Protests," *Guardian*, August 3, 2016, https://www.theguardian.com /us-news/2016/aug/03/uc-berkeley-chancellor-escape-hatch-student-protests#:~ :text=Mogulof%20confirmed%20that%20the%20extra,directly%20in%20the%20 chancellor's%20office.

Teresa Watanabe, "With Money Tight, Chancellor Says UC Berkeley Must 'Reimagine' its Future," *Los Angeles Times*, February 10, 2016, https://www.latimes.com/local/lanow/la-me-ln-uc-berkeley-deficit-20160210-story.html.

Gretchen Kell, "Fasten Your Goggles: New Aquatic Center Is on the Way," *Berkeley News*, September 2, 2016, https://news.berkeley.edu/2016/09/02/fasten-your-goggles-new-aquatic-center-is-on-its-way.

Tina Dupuy, "Occupy Cal Makes Occupy History at Berkeley," *Atlantic*, November 16, 2011, https://www.theatlantic.com/politics/archive/2011/11/occupy-cal-makes-occupy-history-at-berkeley/248555/.

Emily Costanza, "State Must Address the Housing Crisis," *East Bay Times*, October 5, 2016, https://www.eastbaytimes.com/2016/10/05/state-must-address-the-housing-crisis/.

Lillian Dong, "UC Berkeley Student Struggles to Pay Tuition, Faces Homelessness," *Daily Californian*, July 31, 2016, https://www.dailycal.org/2016/07/31/uc-berkeley-student-faces-homelessness.

Jon David Cash, "People's Park: Birth and Survival," *California History* 88, no. 1 (2010): 8–29, 25.

Ann Curthoys and John Docker, *Is History Fiction?* (Sydney: University of New South Wales Press, 2006), 134, 216, 218.

Walter Benjamin, *Illuminations: Essays and Reflections*, trans. Harry Zohn (New York: Schocken Books, 1969), 257–258.

Christopher Clark, *Sleepwalkers: How Europe Went to War in 1914* (New York: HarperCollins, 2013).

Ann Rule, *The Stranger Beside Me* (New York: Gallery Books, 2018).

1. The Idea of Knowing

Dipesh Chakrabarty, "The Climate of History: Four Theses," *Critical Inquiry* 35, no. 2 (2009): 197–222.

Bruno Latour, "Agency at the Time of the Anthropocene," *New Literary History* 45, no. 1 (2014): 1–18.

Georg Wilhelm Friedrich Hegel, *Lectures on the Philosophy of World History*, trans. Hugh Barr Nisbet (New York: Cambridge University Press, 1975); ibid, *Phenomenology of Spirit*, trans. A. V. Miller (Oxford: Oxford University Press, 1977).

Susan Buck-Morss, "Hegel and Haiti," *Critical Inquiry* 26, no. 4 (2000): 821–865.

Robert C. Tucker, ed., *The Marx-Engels Reader* (New York: W.W. Norton & Company, 1978).

2. Deep Play

Robert B. Townsend, "A Grim Year on the Academic Job Market for Historians," *Perspectives on History*, January 1, 2010, https://www.historians.org/research-and-publications/perspectives-on-history/january-2010/a-grim-year-on-the-academic-job-market-for-historians; annual jobs reports released by the American Historical Association at historians.org.

Max Weber, "Politics as Vocation," in *Weber's Rationalism and Modern Society*, ed. and trans. Tony Waters and Dagmar Waters (New York: Palgrave Macmillan, 2015), 129–198.

Clifford Geertz, "Deep Play: Notes on the Balinese Cockfight," *Daedalus* 101, no. 1 (1972): 1–37, 15, 26.

Jean Jacques Rousseau, *Julie, or the New Heloise* (Dartmouth: Stewart & Vache, 1997), 90.

Lynn Hunt, *Inventing Human Rights: A History* (New York: W.W. Norton & Company), 2007.

Edmund Burke, *A Philosophical Inquiry into the Sublime and Beautiful* (New York: Oxford University Press, 2015).

Maximilien Robespierre, "Rapport sur les principes de morale politique" (Paris: Imprimerie National, 1794), translation by author.

3. The Red Sun

Lyrics to "Workers' Marseillaise" (also called "the Russian Marseillaise") by Piotr Lavrov (1875), translation by author. On the song's history see Rustam Fakhretdinov, "'Russkaia marsel'eza': Zhestokii romans Petra Lavrova," *Antropologicheskii forum*, no. 36 (2018): 117–153.

On Russian intelligentsia radicalism and the road to revolution see Orlando Figes, *A People's Tragedy: The Russian Revolution, 1891–1924* (New York: Viking, 1996); Sheila Fitzpatrick, *The Russian Revolution*, 3rd ed. (Oxford, New York: Oxford University Press, 2008); Abbott Gleason, *Young Russia: The Genesis of Russian Radicalism in the 1860s* (New York: The Viking Press, 1980); Susan Morrissey, *Heralds of Revolution: Russian Students and the Mythologies of Radicalism* (New York: Oxford University Press, 1998); Richard Pipes, *The Russian Revolution* (New York: Knopf, 1991).

Jay Bergman, *The French Revolutionary Tradition in Russian and Soviet Politics, Political Thought, and Culture* (New York: Oxford University Press, 2019), Chapter 6: "1917: Russian Jacobins Come to Power," 139–169.

Isaac Babel, *The Collected Stories of Isaac Babel*, ed. Nathalie Babel and trans. Peter Constantine (New York: Penguin, 1994), "My First Goose," 230–233.

On Russian culture in the wake of the October Revolution see Nikolai Krementsov, *Revolutionary Experiments: The Quest for Immortality in Bolshevik Science and Fiction* (New York: Oxford University Press, 2014) and Richard Stites, *Revolutionary Dreams: Utopian Vision and Experimental Life in the Russian Revolution* (New York: Oxford University Press, 1989).

Charles Darwin, *The Expression of the Emotions in Man and Animals*, ed. Paul Ekman (New York: Oxford University Press, 2002).

Mark Peterson, "Chair's Letter," in UC Berkeley Department of History winter 2016 newsletter, https://www.history.berkeley.edu/sites/default/files/2016_winter_newsletter.pdf, 5.

4. "Es schwindelt"

Leon Trotsky, *My Life: An Attempt at an Autobiography* (New York: Pathfinder Press, 1970), 337.

Stephen Kotkin, *Magnetic Mountain: Stalinism as a Civilization* (Berkeley: University of California Press, 1995).

Robert Conquest, *Harvest of Sorrow: Soviet Collectivization and the Terror-Famine* (New York: Oxford University Press, 1986).

Lev Kopelev, *The Education of a True Believer*, trans. Gary Kern (New York: Harper and Row, 1980), 250.

Stephen F. Cohen, *Bukharin and the Bolshevik Revolution: A Political Biography, 1888–1938* (New York: Oxford University Press, 1980).

Rhea Mahbubani, "'They're Absolutely Petrified': Milo Yiannopoulos Lashes Out After UC Berkeley Event Due to Protests," NBC Bay Area, February 1, 2017, https://www.nbcbayarea.com/news/local/theyre-absolutely-petrified-milo-yiannopoulos-lashes-out-after-uc-berkeley-event-nixed-after-protests/34872/.

"Materialy fevral'sko-martovskogo Plenuma TsK VKP(b) 1937 goda. 25 fevralia 1937 g. Vechernee zasedaniie" [Materials from the February-March Plenum of the Central Committee of the All-Union Communist Party of Bolsheviks. February 25, 1937. Evening session], in *Voprosy istorii*, no. 10 (1992): 23–24.

Jochen Hellbeck, "With Hegel to Salvation: Bukharin's Other Trial," *Representations* 107, no. 1 (2009): 59–90, 69, 71.

For various interpretations of the Terror see Robert Conquest, *The Great Terror: A Reassessment* (New York: Oxford University Press, 1990); Robert V. Daniels, ed., *The Stalin Revolution: Foundations of the Totalitarian Era*, 4th ed. (Boston: Houghton Mifflin Company, 1997); Sheila Fitzpatrick, "New Perspectives on Stalinism," *Russian Review* 45, no. 4 (1986): 357–373; J. Arch Getty, *Origins of the Great Purges: The Soviet Communist Party Reconsidered, 1993–1938* (New York: Cambridge University Press, 1985); J. Arch Getty and Oleg Naumov, eds., *The Road to Terror: Stalin and the Self-Destruction of the Bolsheviks, 1932–1939* (New Haven: Yale University Press, 1999).

Arthur Koestler, *Darkness at Noon*, trans. Daphne Hardy (London: The Camelot Press, 1940), 243.

5. The Captive Mind

Joy Neumeyer, "Miłosz's Magic Mountain," *Baffler*, May 2, 2022, https://thebaffler.com/latest/miloszs-magic-mountain-neumeyer.

Cynthia L. Haven, *Czesław Miłosz: A California Life* (Berkeley, CA: Heyday, 2021).

Czesław Miłosz, *The Captive Mind*, trans. Jane Zielonko (New York: Vintage Books, 1955), 6, 76.

Czesław Miłosz, *New and Collected Poems, 1931–2001* (New York: Harper Collins, 2001), "A Magic Mountain," 335.

Andrzej Franaszek, *Miłosz: A Biography*, ed. and trans. Aleksandra and Michael Parker (Cambridge, MA: The Belknap Press of Harvard University Press, 2017), 285–310.

Czesław Miłosz, *To Begin Where I Am: Selected Essays*, ed. Bogdana Carpenter and Madeline G. Levine (New York: Farrar, Straus, and Giroux, 2001), 15.

6. Drop by Drop

Kopelev, *The Education of a True Believer*, 123, 266–267.

Miłosz, *The Captive Mind*, x.

Czesław Miłosz, *Native Realm: A Search for Self-Definition*, trans. Catherine S. Leach (New York: Farrar, Straus & Giroux, 2002), 284.

Lundy Bancroft, *Why Does He Do That? Inside the Minds of Angry and Controlling Men* (New York: Berkley Books, 2003), "Introduction," Chapter 1: "The Mystery," Chapter

2: "The Mythology," Chapter 4: "The Types of Abusive Men," Chapter 6: "The Abusive Man in Everyday Life," Chapter 14: "The Process of Change."

Part 2

7. Targeted Risk

Rebecca Solnit, *Men Explain Things to Me* (Chicago: Haymarket Books, 2014).

Roxane Gay, *Bad Feminist: Essays* (New York: HarperCollins, 2014).

Sigmund Freud, *Beyond the Pleasure Principle*, trans. and ed. James Strachey (New York: W.W. Norton & Company, 1961), 8–11.

Leticia Glocer Fiorini, Thierry Bokanowski, and Sergo Lewkowicz, eds., *On Freud's "Mourning and Melancholia"* (New York: Routledge, 2018).

8. Due Process

Sam Levin, "UC Berkeley Students to File Sexual Harassment Complaint Against Professor," *Guardian*, April 10, 2016, https://www.theguardian.com/us-news/2016/apr/10/uc-berkeley-students-professor-sexual-harassment-complaint.

Nanette Asimov, "UC Berkeley Has History of Tolerating Sexual Misconduct," *San Francisco Chronicle*, March 12, 2016, https://www.sfchronicle.com/education/article/UC-Berkeley-has-history-of-tolerating-sexual-6886611.php.

Sam Levin, "Disturbing Details of Sexual Harassment Scandal at UC Berkeley Revealed in Files," *Guardian*, April 6, 2016, https://www.theguardian.com/us-news/2016/apr/06/uc-berkeley-staff-sexual-harassment-scandal.

Sam Levin, "'Honey Bear': Berkeley Student Details Alleged Sexual Advances by Professor," *Guardian*, May 27, 2016, https://www.theguardian.com/us-news/2016/may/27/uc-berkeley-sexual-harassment-scandal-blake-wentworth.

Bernice Resnick Sandler, "Title IX: How We Got It and What a Difference It Made," *Cleveland State Law Review* 55, no. 4 (2007): 473–489.

Sherry Boschert, *37 Words: Title IX and Fifty Years of Fighting Sex Discrimination* (New York: The New Press, 2022), 1–46, 96–97.

William Celis, "Date Rape and a List at Brown," *New York Times*, November 18, 1990, 26, https://www.nytimes.com/1990/11/18/us/date-rape-and-a-list-at-brown.html.

Helaine Olen and Ronald J. Ostrow, "Date-Rape Gains Attention After Years as Taboo Topic," *Los Angeles Times*, April 23, 1991, https://www.latimes.com/archives/la-xpm-1991-04-23-mn-643-story.html.

Gordon Witkin and David Donald, eds., "Sexual Assault on Campus: A Frustrating Search for Justice" (digital newsbook), The Center for Public Integrity, 2010, https://www.publicintegrity.org/documents/pdfs/Sexual%20Assault%20on%20Campus.pdf, 7, 13.

Jackie Calmes, "Obama Seeks to Raise Awareness of Rape on Campus," *New York Times*, January 22, 2014, https://www.nytimes.com/2014/01/23/us/politics/obama-to-create-task-force-on-campus-sexual-assaults.html.

"Dear Colleague Letter," U.S. Department of Education, April 4, 2011, https://www2.ed.gov/print/about/offices/list/ocr/letters/colleague-201104.html.

On OCR's unwillingness to cut off federal funds see Boschert, *37 Words*, 272.

Vanessa Grigoriadis, "A Revolution Against Campus Sexual Assault," *New York Magazine*, September 21, 2014, https://www.thecut.com/2014/09/emma-sulkowicz-campus-sexual -assault-activism.html#_ga=2.110019532.832418233.1699897687-1225113284.1699897687.

Richard Pérez-Peña, "College Groups Connect to Fight Sexual Assault," *New York Times*, March 19, 2013, https://www.nytimes.com/2013/03/20/education/activists -at-colleges-network-to-fight-sexual-assault.html.

"Title IX: Tracking Sexual Assault Investigations," *Chronicle of Higher Education*, https://projects.chronicle.com/titleix/#:~:text=In%20this%20era%20of%20 enforcement,resolved%20and%20305%20remain%20open.

Danielle Paquette, "How Lady Gaga and Hollywood Unexpectedly Tackled Rape at the Oscars," *Washington Post*, February 29, 2016, https://www.washingtonpost.com /news/wonk/wp/2016/02/29/how-lady-gaga-and-hollywood-unexpectedly-tackled-rape -at-the-oscars/.

Colby Itkowitz, "There's a Moving Story Behind This Powerful Photo of Biden and a Sexual Assault Survivor at the Oscars," *Washington Post*, March 7, 2016, https://www .washingtonpost.com/news/inspired-life/wp/2016/03/07/the-amazing-story-behind -this-photo-of-a-sexual-assault-survivor-and-joe-biden-at-the-oscars/.

Sofie Karasek, "Sexual Assault and Injustice at UC Berkeley: A Story of Bearing the Path to Cloud IX," *Huffington Post*, July 8, 2013, https://www.huffpost.com/entry /sexual-assault-and-injustice_b_3563918.

Sofie Karasek, "America's Universities: Where You're All Too Likely to Be Assaulted," *Guardian*, March 4, 2014, https://www.theguardian.com/commentisfree/2014/mar/04 /sexual-health-sex.

Jessica Testa, "UC Berkeley Accused of 'Deliberate Indifference' by 31 Sexual Assault Survivors," *BuzzFeed News*, February 26, 2014, https://www.buzzfeednews.com/article /jtes/31-sexual-assault-survivors-file-federal-complaints-against.

Kimberly Veklerov, "Federal Probe into UC Berkeley's Handling of Sexual Violence Cases Underway," *Daily Californian*, April 20, 2014, https://www.dailycal.org/2014/04/20 /federal-probe-uc-berkeleys-handling-sexual-violence-cases-underway.

Jessica Lynn and Cassandra Vogel, "Flexibility in Title IX Policy Leads to Allegations of Mishandled Cases," *Daily Californian*, March 6, 2017, https://www.dailycal .org/2017/03/06/flexibility-title-ix-policy-leads-allegations-mishandled-cases.

Eliana Dockterman, "*The Hunting Ground* Reignites the Debate over Campus Rape," *Time*, March 5, 2015, https://time.com/3722834/the-hunting-ground-provocative -documentary-reignites-campus-rape-debate/.

Sheila Coronel, Steve Coll, and Derek Kravitz, "*Rolling Stone*'s Investigation: A Failure That Was Avoidable," *Columbia Journalism Review*, April 5, 2015, https://www .cjr.org/investigation/rolling_stone_investigation.php.

Doreen McCallister, "*Rolling Stone* Settles Defamation Case with Former U.Va. Associate Dean," NPR, April 12, 2017, https://www.npr.org/sections/thetwo-way/2017/04/12 /523527227/rolling-stone-settles-defamation-case-with-former-u-va-associate-dean.

Michael Stratford, "U.S. Faults Virginia's Handling of Sexual Assault," *Inside Higher Ed*, September 21, 2015, https://www.insidehighered.com/news/2015/09/22/feds -say-uva-mishandled-sexual-violence-cases.

T. Rees Shapiro, "U-Va. Rape Survivor, Author Now Doubts *Rolling Stone* Account," *Washington Post*, January 16, 2015, https://www.washingtonpost.com/local/education /u-va-rape-survivor-author-questions-rolling-stone-account/2015/01/16/a50f0560 -9cfe-11e4-a7ee-526210d665b4_story.html.

Liz Seccuro, "Dear Rapist . . . ," *Guardian*, April 29, 2011, https://www.theguardian .com/society/2011/apr/30/rape-justice-after-20-years.

Katie J. M. Baker, "A Former Student Says UC Berkeley's Star Philosophy Professor Groped Her and Watched Porn at Work," *BuzzFeed News*, March 23, 2017, https://www.buzzfeednews.com/article/katiejmbaker/famous-philosophy-professor -accused-sexual-harassment.

Katie J. M. Baker, "UC Berkeley Was Warned About Its Star Professor Years Before Sexual Harassment Lawsuit," *BuzzFeed News*, April 7, 2017, https://www .buzzfeednews.com/article/katiejmbaker/john-searle-complaints-uc-berkeley.

Dennis Overbye, "Geoffrey Marcy to Resign from Berkeley Astronomy Department," *New York Times*, October 14, 2015, https://www.nytimes.com/2015/10/15/science /geoffrey-marcy-to-resign-from-berkeley-astronomy-department.html#:~:text=Marcy's %20resignation%20came%20two%20days,the%20department's%20graduate %20students%20and.

Sam Levin, "UC Berkeley Professor Fired Nearly Two Years After Sexual Harassment Claims Substantiated," *Guardian*, May 24, 2017, https://www.theguardian.com/world /2017/may/24/sexual-harassment-university-california-berkeley-blake-wentworth.

"Ex-Dean Accused of Sexual Harassment Sues Berkeley for Racial Discrimination," *Guardian*, September 15, 2016, https://www.theguardian.com/us-news/2016/sep/15 /sujit-choudhry-sexual-harassment-racial-discrimination.

Sam Levin, "UC Berkeley Dean in Sexual Harassment Case Keeps Tenure and Avoids Charges," *Guardian*, April 18, 2017, https://www.theguardian.com/us-news/2017/apr /18/uc-berkeley-sexual-harassment-dean-sujit-choudhry-deal.

Sasha Langholz, "Former Professor John Searle Loses Emeritus Status over Violation of Sexual Harassment, Retaliation Policies," *Daily Californian*, July 2, 2019, https:// dailycal.org/2019/07/02/former-professor-john-searle-loses-emeritus-status-over -violation-of-sexual-harassment-retaliation-policies.

"Chancellor Dirks Issues an Update on Sexual Assault Prevention, Response," *Berkeley News*, February 25, 2014, https://news.berkeley.edu/2014/02/25/chancellor-dirks -issues-an-update-on-sexual-assault-prevention-response/.

"Chancellor Announces New Committee on Sexual Violence, Harassment and Assault," *Berkeley News*, April 5, 2016, https://news.berkeley.edu/2016/04/05 /chancellor-announces-new-committee-on-sexual-violence-harassment-and-assault.

"Chancellor's Senate/Administration Committee on Sexual Violence and Sexual Harassment: Report of Findings and Recommendations," January 2017, https:// chancellor.berkeley.edu/sites/default/files/svsh_full_report_1-31-2017.pdf.

"Faculty Adviser on Sexual Harassment/Violence Named," *Berkeley News*, June 5, 2017, https://news.berkeley.edu/2017/06/05/faculty-adviser-on-sexual-harassmentviolence -named#:~:text=We%20are%20very%20pleased%20to,term%2C%20beginning%20 on%20July%2024%20.

Bobby Lee, "Carol Christ Becomes UC Berkeley's 11th Chancellor," *Daily Californian*, July 1, 2017, https://www.dailycal.org/2017/07/01/carol-christ-becomes-uc-berkeleys-11th-chancellor.

Anna Akhmatova, "Requiem," trans. Alex Cigale, *Hopkins Review* 9, no. 3 (2016): 339–347, 339.

Jochen Hellbeck, *Revolution on My Mind: Writing a Diary Under Stalin* (Cambridge, MA: Harvard University Press, 2006).

Gavin De Becker, *The Gift of Fear: Survival Signs That Protect Us from Violence* (Boston: Little, Brown, 1997).

Sophie Tatum, "Education Department Withdraws Obama-Era Sexual Assault Guidance," CNN, September 22, 2017, https://www.cnn.com/2017/09/22/politics/betsy-devos-title-ix/index.html#:~:text=Education%20Department%20withdraws%20Obama%2Dera%20campus%20sexual%20assault%20guidance,-By%20Sophie%20Tatum&text=The%20Education%20Department%20announced%20Friday,under%20Title%20IX%20federal%20law.

Jane Mayer, "Betsy DeVos, Trump's Big-Donor Education Secretary," *New Yorker*, November 23, 2016, https://www.newyorker.com/news/news-desk/betsy-devos-trumps-big-donor-education-secretary.

Ben Miller and Laura Jimenez, "Inside the Financial Holdings of Billionaire Betsy DeVos," Center for American Progress, January 27, 2017, https://www.americanprogress.org/article/inside-the-financial-holdings-of-billionaire-betsy-devos/.

"2016 Republican Party Platform," July 18, 2016, The American Presidency Project, https://www.presidency.ucsb.edu/documents/2016-republican-party-platform.

Erica L. Green and Sheryl Gay Stolberg, "Campus Rape Policies Get a New Look as the Accused Get DeVos's Ear," *New York Times*, July 12, 2017, https://www.nytimes.com/2017/07/12/us/politics/campus-rape-betsy-devos-title-iv-education-trump-candice-jackson.html.

Molly Redden, "Betsy DeVos Meets Sexual Assault Survivors After Her Deputy Apologizes," *Guardian*, July 13, 2017, https://www.theguardian.com/society/2017/jul/13/betsy-devos-meets-sexual-assault-survivors-deputy-apologizes.

Emily Yoffe, "The College Rape Overcorrection," *Slate*, December 7, 2014, https://www.slate.com/articles/double_x/doublex/2014/12/college_rape_campus_sexual_assault_is_a_serious_problem_but_the_efforts.html. For another example of how Title IX critics invoke the UVA case see Aya Gruber, *The Feminist War on Crime: The Unexpected Role of Women's Liberation in Mass Incarceration* (Oakland: University of California Press, 2020), 154.

Risa L. Lieberwitz, Rana Jaleel, Tina Kelleher, Joan Wallach Scott, Donna Young, Henry Reichman, Anne Sisson Runyan, and Anita Levy, "The History, Uses, and Abuses of Title IX," American Association of University Professors, June 2016, https://www.aaup.org/report/history-uses-and-abuses-title-ix.

Jeannie Suk Gersen, "Laura Kipnis's Endless Trial by Title IX," *New Yorker*, September 20, 2017, https://www.newyorker.com/news/news-desk/laura-kipniss-endless-trial-by-title-ix.

Laura Kipnis, "Sexual Paranoia Strikes Academe," *Chronicle of Higher Education*, February 27, 2015, https://www.chronicle.com/article/sexual-paranoia-strikes-academe/.

Laura Kipnis, "My Title IX Inquisition," *Chronicle of Higher Education*, May 29, 2015, https://www.chronicle.com/article/my-title-ix-inquisition/.

Laura Kipnis, *Unwanted Advances: Sexual Paranoia Comes to Campus* (New York: HarperCollins, 2017), 1, 17, 37–38, 44, 65, 75, 96, 150–151, 186–187, 221, 225, 229, 234.

Green and Stolberg, "Campus Rape Policies."

"Transcript: Betsy DeVos's Remarks on Campus Sexual Assault," *Washington Post*, September 7, 2017, https://www.washingtonpost.com/news/grade-point/wp/2017/09/07/transcript-betsy-devoss-remarks-on-campus-sexual-assault/.

9. The Flood

A 2002 study funded by the Department of Justice found that less than 5 percent of women who said they had been raped on campus reported it to the police or campus officials. Witkin and Donald, eds., "Sexual Assault on Campus," 51.

Jodi Kantor and Megan Twohey, "Harvey Weinstein Paid Off Sexual Harassment Accusers for Decades," *New York Times*, October 5, 2017, https://www.nytimes.com/2017/10/05/us/harvey-weinstein-harassment-allegations.html.

Rebecca Solnit, "Rebecca Solnit: Let This Flood of Women's Stories Never Cease," *Lithub*, November 14, 2017, https://lithub.com/rebecca-solnit-let-this-flood-of-womens-stories-never-cease/.

Roxane Gay, "Roxane Gay: Why the #MeToo Movement Has a Lot Left to Do," *Refinery29*, October 4, 2018, https://www.refinery29.com/en-us/2018/10/212802/me-too-change-women-2018-roxane-gay.

Masha Gessen, "When Does a Watershed Become a Sex Panic?," *New Yorker*, November 14, 2017, https://www.newyorker.com/news/our-columnists/when-does-a-watershed-become-a-sex-panic.

Boschert, *37 Words*, 204 ("Approximately 61 percent of higher education institutions already used the preponderance standard, according to a study conducted shortly before the Dear Colleague letter.").

MJ Lee and Kevin Liptak, "Former White House Aide's Ex-Wives Detail Abuse Allegations," CNN, February 8, 2018, https://www.cnn.com/2018/02/07/politics/rob-porter-ex-wives-white-house/index.html.

Elise Viebeck, "Second White House Official Departs amid Abuse Allegations, Which He Denies," *Washington Post*, February 9, 2018, https://www.washingtonpost.com/politics/second-white-house-official-departs-amids-abuse-allegations-which-he-denies/2018/02/09/72ba47e6-0d0d-11e8-8b0d-891602206fb7_story.html?hpid=hp_no-name_no-name%3Apage%2Fbreaking-news-bar.

Ben Jacobs, "Trump Appears to Issue New Defense of Aide Accused of Domestic Abuse," *Guardian*, February 10, 2018, https://www.theguardian.com/us-news/2018/feb/10/trump-tweet-domestic-abuse-rob-porter.

10. Sweet as Always

Natal'ia Galadzheva and Elizaveta Dal', eds., *Oleg Dal': Dnevniki. Pis'ma. Vospominaniia* (Moscow: Tsentrpoligraf, 1998), 51, 111, 136, 144, 304.

On the history of Russian and Soviet feminism see Richard Stites, *The Women's Liberation Movement in Russia: Feminism, Nihilism, and Bolshevism, 1860–1930*, 2nd ed.

(Princeton: Princeton University Press, 1991); Barbara Clement Evans, "The Utopianism of the Zhenotdel," *Slavic Review* 51, no. 3 (1992): 485–496; Barbara Engel, *Women in Russia, 1700–2000* (New York: Cambridge University Press, 2004). On the late Soviet "crisis of masculinity" see Elena Zdravomyslova and Anna Temkina, "Krizis maskulinnosti v pozdnesovetskom diskurse," in *O muzhe(n)stvennosti: Sbornik statei*, ed. Sergei Ushakin (Moscow, 2002), 432–451.

Quotes from letters in A. G. Ivanova, ed. *Oleg Dal': 'Govoriu to, chto dumaiu . . .'* (Moscow, 2001), 19; Galadzheva and Elizaveta Dal', eds., *Oleg Dal': Dnevniki. Pis'ma. Vospominaniia*, 111, 404–405, 412.

Description of Oleg's violence by Olga Eikhenbaum in Galadzheva and Dal', eds., *Oleg Dal'*, 206–209.

Dal's notebooks at the Bakhrushin Theater Museum archive, Gosudarstvennyi tsentral'nyi teatral'nyi muzei im. A. A. Bakhrushina (GTsTM im. A.A. Bakhrushina) f. 633 op. 1 d. 318988/36, 37, 40–42; letter to Anatolii Efros about geniuses of centuries past in Galadzheva and Dal', eds., *Oleg Dal'*, 394.

Imagined sequence includes details from Elizaveta (Apraksina) Dal's 1977–1978 correspondence with Olga Eikhenbaum at GTsTM im. A.A. Bakhrushina f. 633 op. 1 d. 318988/154-156 and "Elizaveta Dal': Ia provotsirovala Olega na skandaly," *Komsomol'skaia pravda*, May 23, 2003, https://www.kp.ru/daily/23037/3861/.

Cause of Oleg's death in Aleksandr Ivanov, *Moi drug–Oleg Dal'. Mezhdu zhizn'iu i smert'iu* (Moscow: Algoritm, 2017), 349; details of Liza's death in "Elizaveta Dal': Ia provotsirovala Olega na skandaly."

Saidiya Hartman, "Venus in Two Acts," *Small Axe* 12, no. 2 (2008): 1–14.

Saidiya Hartman, *Lose Your Mother* (New York: Farrar, Straus, and Giroux, 2007), 17.

Hayden White, *Tropics of Discourse: Essays in Cultural Criticism* (Baltimore: John Hopkins University Press, 1978); Hayden White, *The Content of the Form: Narrative Discourse and Historical Representation* (Baltimore: John Hopkins University Press, 1987).

Christopher R. Browning, "German Memory, Judicial Interrogation, and Historical Reconstruction: Writing Perpetrator History from Postwar Testimony," Hayden White, "Historical Emplotment and the Problem of Truth," Carlo Ginzburg, "Just One Witness," and Martin Jay, "Of Plots, Witnesses, and Judgements," in Saul Friedlander, ed., *Probing the Limits of Representation: Nazism and the "Final Solution"* (Cambridge, MA: Harvard University Press, 1992), 22–36, 37–53, 82–96, 97–107.

12. The Real Daniel

Coronel, Coll, and Kravitz, "*Rolling Stone*'s Investigation."

Margalit Fox, "Carolyn Bryant Donham Dies at 88; Her Words Doomed Emmett Till," *New York Times*, April 27, 2023, https://www.nytimes.com/2023/04/27/us/carolyn-bryant-donham-dead.html.

13. Preponderance of Evidence

Elizabeth Williamson, Rebecca R. Ruiz, Emily Steel, Grace Ashford, and Steve Eder, "For Christine Blasey Ford, a Drastic Turn from a Quiet Life in Academia," *New York Times*, September 19, 2018, https://www.nytimes.com/2018/09/19/us/politics/christine-blasey-ford-brett-kavanaugh-allegations.html.

"Statements of Support for Judge Brett Kavanaugh Pour In," archives.org, July 13, 2018, https://trumpwhitehouse.archives.gov/briefings-statements/statements-support -judge-brett-kavanaugh-pour/.

Jamelle Bouie, "No One Could Be Further from Atticus Finch," *Slate*, October 4, 2018, https://slate.com/news-and-politics/2018/10/atticus-finch-brett-kavanaugh -john-cornyn-rich-lowry.html.

Oliver Laughland, "Kavanaugh Accuser Julie Swetnick to Be Excluded from FBI Investi- gation," *Guardian*, September 30, 2018, https://www.theguardian.com/us-news/2018 /sep/30/fbi-investigation-brett-kavanaugh-julie-swetnick-kellyanne-conway.

"FBI Failed to Fully Investigate Kavanaugh Allegations, Say Democrats," *Guardian*, July 22, 2021, https://www.theguardian.com/us-news/2021/jul/22/brett-kavanaugh -sexual-misconduct-allegations-fbi-senators.

Julia Jacobs, "Anita Hill's Testimony and Other Key Moments from the Clarence Thomas Hearings," *New York Times*, September 20, 2018, https://www.nytimes .com/2018/09/20/us/politics/anita-hill-testimony-clarence-thomas.html.

"Notice of Proposed Rulemaking," Department of Education, November 18, 2018, https://www2.ed.gov/about/offices/list/ocr/docs/title-ix-nprm.pdf.

Hélène Barthélemy, "How Men's Rights Groups Helped Rewrite Regulations on Cam- pus Rape," *Nation*, August 14, 2020, https://www.thenation.com/article/politics /betsy-devos-title-ix-mens-rights/.

14. The Hammer

Friedrich Nietzsche, *The Gay Science*, trans. Walter Kaufmann (New York: Vintage Books, 1974), 354.

Browning, "German Memory," in Friedlander, ed., *Probing the Limits of Representa- tion*, 30.

Part 3

15. Mastering the Past

"Reverting to Original Name, Sverdlovsk Is Yekaterinburg," September 24, 1991, *New York Times*, https://www.nytimes.com/1991/09/24/world/reverting-to-original -name-sverdlovsk-is-yekaterinburg.html.

"Nicholas II and Family Canonized for Passion," *New York Times*, August 15, 2000, https://www.nytimes.com/2000/08/15/world/nicholas-ii-and-family-canonized-for -passion.html.

Anna North, "When the Accused Is a Woman: A #MeToo Story's Lessons on Gen- der and Power," *Vox*, August 14, 2018, https://www.vox.com/2018/8/14/17688144 /nyu-me-too-movement-sexual-harassment-avital-ronell.

Nell Gluckman, "How a Letter Defending Avital Ronell Sparked Confusion and Con- demnation," *Chronicle of Higher Education*, June 12, 2018, https://www.chronicle.com /article/how-a-letter-defending-avital-ronell-sparked-confusion-and-condemnation/.

"NYU Response to Open Letter Concerning Avital Ronell," NYU news release, Sep- tember 5, 2019, https://www.nyu.edu/about/news-publications/news/2019/september /NYU_Ronell_Response.html.

"History Unclassified," *American Historical Review*, https://academic.oup.com/ahr /pages/history_unclassified.

Yuri Trifonov, *Another Life and The House on the Embankment*, trans. Michael Glenny (New York: Simon and Schuster, 1983).

Hayden White, "The Value of Narrativity in the Representation of Reality," *Critical Inquiry* 7, no. 1 (1980), 5–27.

Joy Neumeyer, "Darkness at Noon: On History, Narrative, and Domestic Violence," *American Historical Review* 126, no. 2 (June 2021): 700–707.

16. Public Peril

Catherine Gallagher, *Telling It Like It Wasn't: The Counterfactual Imagination in History and Fiction* (Chicago: The University of Chicago Press, 2018), 7.

International House at UC Berkeley, accessed November 15, 2023, https://ihouse .berkeley.edu/home/welcome-international-house-0.

Respondent's Brief in the People of the State of California v. Prosenjit Poddar, https:// www.law.berkeley.edu/files/Tarasoff_prosecutor_brief.pdf, 3–8.

Appellant's Opening Brief in the People of the State of California v. Prosenjit Poddar, https://www.law.berkeley.edu/files/Tarasoff_defense_opening_brief.pdf, 2, 6–12.

Deborah Blum, *Bad Karma: A True Story of Obsession and Murder* (ReAnimus Press: 1986, 2012), I: "Somebody to Love," III: "Karma," Kindle.

"UC Coed Slain—Savage Attack at Her Home," *San Francisco Chronicle*, October 28, 1969, 1.

"Student Faces Murder Charge in Coed's Death Here," *Daily Californian*, October 29, 1969, 12.

William Moore, "An Advance Tip in Coed Killing," *San Francisco Chronicle*, October 29, 1969, 3.

"Penalty Reduced in Knife Slaying," *San Francisco Chronicle*, June 28, 1972, 21.

Julie Smith, "Coed Slaying Case Reversed," *San Francisco Chronicle*, February 8, 1974, 4.

Michael Taylor, "State Court Rule Shocks Doctors," *San Francisco Chronicle*, December 24, 1974, 1.

Andrew Malcolm, "California Court Limits Patient-Doctor Privilege," *New York Times*, December 24, 1974, 15.

"Rehearing on Disclosure by Doctors," *San Francisco Chronicle*, March 13, 1975, 4.

Harry Jupiter, "Doctors Must Report Mental Patient Threats," *San Francisco Chronicle*, July 2, 1976, 1.

Jamie R. Abrams, "Commentary on 'Tarasoff v. Regents of University of California,'" in Martha Chamallas and Lucinda M. Finley, *Feminist Judgments: Rewritten Tort Opinions* (New York: Cambridge University Press, 2020), 93–118.

Blum, *Bad Karma*, "Author's Note."

Curthoys and Docker, *Is History Fiction?*, 13–30, 155–179.

Blum, *Bad Karma*, I: "Somebody to Love."

Natalie Zemon Davis, *Women on the Margins: Three Seventeenth-Century Lives* (Cambridge, MA: Harvard University Press, 1995).

Hartman, "Venus in Two Acts," 11.

Blum, *Bad Karma*, III: "Karma."

Miłosz, *The Captive Mind*, 77.

17. No Major Problem

"Pot Should Be Legal," Mark Goldenson, "Frisbee Throwing Popular Here," *Daily Californian*, October 28, 1969, 2.

Ruth Rosen, *The World Split Open: How the Modern Women's Movement Changed America* (New York: Penguin Books, 2006), 206.

On the Free Speech Movement, the New Left, and women see W. J. Rorabaugh, *Berkeley at War: The 1960s* (New York: Oxford University Press, 1989), 132; Robert Cohen and Reginald E. Zelnik, eds., *The Free Speech Movement: Reflections on Berkeley in the 1960s* (Berkeley and Los Angeles: University of California Press, 2002), 28, 125–137; Sara Evans, *Personal Politics: The Roots of Women's Liberation in the Civil Rights Movement and the New Left* (New York: Vintage Books, 1980), 176–209.

Lisa Gerrard, "Berkeley, 1969: A Memoir," *Women's Studies Quarterly* 30, nos. 3 and 4 (2002): 60–72, 62.

Rosen, *The World Split Open*, 129–138; 181–186; 197–198; 206–207.

Kathleen J. Tierney, "The Battered Women Movement and the Creation of the Wife Beating Problem," *Social Problems* 29, no. 3 (1982): 207–220.

Boschert, *37 Words*, 13, 96.

Title IX self-study, University Archives, The Bancroft Library, University of California at Berkeley, CU-509 carton 1, folder 12, letter to Roderic B. Park, Provost, College of Letters and Sciences from Janette Richardson, chairman, May 21, 1976; folder 7, letter to Dean Sanford H. Kadish from Professor John K. McNulty, May 11, 1976; folder 12, letter to Provost and Dean Roderic B. Park from Benson Mates, chairman, May 13, 1976; folder 3, Title IX Statistics: Departmental Comparison of Female Doctoral Students and Female Ladder-Rank Faculty, Fall 1975.

On Searle see Cohen and Zelnik, eds., *The Free Speech Movement*, 9–10; Baker, "UC Berkeley Was Warned About Its Star Professor Years Before Sexual Harassment Lawsuit," *BuzzFeed News*.

Statistics on women faculty at the University of California from Online Archive of California (OAC), courtesy of University Archives, The Bancroft Library, University of California at Berkeley, Notice of Meeting of the Assembly of the Academic Senate, The University of California, March 28, 1979, Appendix 1—Annual Report, 1977–1978: Committee on Affirmative Action, Table I. University of California: Work Force Data, Table II. University of California: Ladder Rank Faculty Headcount, 1973–1977, 20.

Bancroft CU-509 carton 1, folder 12, letter to Ira Michael Heyman, Vice Chancellor, from the Women's Caucus of the Department of Comparative Literature, May 18, 1976, and letter to Roderic B. Park from Janette Richardson, May 21, 1976; folder 6, letter to Provost Maslach from Dean William L.C. Wheaton, May 19, 1976; folder 11, letter to Vice Chancellor Ira Heyman from Daniel E. Koshland, Jr., Chairman, June 2, 1976, letter to VC Heyman from Mary Luckey, June 11, 1976, Title IX Evaluation of Biochemistry Department, and For the Title IX Self-Evaluation of the

Biochemistry Department; folder 3, Title IX Statistics: Departmental Comparison of Female Doctoral Students and Female Ladder-Rank Faculty, Fall 1975, Office of Institutional Research, May 1976; folder 1, letter to Chancellor Bowker from the advisory committee, July 16, 1976; folder 11, letter to VC Heyman from Koshland, Jr., June 2, 1976; letter to Provost and Dean Roderic Park from Robert K. Mortimer with Report on the Division of Medical Physics Self-Evaluation, May 14, 1976; folder 14, handwritten note and note attached to copy of letter to All Students, Staff and Faculty at the Center for South and Southeast Asia Studies from Bruce R. Pray, Chairman, May 12, 1976; folder 6, letter from Virginia Barker, Women of Wurster, Re: Sex Discrimination in the Department of Architecture to Richard Bender, May 13, 1976.

Boschert, *37 Words*, 72–79, 83–89.

Carrie N. Baker, *The Women's Movement Against Sexual Harassment* (New York: Cambridge University Press, 2007), 27–48.

Linda M. Blum and Ethel L. Mickey, "Women Organized Against Sexual Harassment: A Grassroots Struggle for Title IX Enforcement, 1978–1980," *Feminist Formations* 30, no. 2 (2018): 175–201, 178–180, 189.

"Notice of Meeting of the Assembly of the Academic Senate," March 3, 1979, 25–26.

Jessica Campbell, "The First Brave Woman Who Alleged 'Sexual Harassment,'" *Legacy*, December 7, 2017, https://www.legacy.com/news/culture-and-history/the-first-brave-woman-who-alleged-sexual-harassment/.

Blaine Friedlander, "Boyce D. McDaniel, Cornell Physicist Who Gave First Atomic Bomb Final Check Before Test at Trinity Site in 1945, Dies at 84," *Cornell Chronicle*, May 15, 2002, https://news.cornell.edu/stories/2002/05/physicist-boyce-d-mcdaniel-veteran-trinity-atomic-bomb-test-1945-dies-84.

Baker, *The Women's Movement Against Sexual Harassment*, 36–37.

Blum and Mickey, "Women Organized Against Sexual Harassment," 176–177, 182–184, 190–191, 195–196; Boschert, *37 Words*, 86–88.

On racial divisions in the women's liberation movement see Winifred Breines, *The Trouble Between Us: An Uneasy History of White and Black Women in the Feminist Movement* (New York: Oxford University Press, 2006); Audre Lorde, *Sister Outsider: Essays and Speeches* (Trumansburg, NY: Crossing Press, 1984); Benita Roth, *Separate Roads to Feminism: Black, Chicana, and White Feminist Movements in America's Second Wave* (New York: Cambridge University Press, 2004).

Gruber, *The Feminist War on Crime*, 43–47, 64–68.

Sam Whiting, "3 Killed in One Market Plaza in 1982," *San Francisco Chronicle*, December 6, 2012, https://www.sfchronicle.com/entertainment/article/3-killed-in-One-Market-Plaza-in-1982-4097304.php.

Barbara Mahan, "Most Abused Women Suffer in Silence," *Daily Californian*, February 10, 1982, 1.

Gene A. Brucker, Henry F. May, and David A. Hollinger, *History at Berkeley: A Dialog in Three Parts* (Berkeley: Center for the Studies in Higher Education and Institute of Governmental Studies, 1998), 14, 19.

Bancroft CU-509, carton 1, folder 13, letter to Vice Chancellor Ira M. Heyman from Robert Brentano, chairman of the History Department, July 29, 1976.

"Mary Elizabeth Berry, 1978–2017," https://history.berkeley.edu/sites/default/files/150w_meb_final.pdf, 8–13.

Interview with Natalie Zemon Davis, conducted by Ann Lage, 2003, Regional Oral History Office, The Bancroft Library, https://digicoll.lib.berkeley.edu/record/218555?ln=en, 48–49.

Interview with Robert Brentano, conducted by Frances Starn, 2002, Regional Oral History Office, The Bancroft Library, https://digicoll.lib.berkeley.edu/record/218189?ln=en, 137; "Mary Elizabeth Berry," 13.

Interview with Lawrence W. Levine, conducted by Ann Lage, 2004–2005, Regional Oral History Office, The Bancroft Library, https://digicoll.lib.berkeley.edu/record/218887?ln=en, 455.

Wolfgang Sauer, "Die Mobilmachung der Gewalt," in Karl Dietrich Bracher, Gerhard Schulz, and Wolfgang Sauer, *Die nationalsozialistische Machtergreifung. Studien zur Errichtung des totalitären Herrschaftssystems in Deutschland 1933/34* (Köln: Westdeutscher Werlag, 1960), 683–966.

Interview with Davis, 48–49.

Interview with Levine, 452–455.

Interview with Lynn A. Hunt, conducted by Ann Lage, 2012, Regional Oral History Office, The Bancroft Library, https://digicoll.lib.berkeley.edu/record/103664?ln=en, 30–31.

C. P. Smith and J. J. Freyd, "Institutional Betrayal," *American Psychologist* 69, no. 6 (2014): 575–587.

18. Patterns

Deborah Wood, "Opinion: When Is Sexual Conduct 'Severe' or 'Pervasive' Enough for UC?," *Berkeleyside*, July 3, 2018, https://www.berkeleyside.org/2018/07/03/opinion-when-is-sexual-misconduct-severe-or-pervasive-enough-for-uc.

Erik Ortiz, "Public Comments Reopen for DeVos' Campus Sexual Assault Rules—But Only for One Day," NBC News, February 13, 2019, https://www.nbcnews.com/news/us-news/public-comments-reopen-devos-campus-sexual-assault-rules-only-one-n970956.

Greta Anderson, "U.S. Publishes New Regulations on Campus Sexual Assault," *Inside Higher Ed*, May 7, 2020, https://www.insidehighered.com/news/2020/05/07/education-department-releases-final-title-ix-regulations.

Annie Grayer and Veronica Stracqualursi, "DeVos Finalizes Regulations That Give More Rights to Students Accused of Sexual Assault on College Campuses," CNN, May 6, 2020, https://www.cnn.com/2020/05/06/politics/education-secretary-betsy-devos-title-ix-regulations/index.html#:~:text=%E2%80%9CThis%20new%20regulation%20requires%20schools,of%20sexual%20misconduct%20on%20campuses.

"Summary of Major Provisions of the Department of Education's Final Title IX Rule," Department of Education, 2020, https://www2.ed.gov/about/offices/list/ocr/docs/titleix-summary.pdf.

"Executive Order on Guaranteeing an Educational Environment Free from Discrimination on the Basis of Sex, Including Sexual Orientation and Gender Identity,"

The White House, March 8, 2021, https://www.whitehouse.gov/briefing-room
/presidential-actions/2021/03/08/executive-order-on-guaranteeing-an-educational
-environment-free-from-discrimination-on-the-basis-of-sex-including-sexual
-orientation-or-gender-identity/.

"Federal Register Notice of Proposed Rulemaking," Department of Education, 2022,
https://www2.ed.gov/about/offices/list/ocr/docs/t9nprm.pdf.

Tyler Kingkade, "Biden Administration Proposes Sweeping Changes to Title IX to Undo
Trump-Era Rules," NBC News, June 23, 2022, https://www.nbcnews.com/politics
/biden-admin-proposes-sweeping-changes-title-ix-undo-trump-era-rules-rcna34915.

Sara Nesbitt and Sage Carson, "The Cost of Reporting: Perpetrator Retaliation, Institutional Betrayal, and Student Survivor Pushout," Know Your IX/Advocates for Youth,
2021, https://knowyourix.org/thecostofreporting/.

Anne Applebaum, "The New Puritans," *Atlantic*, August 31, 2021, https://www.the
atlantic.com/magazine/archive/2021/10/new-puritans-mob-justice-canceled/619818/.

"2018 Annual Report on Sexual Violence/Sexual Harassment: Incidence, Prevention,
and Response," University of California at Berkeley, UC Regents, 2018, https://svsh
.berkeley.edu/sites/default/files/2017-18_ucb_svshannualreport.pdf, 50, 61–62. Some
cases may have started during the previous year, while others continued into the following year.

"Sexual Misconduct Data Report, September 1, 2017–August 31, 2018," Northwestern University Office of Equity, http://www.northwestern.edu/sexual-misconduct
/about-us/Annual%20Data%20Report%202017-2018.pdf, 6–7, 9–10. Some cases
remained unresolved at the end of the reporting period.

Linda Qui, "Trump Stretches Facts by Claiming Record Successes During 'Greatest Witch Hunt' in U.S. History," *New York Times*, May 17, 2018, https://www
.nytimes.com/2018/05/17/us/politics/fact-check-trump-witch-hunt-successful
-presidency.html.

Jeannie Suk Gersen, "Shutting Down Conversations About Rape at Harvard Law,"
New Yorker, December 11, 2015, https://www.newyorker.com/news/news-desk
/argument-sexual-assault-race-harvard-law-school. See also Laura Bazelon, "I'm a Dem-
ocrat and a Feminist. And I Support Betsy DeVos's Title IX Reforms.," *New York
Times*, December 4, 2018, https://www.nytimes.com/2018/12/04/opinion/-title-ix
-devos-democrat-feminist.html; "The History, Uses, and Abuses of Title IX," 79;
Amia Srinivasan, *The Right to Sex* (London: Bloomsbury Publishing, 2021), 11, 146.

For studies on the impact of campus sexual assault on queer students and women of color
see David Cantor, Bonnie Fisher, Susan Chibnall, Shauna Harps, Reanne Townsend,
Gail Thomas, Hyunshik Lee, Vanessa Kranz, Randy Herbison, and Kristin Madden,
"Report on the AAU Campus Climate Survey on Sexual Assault and Misconduct,"
Association of American Universities, 2020, https://www.aau.edu/sites/default/files
/AAU-Files/Key-Issues/Campus-Safety/Revised%20Aggregate%20report%20%20
and%20appendices%201-7_(01-16-2020_FINAL).pdf; Robert W. S. Coulter and
Susan R. Rankin, "College Sexual Assault and Campus Climate for Sexual- and
Gender-Minority Undergraduate Students," *Journal of Interpersonal Violence* 34, no.
5–6 (2020): 1351–1366; Kathryn K. O'Neill, Kerith J. Conron, Abbie E. Goldberg,

and Rubeen Guardado, "Experiences of LGBTQ People in Four-Year Colleges and Graduate Programs," University of California Los Angeles School of Law, Williams Institute, May 2022, https://williamsinstitute.law.ucla.edu/wp-content/uploads/LGBTQ -College-Grad-School-May-2022.pdf; "Campus Sexual Assault: Fact Sheet from an Intersectional Lens," American Psychological Association, June 2023, https://www.apa .org/apags/resources/campus-sexual-assault-fact-sheet.

Smokey Fontaine, "Spelman, Morehouse Address Issues of Sexual Assault," *Newsone*, March 3, 2009, https://newsone.com/125181/video-covers-rape-at-spelman-and-morehouse/.

Anita Badejo, "What Happens When Students at Historically Black Colleges Report Their Assaults," *BuzzFeed News*, January 21, 2016, https://www.buzzfeednews.com /article/anitabadejo/where-is-that-narrative.

Clarissa Brooks, "How HBCUs Can Make It Hard for Sexual Assault Survivors to Speak Up," *Teen Vogue*, December 21, 2017, https://www.teenvogue.com/story/hbcus -and-sexual-assault-op-ed.

Wagatwe Wanjuki, "Stop Telling Survivors They Must Report to the Police," *Feministing*, April 11, 2014, https://www.feministing.com/2014/04/11/stop-telling-survivors -they-must-report-to-the-police/.

"Faculty Discipline Process," presentation made to the UC Berkeley Academic Senate by Erin Rakowski, April 7, 2016, https://www.academic-senate.berkeley.edu/sites /default/files/faculty_discipline_process_160405.pdf.

Sam Levin, "Berkeley Professor at Center of Sexual Harassment Scandal Sues His Accusers," *Guardian*, September 29, 2016, https://www.theguardian.com/us-news/2016/sep /29/uc-berkeley-sexual-harassment-blake-wentworth-sues-victims.

Kipnis, *Unwanted Advances*, 1, 186–187, 215.

Rudyard Kipling, "Danny Deever," in *A Choice of Kipling's Verse* (New York: Charles Scribner's Sons, 1943), https://www.poetryfoundation.org/poems/46782/danny -deever#:~:text=They%20are%20hangin'%20Danny%20Deever%2C%20you%20 must%20mark%20'im,Danny%20Deever%20in%20the%20mornin'.

19. War

Joy Neumeyer, "The View from Warsaw," *Baffler*, March 21, 2022, https://thebaffler .com/latest/the-view-from-warsaw-neumeyer.

Mike Eckel, "How Did Everybody Get the Ukraine Invasion Predictions So Wrong," Radio Free Europe/Radio Liberty, February 17, 2023, https://www.rferl.org/a /russia-ukraine-invasion-predictions-wrong-intelligence/32275740.html.

For examples of the Russia-Ukraine domestic violence comparison see John Feffer, "Russia Is from Mars, Ukraine Is from Venus," *Foreign Policy in Focus*, April 27, 2022, https://www.fpif.org/russia-is-from-mars-ukraine-is-from-venus/; Alaric Dearment, "How Russian Colonialism Took the Western Anti-imperialist Left for a Ride," *Salon*, July 29, 2023, https://www.salon.com/2023/07/29/how-russian-colonialism -took-the-western-anti-imperialist-left-for-a-ride/.

Amie Ferris-Rotman, "Gender Is Front and Center in Moscow's Invasion of Ukraine," *New Lines Magazine*, January 23, 2023, https://www.newlinesmag.com/spotlight/russia -and-ukraines-battle-of-the-sexes/.

For examples of the argument that Russia was provoked see John J. Mearsheimer, "Why the Ukraine Crisis Is the West's Fault: The Liberal Delusions That Provoked Putin," *Foreign Affairs*, August 18, 2014; Isaac Chotiner, "Why John Mearsheimer Blames the U.S. for the Crisis in Ukraine," *New Yorker*, March 1, 2022, https://www.newyorker.com/news/q-and-a/why-john-mearsheimer-blames-the-us-for-the-crisis-in-ukraine; Benjamin Schwarz and Christopher Layne, "Why Are We in Ukraine? On the Dangers of American Hubris," *Harper's*, June 2023, https://www.harpers.org/archive/2023/06/why-are-we-in-ukraine/.

"Exclusive: As War Began, Putin Rejected a Peace Deal Recommended by an Aide," Reuters, September 14, 2022, https://www.reuters.com/world/asia-pacific/exclusive-war-began-putin-rejected-ukraine-peace-deal-recommended-by-his-aide-2022-09-14/.

On growing divisions among Ukraine's allies see Phillip Meng, "Europeans Continue to Back Ukraine, but Disagree on the Endgame," The Chicago Council on Global Affairs, February 14, 2023, https://www.globalaffairs.org/commentary-and-analysis/blogs/europeans-continue-back-ukraine-disagree-endgame; Mitchell McCluskey, "Poland Will Stop Providing Weapons to Ukraine as Dispute over Grain Imports Deepens," CNN, September 21, 2023, https://www.cnn.com/2023/09/20/europe/poland-ukraine-weapons-grain-intl-hnk/index.html; Karoun Demirjian, "Opposition to Ukraine Aid Becomes a Litmus Test for the Right," *New York Times*, October 5, 2023, https://www.nytimes.com/2023/10/05/us/politics/republicans-ukraine-aid.html.

Itkowitz, "There's a Moving Story Behind This Powerful Photo."

"Sofie Karasek," accessed November 15, 2023, https://www.sofiekarasek.com/.

State-Level Laws "Enough Is Enough" (New York, signed into law in 2015), "Yes Means Yes" (California, signed into law in 2014), https://www.endrapeoncampus.org/laws/#:~:text=This%20legislation%20was%20signed%20into%20law%20in%202015.&text=Affirmative%20consent%20can%20be%20given,Yes%E2%80%9D%20is%20a%20groundbreaking%20effort.

As of November 2023, the Know Your IX website says that it supports "campus-based adjudication of sexual and dating violence cases as a non-carceral alternative to the criminal legal system" (without language about prison abolition or rejecting punitive measures). "Our Values," accessed November 15, 2023, https://www.knowyourix.org/our-values/.

Karasek, "America's Universities: Where You're All Too Likely to Be Assaulted." For more on the evolution of her views see Sofie Karasek, "I'm a Campus Sexual Assault Activist. It's Time to Reimagine How We Punish Sex Crimes.," *New York Times*, February 22, 2018, https://www.nytimes.com/2018/02/22/opinion/campus-sexual-assault-punitive-justive.html.

For examples of the Title IX-incarceration comparison see Yoffe, "The College Rape Overcorrection"; Barthélemy, "How Men's Rights Groups Helped Rewrite Regulations on Campus Rape"; Kipnis, *Unwanted Advances*, 18; Gruber, *The Feminist War on Crime*, 17, 169. Definition of "carceral feminism" in Elizabeth Bernstein, "The Sexual Politics of the 'New Abolitionism,'" *Differences* 18, no. 3 (2017): 128–151, 128, 143.

David Hirschel and Philip D. McCormack, "Same-Sex Couples and the Police: A 10-Year Study of Arrest and Dual Arrest Rates in Responding to Incidents of Intimate Partner Violence," *Violence Against Women* 27, no. 9 (2021): 1119–1149.

Christine Hauser, "Florida Woman Whose 'Stand Your Ground' Defense Was Rejected Is Released," *New York Times*, February 7, 2017, https://www.nytimes .com/2017/02/07/us/marissa-alexander-released-stand-your-ground.html.

Gruber, *The Feminist War on Crime*, 151–169.

F. A. Hayek, *The Road to Serfdom: Text and Documents: The Definitive Edition*, ed. Bruce Caldwell (New York: Routledge, 2014).

Mariame Kaba, *We Do This 'Til We Free Us: Abolitionist Organizing and Transforming Justice*, ed. Tamara K. Nopper (Chicago: Haymarket Books, 2021), ebook, 357.

James Ptacek, ed., *Restorative Justice and Violence Against Women* (New York: Oxford University Press, 2010).

Shauntey James and Melanie D. Hetzel-Riggin, "Campus Sexual Violence and Title IX: What Is the Role of Restorative Justice Now?," *Feminist Criminology* 17, no. 3 (2002): 407–420.

"The Criminal Justice System: Statistics," Rape, Abuse, and Incest National Network (RAINN), accessed November 15, 2023, https://www.rainn.org/statistics /criminal-justice-system; "What to Expect from the Criminal Justice System," RAINN, accessed November 15, 2023, https://www.rainn.org/articles/what-expect -criminal-justice-system. See more statistics on domestic violence rates reporting, arrest, and prosecution rates at "Domestic Violence Prevalence," U.S. Department of Justice, accessed November 15, 2023, https://www.ojp.gov/feature/domestic-violence /prevalence.

For more on Title IX administrators see Vanessa Grigoriadis, *Blurred Lines: Rethinking Sex, Power, and Consent on Campus* (Boston and New York: Houghton Mifflin Harcourt, 2017).

"Russian Advance to the Vistula (Summer 1944)," *Encyclopedia Britannica*, https://www .britannica.com/event/Eastern-Front-World-War-II/Russian-advance-to-the-Vistula -summer-1944.

Elena Flores Ruíz, "The Secret Life of Violence," in Dustin J. Byrd and Seyed Javad Miri, *Frantz Fanon and Emancipatory Social Theory: A View from the Wretched* (Boston: Brill Press, 2020): 231–250. Fanon quote from Félix F. Germain, *Decolonizing the Republic: African and Caribbean Migrants in Postwar Paris, 1946–1974* (East Lansing: Michigan State University Press, 2016), 90.

Gruber, *The Feminist War on Crime*, 16, 52, 65–66; Srinivasan, *The Right to Sex*, 165, 171–177.

On Adorno and negative dialectics see Martin Jay, *Refractions of Violence* (New York: Routledge, 2012), 186–187; Martin Jay, *Permanent Exiles: Essays on the Intellectual Migration from Germany to America* (New York: Columbia University Press, 1985), Chapter 9: "Adorno in America," 120–137; Martin Jay, *The Dialectical Imagination: A History of the Frankfurt School and the Institute of Social Research 1923–1950* (Boston: Little, Brown and Company, 1973), 296.

20. Lessons in Forgetting

Jackie Willis, "Amber Heard's Texts from 2014 Detail Alleged Assault by Johnny Depp: 'He's Done This Many Times,'" *Entertainment Tonight*, June 1, 2016, https://www.etonline.com/news/190049_amber_heard_texts_from_2014_detail_alleged _assault_by_johnny_depp_exclusive.

Amber Heard, "Amber Heard: I Spoke Up Against Sexual Violence—and Faced Our Culture's Wrath. That Has to Change.," *Washington Post*, December 18, 2018, https://www.washingtonpost.com/opinions/ive-seen-how-institutions-protect-men -accused-of-abuse-heres-what-we-can-do/2018/12/18/71fd876a-02ed-11e9-b5df -5d3874f1ac36_story.html.

Alice McCool, "The Daily Wire Spent Thousands of Dollars Promoting Anti-Heard Propaganda," *Vice*, May 19, 2022, https://www.vice.com/en/article/3ab3yk/daily-wire -amber-heard-johnny-depp.

Jessica Wang, "Johnny Depp Wins Defamation Trial Against Amber Heard, Jury Awards Him $15 Million in Damages," *Entertainment Weekly*, June 1, 2022, https://ew.com /celebrity/johnny-depp-v-amber-heard-verdict/.

"Amber Heard GETS WRECKED LIVE in New TV Interview About Her Appeal!," accessed November 15, 2023, https://www.youtube.com/watch?v=EF0t3RlrHIo.

Christopher Ying, "Campus Alumnus Sues UC, Alleges Title IX Violations," *Daily Californian*, June 13, 2022, https://www.dailycal.org/2022/06/13/campus-alumnus -sues-uc-alleges-title-ix-violations.

Greta Anderson, "More Title IX Lawsuits by Accusers and Accused," *Inside Higher Ed*, October 2, 2019, https://www.insidehighered.com/news/2019/10/03/students -look-federal-courts-challenge-title-ix-proceedings.

James A. Johnson and Julie A. Gafkay, "Title IX's 'Deliberate Indifference' Hurtle," New York State Bar Association, March 28, 2022, https://www.nysba.org/title-ixs -deliberate-indifference-hurdle/.

Equal Rights Advocates, "Title IX Defamation 101," accessed November 15, 2023, https://www.equalrights.org/title-ix-defamation-101/.

Vimal Patel, "How a Yale Student's Rape Accusation Exposed Her to a Defamation Lawsuit," *New York Times*, September 17, 2023, https://www.nytimes.com/2023/09 /17/us/yale-rape-case-defamation.html.

Czerwienski et al. v. Harvard University, U.S. District Court of the State of Massachusetts, filed February 8, 2022, https://www.thecrimson.com/PDF/2022/2/9/Czerwienski -et-al-v-harvard-filing/, 5, 33, 63.

Anemona Hartocollis, "A Lawsuit Accuses Harvard of Ignoring Sexual Harassment by a Professor," *New York Times*, February 8, 2022, https://www.nytimes.com/2022 /02/08/us/harvard-sexual-harassment-lawsuit.html.

Isabella B. Cho and Ariel H. Kim, "38 Harvard Faculty Sign Open Letter Questioning Results of Misconduct Investigations into Prof. John Comaroff," *Harvard Crimson*, February 4, 2022, https://www.thecrimson.com/article/2022/2/4/comaroff -sanctions-open-letter/.

Vincent A. Brown, Alison F. Johnson, and Kristen A. Weld, "A Response Letter from 37 Faculty Members," *Harvard Crimson*, February 9, 2022, https://www.thecrimson .com/article/2022/2/9/letter-73-faculty-response/.

Ariel H. Kim and Meimei Xu, "35 Harvard Professors Retract Support for Letter Questioning Results of Comaroff Investigation," *Harvard Crimson*, February 10, 2022, https://www.thecrimson.com/article/2022/2/10/comaroff-faculty-letter-retraction/.

Caitlín Doherty, "A Feminist Style," *New Left Review*, July 7, 2023, https://www.new leftreview.org/sidecar/posts/a-feminist-style.

Christa Hillstrom, "The Hidden Epidemic of Brain Injuries from Domestic Violence," *New York Times*, March 1, 2022, https://www.nytimes.com/2022/03/01/magazine /brain-trauma-domestic-violence.html; Rachel Louise Snyder, *No Visible Bruises: What We Don't Know About Domestic Violence Can Kill Us* (New York: Bloomsbury, 2019).

Emiko Petrosky, Janet M. Blair, Carter J. Betz, Katherine A. Fowler, Shane P. D. Jack, and Bridget H. Lyons, "Racial and Ethnic Differences in Homicides of Adult Women and the Role of Intimate Partner Violence—United States, 2003–2014," Centers for Disease Control and Prevention, *Morbidity and Mortality Weekly Report* 28, no. 66 (2017): 741–746.

Lisa B. Geller, Marisa Booty, and Cassandra K. Crifasi, "The Role of Domestic Violence in Fatal Mass Shootings in the United States, 2014–2019," *Injury Epidemiology* 8, no. 38 (2021), https://www.injepijournal.biomedcentral.com/articles/10.1186 /s40621-021-00330-0#citeas.

Theresa K. Vescio and Nathaniel E. C. Schermerhorn, "Hegemonic Masculinity Predicts 2016 and 2020 Voting and Candidate Evaluations," *PNAS Proceedings of the National Academy of Sciences of the United States of America* 118, no. 2 (2021): 1–10.

On domestic violence in Russia since 2017 see Marianna Spring, "Decriminalisation of Domestic Violence in Russia Leads to Fall in Reported Cases," *Guardian*, August 16, 2018, https://www.theguardian.com/world/2018/aug/16/decriminalisation-of -domestic-violence-in-russia-leads-to-fall-in-reported-cases; "'I Could Kill You and No One Would Stop Me': Weak State Response to Domestic Violence in Russia," Human Rights Watch, October 2018, https://www.hrw.org/sites/default/files /report_pdf/russia1018_web3.pdf; Marina Pisklakova-Parker, "Gender Issues in Russia," *Istituto Affari Internazionali Papers* 22, no. 19 (June 2022): 1–14, 3; Kay Rollins, "Putin's Other War: Domestic Violence, Traditional Values, and Masculinity in Modern Russia," *Harvard International Review*, August 3, 2022, https://www.hir.harvard .edu/putins-other-war/; "'Eto budet rasti'. Anna Rivina—o domashnem nasiliii vo vremia voiny," *Svoboda*, February 14, 2023, https://www.svoboda.org/a/eto-budet -rasti-anna-rivina-o-domashnem-nasilii-vo-vremya-voyny/32269669.html; Dhruti Shash and Yaroslava Kiryukhina, "'I Didn't Want to Die': Why Are Russians Using Bloody Makeup to Tackle Domestic Abuse?," BBC, July 23, 2019, https://www.bbc .com/news/blogs-trending-49081045.

Rachel B. Vogelstein and Meighan Stone, *Awakening: #MeToo and the Global Fight for Women's Rights* (New York: PublicAffairs, 2021).

Srinivasan, *The Right to Sex*, 167.

E. P. Thompson, *The Making of the English Working Class* (New York: Pantheon Books, 1963), 12.

A. A. Brill, ed., *The Basic Writings of Sigmund Freud* (New York: Modern Library, 1938).

Michael Feola, "'You Will Not Replace Us': The Melancholic Nationalism of Whiteness," *Political Theory* 49, no. 4 (2021): 528–553.

Sara Ahmed, *Living a Feminist Life* (Durham: Duke University Press, 2017), 22; Sara Ahmed, "Resignation," May 30, 2016, Feminist Killjoys blog, https://www.feminist killjoys.com/2016/05/30/resignation/.

On historians and "memory" see Kerwin Klein, *From History to Theory* (Berkeley and Los Angeles: University of California Press, 2011), Chapter Five: "On the Emergence of *Memory* in Historical Discourse," 112–137; Enzo Traverso, *Singular Pasts: The 'I' in Historiography*, trans. Adam Schoene (New York: Columbia University Press, 2023).

Leila J. Rupp, *Worlds of Women: The Making of an International Women's Movement* (Princeton: Princeton University Press, 1997), Chapter Six: "How Wide the Circle of the Feminist 'We,'" 130–156.

Koestler, *Darkness at Noon*, 244.

Neumeyer, "The View from Warsaw."

Walter Benjamin, "Über den Begriff der Geschichte" [On the Concept of History], in *Gesammelte Schriften*, 6 vols, in 12 (Frankfurt am Main: Suhrkamp, 1974–1985), I, 2, 695, translation from Charles S. Maier, *The Unmasterable Past: History, Holocaust, and German National Identity* (Cambridge, MA: Harvard University Press, 1988), 99.

Epilogue: A Long Time Ago

"Respondent's Brief," 4–5.

INDEX

abuse, abusive partners and. *See also*
  Daniel; domestic violence; emotional
  abuse; intimate partner violence;
  physical abuse
archetypes of, 67
Bancroft on, 66–68, 73
boundary-setting and, 72
choking and, 77
conflicting behaviors of, 66–67
cycles of, 67, 74
de-escalation strategies in, 74, 157
emotional, 40, 144
family of perpetrator involvement in, 77
"flipping" and, 71
misogyny and, 67
promises of, 68
safety checklist for, 104
therapy as element of, 67, 70–74
under Univ. of California Policy
    on Sexual Violence and Sexual
    Harassment, 85–86
verbal, 75
"the Victim" in, 67
abuse survivors
anxiety response for, 146
archetypes of, 67
boundary-setting for, 72
de-escalation strategies for, 74, 157

distancing strategies for, 71–73
divided consciousness of, 77, 156–157
homicide and, 77–78
in literature, 67
paper trails for, 97–98
personal accountability strategies, 73
safety checklist for, 104
therapy after domestic violence,
    67, 70–74
activism, political, after election of
    Trump, 39
acute stress reaction, domestic violence
    and, 81
Adam (History Department teaching
    assistant), 39, 41
Adorno, Theodor, 240
advisors. *See specific people*
affirmative consent, legislation for,
    234–235
afterlife, mysteries of, 14
Aguilera, Christina, 14
Ahmed, Sara, 250
Akhmatova, Anna, 94–96
Alex (brother of Tanya Tarasoff), 197,
    259–260
Alexander (UC Berkeley advisor/
    professor)
on "Darkness at Noon" essay, 189–194

Alexander *(Continued)*
  Es schwindelt and, 41–43
  in Moscow, 158–159
  personal detachment from assault
    claims, 155, 158–159
  on pitfalls of historical research, 21
  support for Daniel, 151–152, 159,
    162–163
  on the Terror, 52–53
Alexander, Marissa, 236
Alexandra (family of Tsar Nicholas
    II), 182
Alexei (family of Tsar Nicholas II), 182
"Alpha, the Moralist" (Miłosz), 56
alternative resolution process, for
    OPHD, 220
Amanda (UC Berkeley graduate
    student), 70
American Association of University
    Professors, 105
American Historical Association, 24
American Historical Review, 185
Anastasia (family of Tsar Nicholas II), 182
Anna (UC Berkeley professor), 29, 66, 69,
    83–84, 157–158, 182
Anna Karenina (novel) (Dostoyevsky), 124
Anthropocene era, 19
antisemitism. *See* Final Solution;
    Holocaust; Nazi Germany
anxiety response, for domestic violence
    survivors, 146
Apollo (myth of), 181
Applebaum, Anne, 224–225
Apraksina, Liza, 121–128, 243,
    250, 259
Argentina, 249
art, of Soviet Union, 17
assault. *See* physical abuse and assault
Atlantic, 224–225

Austin, Texas, physical abuse in, 75–76
authority, power and, 25–26

Babel, Isaac, 32
Bad Feminist (Gay), 82
Bad Karma (Blum), 200–203
Bancroft, Lundy, 66–68, 73
Bannon, Steve, 36
battering, 209
beigeocracy, of Berkeley History
    Department, 8, 57
Bella (friend of Daniel), 60–61, 84
Benjamin, Walter, 10, 256–257
Bennett, Erin, 89–90
Berkeley, California, People's Park, 6–7
Berkeley, University of California at
    (UC Berkeley). *See also* History
    Department; Office for the
    Prevention of Harassment and
    Discrimination; Title IX system
  "Bloody Thursday," 6
  bureaucracy of, 9–10
  Center for Student Conduct, 87,
    164–165, 167, 172, 178, 192
  Christ as Chancellor at, 94
  Code of Student Conduct at, 85,
    164, 167
  Daily Cal, 198–199, 208, 215
  Dirks as Chancellor at, 5
  Free Speech Movement at, 6, 208–209
  History at Berkeley, 215–216
  information about domestic violence
    protocols, 84
  investigation by Office for Civil
    Rights, 90–91
  neoliberal transformation of, 6
  protests against sexual violence
    at, 89–90
  protests against Yiannopoulos at, 45

sexual assault claims at, 93–94
Sexual Violence and Sexual
    Harassment Policy, 164
social codes at, 8–9
Title IX claims, 84–86, 212–214, 216
Trump and, 45
Berlin Wall, fall of, 25
Bernstein, Elizabeth, 236
Berry, Mary Elizabeth "Beth," 216–218
"Beta, the Disappointed Lover"
    (Miłosz), 56
Biden, Joe, 223, 234
Big Little Lies, 72
Black Lives Matter movement, 235
Black women, intimate partner violence
    against, 248
Black Women's and Chicana caucuses,
    213–214
Blasey Ford, Christine, 165–166
Blum, Deborah, 200–203
Blum, Linda M., 214
Bolsheviks
    October Revolution and, 122
    during Russian Revolution, 31–32
    the Terror and, 52–53
boundary-setting, in abusive
    relationships, 72
Bouwsma, William, 215–216
"Brand New Person, Same Old
    Mistakes," 4
Broken Social Contracts, 226–227
Browning, Christopher, 130
Brown University, 91
Brucker, Gene A., 215–216
Bryant, Carolyn, 153
Bukharin, Nikolai, 156, 182, 213, 249–250
    arrest of, 49
    divided consciousness of, 77
    execution of, 51

false accusations against, 50–51
    guilty pleas by, 50–51
    Stalin and, 43, 48–49
Bundy, Ted, 11
Butler, Judith, 184
Buzzfeed, 94
by-products, cultural, of feminism, 247

Campanile, 229
Campus Sexual Assault Victims' Bill of
    Rights, 91
Candide (Voltaire), 195
The Captive Mind (Miłosz), 55–56,
    204–205
carceral feminism, 236
Carol (student), 103
Carr, E. H., 10
Cassandra (friend), 85, 104–105,
    195, 200
Castorp, Hans (fictional character in *The
    Magic Mountain*), 3
Catholic Church, 193, 238
Ceaușescu, Nicolae, 25
Center for Public Integrity, 110–111
Center for Student Conduct, at UC
    Berkeley, 87, 164–165, 167, 172,
    178, 192
Charles V (king), 25
Cheney, Dick, 36
choking, 77
Choudhry, Sujit, 94
Christ, Carol T., 94
Christianity, afterlife and, 14
Chronicle of Higher Education, 105
civil rights, 90–91, 116
Clark, Annie, 92
Clinton, Bill, 33
Clinton, Hillary, 7
    2016 presidential election and, 33–35

Code of Student Conduct, at UC
  Berkeley, 85, 164, 167
Columbia Journalism Review, 153
Columbia University, 92
Comaroff, John, 246
communism, 239, 248
  doublethink, 56
  in Eastern Europe, 25
  fall of, 25
  in Russia, 31
Complainant
  claims of economic privilege
    for, 144–145
  claims of racial privilege for, 144–145
  in Office for the Prevention of
    Harassment and Discrimination
    claim, 85–86, 132–147, 175–177
  in Title IX system, 85–86
complainant, in Title IX system, 111–112
confirmation bias, 155–156
conservative religious movement, in US, 14
Cornell University, 212–213
counterfactual history, 195
Covid-19 pandemic, 204
critical fabulation, 201
cultural rituals, in Soviet Union, 17

Daily Cal (UC Berkeley newspaper),
  198–199, 208, 215
Daily Wire, 244
Dal, Oleg, 121–128, 187, 250
Daniel (abusive boyfriend)
  Alexander as support for, 151–152, 159,
    162–163
  Anna as support for, 191
  apologetic behaviors, 63
  attacks while in "fugue state," 172
  behaviors on domestic violence safety
    checklist, 104

character references for, 152–153, 152
  (photo), 155–156
childhood trauma claims, 37–38, 133,
  150, 162
claimed suicide attempts by, 61
claims of racial discrimination, 139–140
claims of victimhood by, 63, 69–70,
  140, 154, 169
under Code of Student Conduct, 85,
  164–165, 167
contextualization of behavior by,
  240–241
counseling and therapy for, 51
decision to attend UC Berkeley, 17
depression and, 58
destruction of personal property
  by, 59–60
development of romantic feelings
  for, 34–35
early relationship with, 4–12
emotional abuse by, 40, 144
emotional manipulation by, 40, 144, 148
expulsion from Berkeley campus, 165
on Facebook, 63
"flipping" by, 71
history of aggressiveness, 70
history of emotions seminar, 29–30
incident report for, 98–99, 98 (photo)
jealous behaviors, 44–45
legal representation for, 115
love-hurt dialectic with, 50, 59–60
mental health issues for, 51, 58, 61–62,
  73, 154–155
misogyny of, 56–57, 133
monitoring of FlightWire trip, 38
OkCupid and, 7
OPHD claim report, 161–166
OPHD Notice of Allegations for,
  87–88, 111, 114

paper trails as evidence against, 97–101,
    150 (photo), 151 (photo)
past abuse history for, 110–111
physical abuse and assaults by, 40,
    46–48, 57, 74–76, 136–137
post-traumatic stress disorder
    claims, 162
psychiatric evaluation of, 61–62, 73
public face of, 69–70
public support of, 63, 73
sanctions against, 173
self-abuse of, 57–58
temporary restraining order
    against, 96–97
therapy as manipulative tool for, 88
threats of suicide by, 46–47, 50, 58
verbal abuse by, 75, 102–103
"Danny Deever" (Kipling), 229
Daphne (myth of), 181
Darkness at Noon (Koestler), 52–53,
    251–252
"Darkness at Noon" (historical essay
    about domestic violence),
    185–194
Darwin, Charles, 34
date rape, sexual assault and, at colleges
    and universities, 94. *See also specific
    colleges and universities*
affirmative consent legislation for,
    234–235
Campus Sexual Assault Victims' Bill of
    Rights, 91
End Rape on Campus, 92, 234–235
global scope of, 113
The Hunting Ground, 92–93, 234
as imaginary problem, 105
Obama administration response
    to, 91
protests against, 89–90

in *Rolling Stone*, 93, 105, 153
Davis, Natalie Zemon, 201, 216–217
death, childhood questions about, 13
"Deep Play" (Geertz), 26, 28
democratic socialism, in US, 33
Democratic Socialists of America, 39
Department of Education, US. *See also*
    Title IX system
DeVos and, 105, 107, 115
Office for Civil Rights, 116
withdrawal of sexual assault guidelines,
    104–105
Depp, Johnny, 244–245
depression, depressive states and, Daniel
    and, 58
DeVos, Betsy, 105, 107, 115, 223
Dirks, Nicholas (Chancellor of UC
    Berkeley), 5
diversity, equity, and inclusion
    programs, 224
divided consciousness, of abuse survivors,
    77, 156–157
Doherty, Caitlín, 247
domestic violence. *See also* abuse; abuse
    survivors; intimate partner violence;
    misogyny; physical abuse and assault;
    specific people
acute stress reaction after, 81
affidavits for, 95 (photo), 96 (photo)
anxiety response after, 146
Apraksina and, 121–128
Dal and, 121–128
"Darkness at Noon," 185–194
inappropriate affect and, 81–82
lack of eyewitnesses for, 110
"no contact directives," 84
patterns of, 68–69
safety checklist for, 104
self-denial about, 83

domestic violence *(Continued)*
support groups for, 71
supposed lynch mob mentality
after, 140
as taboo subject, 69
therapy after, 70–74
UC Berkeley information protocols
about, 84
under Univ. of California Policy
on Sexual Violence and Sexual
Harassment, 85–86
victim's sense of reality under,
190–191
Dostoyevsky, Fyodor, 37, 124
doughnuts, as comfort food,
36, 163
Dovlatov, Sergei, 121

East Berlin, demonstrations in, 65
Echo, myth of, 127
The Education of a True Believer
(Kopelev), 43
Eichmann, Adolf, 129
Eikhenbaum, Olga, 123
emotional abuse, manipulation and
by Daniel, 40, 144, 148
as mindboggling, 155
emotions
history of emotions seminar at UC
Berkeley, 29–30
as physiological reflexes, 34
End Rape on Campus, 92, 234–235
Engels, Friedrich, 6, 122
Enlightenment, 29
Eramo, Nicole, 93
Erdely, Sabrina, 93
Es schwindelt, 41–43, 136
Evan (Daniel's roommate), 58,
152–153

evidence, for abuse claims, 174 (photo),
175 (photo)
in emails, 150 (photo), 151 (photo)
for Office for the Prevention of
Harassment and Discrimination,
112–113, 131–143
preponderance of evidence
standard, 130
in texts, 146
under Title IX system, 166–167
*Expression of the Emotions in Man and
Animals* (Darwin), 34

facade, of progressive language, 224
Facebook, 63, 155, 244
falsification principle, 20
Falwell, Jerry, 14
Fanon, Frantz, 239
fascism, 93, 103, 250
Faust (Goethe), 3
fellow travelers, 156
feminism, 115–116
carceral, 236
cultural by-products of, 247
as distraction from socialism, 209
as memory work, 250
second-wave, 159, 236
sexual harassment and, 212–213
Title IX system and, 237
*Voice of the Women's Liberation
Movement*, 209
The Feminist War on Crime (Gruber),
236–237
Ferdinand, Franz, 11
Final Solution, 129. *See also* Holocaust
FlightWire, monitoring of, 38
"flipping," in abusive relationships, 71
Foucault, Michel, 5
Freeman, Jo, 209

Free Speech Movement, at UC Berkeley, 6, 208–209

French Annales school, of history, 20

French Revolution, 29, 31, 32

Freud, Sigmund, 87, 250

Gates, Henry Louis, Jr., 246

Gay, Roxane, 82, 115–116

Geertz, Clifford, 26, 28

gender-based violence, 205, 234

Gender Trouble (Butler), 184

Gentileschi, Artemisia, 113–114

Gerrard, Lisa, 209

Gersen, Jeannie Suk, 105, 226

Gessen, Masha, 116

Gift of Fear, 103

Ginzburg, Carlo, 129–130, 153

global historians, 24

Goethe, Johann Wolfgang von, 3

Goldsmiths College, 250

good ole boy, 93

Good Samaritan parable, 14

Goya, Francisco, 34–35

Grateful Dead, 28

grief, 87

Gruber, Aya, 236–237, 239–240

Guardian, 89–90, 227, 235

Gutierrez, Kathleen "Kat," 89–90, 227

Hamlet (Shakespeare), 3

Hannah (friend), 7, 39, 45, 73, 103, 183
    on alleged sexual assault by Tony, 219
    discussing writing about abuse with, 185
    fear of Daniel's manipulative behaviors, 57–58

Harper's, 213

Hartman, Saidiya, 127, 201

Harvard University, 246

Hayek, Friedrich, 237

Heard, Amber, 244–245, 247

Hegel, Georg Wilhelm Friedrich, 10, 19, 256

hegemonic masculinity, 248

Hellbeck, Jochen, 101–102

Hermassi, Elbaki, 212–214

Herodotus, 201

Hill, Anita, 166

history
    Anthropocene era, 19
    boundary construction as element in, 19
    counterfactual, 195
    economic movements across, 19–20
    fall of Berlin Wall, 25
    French Annales school, 20
    of gender-based violence, 205
    Hegel on, 10
    Klee and, 10
    longue durée, 20, 195
    Marx on, 19–20
    as narrative, 128–130
    owls as symbol of, 10–11
    positivist, 20
    Stalinism and, 55

History at Berkeley, 215–216

History Department, at UC Berkeley, 5.
        See also specific people
    beigeocracy of, 8, 57
    cultural history approach in, 24
    department culture, 18–19
    dissertation analysis in, 27
    diversity statements for, 8
    fellowship at, 17
    history of emotions seminar, 29–30
    masculinity themes as focus in, 9–10
    N-grams and, 24
    PhD program, 23–24, 28–29
    tenured faculty in, 21, 26
    working group in, 28–29

Hitler, Adolf, 65, 239
Hollywood Reporter, 36
Holocaust, 129
Holofernes, slaying of, 113
homicide, of abuse victims
  choking behaviors and, 77
  fears of, 76
  of Shannon, 253–256
The House on the Embankment
  (Trifonov), 187–188
Houston, Texas, physical abuse following
  visit to, 74
Huffington Post, 92
humblebragging, 9
Hume, David, 210
Hungary, demonstrations in, 65
Hunt, Lynn, 217–218
The Hunting Ground, 92–93, 234

#IDidn'tWantToDie campaign, 249
inappropriate affect, 81–82
Indian Institute of Technology, 197
Instagram, 244
intimate partner violence, 169
  battering, 209
  marital rape, 209
  mortality statistics for, 248
  threats of future escalation, 58
  threats of self-abuse in, 57–58
  victim's sense of reality under, 190–191
Isabella I (of Castile), 14
Issa (attorney), 172
Iulia (Ukrainian refugee), 232–233

Jackson, Candice E., 105, 107
Jacobins, French Revolution and, 31
Jay, Martin, 130
Judith, myth of, 113
Julia (friend), 60, 66, 75

Julie (Rousseau), 29
Justitia (goddess), 160

Kaba, Mariame, 237
Kaczynski, Ted, 71
Karasek, Sofie, 92–94, 214, 234, 241
Kavanaugh, Brett, 166
Khan, Saifullah, 245–246
Khrushchev, Nikita, 65
Kidman, Nicole, 72
Kierkegaard, Søren, 4
King Lear (Shakespeare), 121
Kipling, Rudyard, 9, 229
Kipnis, Laura, 105–107, 226, 228,
  236, 251
Klee, Paul, 10
Know Your IX, 223, 235
"Koba" (nickname for Stalin), 50
Koestler, Arthur, 52–53, 56, 248, 251–252
Kollontai, Alexandra, 122
Kopelev, Lev, 43, 65
Kurosawa, Akira, 129

Lady Gaga, 92, 234
Lars (former boyfriend), 18
Lectures on the Philosophy of World History
  (Hegel), 19
Lee, Harper, 166
Leibniz, Gottfried Wilhelm, 195
Lenin, Vladimir
  Bolsheviks and, 31–32
  Bukharin and, 43
  death mask of, 16
  Es schwindelt and, 41–42
  role in Russian Revolution, 31, 41
  Trotsky and, 37, 41
Leninka (Russian State Library in
  Moscow), 110
Lepore, Jill, 246

Levine, Lawrence, 216–217

LGBTQ populations, Title IX protections for, 223

Liberty University, 14

Locke, John, 210

longue durée, 20, 195

lotería card, 8

Louis XVI (king), 32

love-hurt dialectic, 50

Ludlow, Peter, 105–107

Lukács, György, 240

Luxemburg, Rosa, 209

Lynchburg, Virginia, 14

lynch mob mentality (supposed), after accusation of domestic violence, 140

Machiavelli, Niccolò, 25–26

"A Magic Mountain" (poem) (Miłosz), 55

The Magic Mountain (novel) (Mann), 3

Magritte, René, 10

manipulation. *See* emotional abuse

Mann, Thomas, 3

Marcy, Geoff, 94

Maria (family of Tsar Nicholas II), 182

marital rape, 209

Mark (graduate student), 61

Marty (aunt of Shannon), 253–254, 259

Marx, Karl, 6, 10

  on communism in Russia, 31

  on destruction of family structure, 122

  on historical economic movements, 19–20

  on history, 19–20

Marxism, 12

masculinity

  hegemonic, 248

  as theme in UC Berkeley History Department, 9–10

Men Explain Things to Me, 82

men's rights groups, 166, 236, 245

Mephistopheles (in *Faust*), 3

#MeToo movement, 112–113, 235. *See also* Weinstein, Harvey

  critics of, 239–240

  fragmentation of, 236

  as moral panic, 116

  second-wave feminism and, 159

  support for women as core of, 153

  "trauma essays" as result of, 184

  "victims" of, 166

Michelle (graduate student), 221–225

Miłosz, Czesław, 55–56, 204–205, 248

  defection from Poland under Stalinism, 65–66

mindboggling, manipulation as, 155

misogyny. *See also* intimate partner violence; physical abuse and assault

  abuse and, 67

  of Daniel, 56–57, 133

"The Mobilization of Violence" (Sauer), 217

Morehouse College, 226–227

Moscow, Russia, 157–158

  Fulbright grant and, 15

  journalism career in, 15

  Leninka library, 110

Moscow State University, 109–110

MTV, 14

"My First Goose" (Babel), 32

Narcissus, myth of, 127

Nation, 166

National Alliance for Mental Illness, 172

NATO. *See* North Atlantic Treaty Organization

Nazi Germany, 239. *See also* Hitler, Adolf
  Final Solution, 129
  historical narrative of, 129–130
  Holocaust, 129
  nonaggression pact with Soviet
    Union, 65
  Soviet Union invaded by, 65
negative dialectics, 240
New Left movement, 208–209
New Left Review, 247
"The New Puritans" (Applebaum),
  224–225
New Yorker, 105, 116
New York Times, 92, 107, 112
New York University (NYU), 184
N-grams, 24
Nicholas II (Tsar), 181–182
Nicky (Tsar Nicholas II, cousin of Kaiser
  Wilhelm II), 11
Nietzsche, Friedrich, 177
Nikolai (sculptor and interview
  subject), 15–16
Nikolai (Nicholas) II (tsar), 181–182
#NiUnaMenos campaign, 249
"no contact directives," 84
nonaggression pact, 65
nonexistent witnesses, 99
nonprofit organizations, 115, 234. *See also*
  specific organizations
North Atlantic Treaty Organization
  (NATO), 233–234
Northwestern University, 226
NYU. *See* New York University
Nzingha ("Warrior Queen of
  Matamba"), 14

Oakland Tribune, 214
Obama, Barack, 56, 91, 223
Occupy movement, 6

October Revolution, 122
Office for Civil Rights, investigation of
  UC Berkeley, 90–91
Office for the Prevention of Harassment
  and Discrimination (OPHD), UC
  Berkeley, 86 (photo)
  alternative resolution process for, 220
  annual complaints to, 225
  character references, 152–153, 152
    (photo), 155–156
  claim report, 161–166
  Complainant witnesses, 85–86,
    132–147, 175–177
  cross-examination procedures, 115
  economic privilege as factor,
    144–145
  evidence review for, 112–113,
    131–143
  investigations by, 87–88, 111, 114
  nomenclature for, 85
  Notice of Allegations from, 87–88,
    111, 114
  racial privilege as factor, 144–145
  Respondent claims, 86, 117–119,
    132–143, 175–177
  therapist interviews, 141–142
  witness interviews, 132–143
OkCupid, 7
Olga (family of Tsar Nicholas II), 182

Pangloss (in *Candide*), 195
Parton, Dolly, 7
Path to Care Center, 84, 97, 171
people pleasers, people pleasing and,
  57, 158
personal accountability strategies, in
  recognizing and leaving abusive
  relationships, 73
Peter (former romantic partner), 4, 47

physical abuse and assault
  by Daniel, 40, 46–48, 57, 74–76,
    136–137
  under Univ. of California Policy
    on Sexual Violence and Sexual
    Harassment, 85–86
Pino, Andrea, 92
Plato, 210
Poddar, Prosenjit, 196–197, 229,
    259–260
  Bad Karma, 200–203
  mental illness claims by, 199,
    202–203
Poland, 206, 243
  historical relationship with
    Ukraine, 252
  Miłosz defection from, under
    Stalinism, 65–66
  Miłosz return to, 66
  Russian invasion of Ukraine and,
    231–233
  Ukrainian refugees in, 232–233
Poor Folk (Dostoyevsky), 37
Popper, Karl, 20
Porter, Rob, 116
positivism, 20, 178
post-traumatic stress disorder, 162, 169
power, authority and, 25–26
preponderance of evidence
    standard, 91, 105, 116, 130,
    161–169, 245
Price, Pamela, 212–213
psychological coercion, 209
Putin, Vladimir, 111–112, 231–233

race, racism and. *See also* whiteness
  Black Lives Matter movement, 235
  Daniel's claims of, 139–140
  feminism and, 115–116

  in Office for the Prevention of
    Harassment and Discrimination
    claim, 144–145
  Till murder and, 153
von Ranke, Leopold, 20, 178, 183, 215
rape, 209. *See also* date rape
Rape, Abuse, and Incest National
    Network, 224
"A Rape on Campus" (*Rolling Stone*
    article), 93, 105, 153
Rashomon (Kurosawa), 129
Reagan, Ronald, 6
Red Cavalry (Babel), 32
Redford, Robert, 5
Republic (Plato), 210
Requiem (Akhmatova), 94
respondent, in Title IX
    system, 111–112
Respondent claims, to OPHD, 86,
    117–119, 132–143, 175–177
restorative justice, 237–238
restraining orders, 203
Revolution on My Mind (Hellbeck), 101
revolutions. *See* French Revolution;
    October Revolution; Russian
    Revolution
The Right to Sex (Srinivasan), 249
The Road to Serfdom (Hayek), 237
Robespierre, Maximilien, 30
Robinson, Tom (fictional character in *To
    Kill a Mockingbird*), 166
Rolling Stone, 93, 105, 153
Romania, 25
Ronell, Avital, 184
Rose (friend), 45, 66, 75–77, 82, 244
Rousseau, Jean-Jacques, 29
Rubashov (fictional character in *Darkness
    at Noon*), 52–53, 251–252
Rule, Ann, 11

Russia. *See also* Moscow, Russia; Putin, Vladimir
establishment of communism in, 31
#IDidn'tWantToDie campaign, 249
invasion of Ukraine, 231–233
Russian Revolution. *See also* Soviet Union
atmosphere of possibility after, 32–33
Bolsheviks and, 31–32
foundations of, 31–32
Lenin's role in, 31, 41
as "the revolution," 218
"Workers' Marseillaise," 31
Russian State Library. *See* Leninka

safe houses, 62
safety planning, 203
Sand, George, 15
Sanders, Bernie, 33
Sandler, Bernice, 90
San Francisco Chronicle, 89, 106, 198–199
Santa Cruz, University of California at, 227
Sauer, Wolfgang, 216–217
Savio, Mario, 208–209
Schermerhorn, Nathaniel E. C., 248
Scott, Joan Wallach, 184
Searle, John, 94, 210
Seccuro, Liz, 93
second-wave feminism, 159, 236
self-abuse, self-harm and, by Daniel, 57–58
self-calming techniques, 182
sexual assault, sexual assault victims. *See also* date rape; physical abuse and assault; violence
DeVos on, 105, 107
due process for men accused of, 107
as "fake victims," 105
lack of eyewitnesses for, 110
marital rape, 209
race as credibility factor, 115–116
retribution for supporting victims, 188
by Trump, 105
verbal coercion as element of, 220
of Weinstein, 112
sexual harassment, 212–215
Sexual Violence and Sexual Harassment Policy, at UC Berkeley, 164
S.F. Bay Guardian, 214
Shakespeare, William, 3, 121
Shannon (domestic violence victim), 253–256
shelters, 203
She Said, 247
Slate, 105
slavery, slave trade and, Hegel as apologist for, 19
The Sleep of Reason Produces Monsters (Goya), 34–35
social codes, at UC Berkeley, 8–9
social media. *See also* Facebook; Instagram
#MeToo movement on, 112–113
support for Ukraine on, 233–234
social movements
Black Lives Matter, 235
"Bloody Thursday," 6
conservative religious movement, 14
Free Speech Movement, 6, 208–209
Occupy movement, 6
Solnit, Rebecca, 82, 113
Sorensen, David, 116
Sorrell, Tyann, 94
Soviet Union. *See also* Khrushchev, Nikita; Stalin, Joseph
art of, 17
cultural rituals in, 17
death masks of former elite in, 16

demonstrations in Soviet satellite
    countries, 65
Five-Year Plan, 43
industrialization of, 43
invasion by Nazi Germany, 65
nonaggression pact with Nazi
    Germany, 65
October Revolution and, 122
the Terror in, 52–53
Spears, Britney, 14
Spelman College, 226–227
Spivak, Gayatri Chakravorty, 184
Srinivasan, Amia, 239–240, 249
Stalin, Joseph, 65, 239. *See also*
    Soviet Union
    Bukharin and, 43
    Five-Year Plan, 43
    "Koba" as nickname for, 50
    the Terror under, 52–53, 94–96,
        187–188
    women under, 122
Stalinism, 55, 129, 156
stalking laws, 203
standoffs, 6, 191
The Stranger Beside Me (Rule), 11
suicide, suicidal ideation, threats of, by
    Daniel, 46–47, 50, 58, 61
Sulkowicz, Emma, 92
Sun, 244
Sunrise Movement, 235
support groups, for domestic violence, 71
sympathy, as virtue, 29

Tang Center, 134
Tarasoff, Tatiana ("Tanya"), murder
    of, 196–197, 203–204, 229,
        243, 246
    Bad Karma, 200–202
    historical legacy of, 208, 247

lawsuits as result of, 200
    as legal precedent, 200
    in newspapers, 198–199, 198 (photo)
Tatiana (family of Tsar Nicholas II), 182
temporary restraining order (TRO),
    against Daniel, 96–97
the Terror, 52–53, 94–96, 187–188
therapy, therapists and
    after domestic violence, 70–74
    as manipulative tool by abuser, 88
    in Office for the Prevention of
        Harassment and Discrimination
        claims, 141–142
Third World Women's Alliance, 213–214
Thomas, Clarence, 166
Thompson, E. P., 249
"Til It Happens to You" (Lady Gaga), 92
Till, Emmett, 153
Title IX system
    administrative language for, 85–86, 111
    alleged abuses of, 107
    alleged bias against accused in, 228
    backlash against, 116
    Center for Public Integrity, 110–111
    Center for Student Conduct and, 165
    complainant in, 111–112
    Complainant nomenclature, 85–86
    as "crime logic," 237
    critics of, 167–168, 224–225,
        236–237, 239
    under DeVos, 105, 223
    discrimination review, 216
    in Education Amendments bill, 90
    evidence standard for, 116
    feminist criticism of, 237
    fragmentation of, 236
    goal and purpose of, 205
    historical application of, 209–210
    investigations under, 91, 98–99

Title IX system *(Continued)*
 investigators for, 163
 Kipnis critique of, 105–107
 Know Your IX, 223, 235
 lack of national consistency for, 227–228
 language use in claims, 182–183
 media coverage of, 105
 men as victims of, 107
 men's rights under, 245
 "no contact directives," 84
 no-retaliation policy, 105
 "overreach" of, 105
 paper trails for, 97–101
 passage of legislation for, 90
 reporting protocols for, 84–85
 respondent in, 111–112
 restorative justice under, 237–238
 retribution for supporting victims
  under, 188
 revocation of university funding under, 92
 self-reporting by colleges and
  universities in, 210–211
 stricter evidence standards for, 166–167
 transgender protections under, 223
 under Trump, 107, 166, 223, 244
 at UC Berkeley, 84–86, 212–214,
  216, 225
 in University of California schools, 167
 victim's sense of reality under, 190–191
 women's liberation movement and,
  210–211
Tomsky, Mikhail, 44
Tony (accused graduate student),
 219–222, 225
totalitarianism, study of, 55
To Kill a Mockingbird (Lee), 166
transgender populations, Title IX
 protections for, 223
"trauma essays," 184

Trifonov, Yuri, 187–188
TRO. *See* temporary restraining order
Trotsky, Leon, 37, 41, 43, 218
Trump, Donald, 4
 alt-right support for, 35–36
 Clinton, H., and, 7
 DeVos and, 105, 107, 115, 223
 funding threats against UC Berkeley, 45
 political activism after election of, 39
 political disillusionment under, 128
 as political victim, 226
 sexual assault accusations against, 105
 Title IX regulations under, 107, 166,
  223, 244
 2016 presidential election and, 33–35
 withdrawal of sexual assault guidelines
  under, 104–105
T-shirts, 114
Twitter (X), 112–113
2007–2008 global financial crisis, 24
2016 US presidential election, 7, 33–35
 political movements after, 39

UC Berkeley. *See* Berkeley, University of
 California at
UCLA. *See* University of California, Los
 Angeles
Ukraine
 feminization of, 233
 historical relationship with Poland, 252
 Russian invasion of, 231–233
UNC Chapel Hill, 92
United States (US)
 democratic socialism in, 33
 Democratic Socialists of America, 39
 2016 presidential election, 7, 33–35
Unite the Right rally, 93, 103, 250
University of California, Los Angeles
 (UCLA), 129

University of California at Berkeley. *See* Berkeley

University of California system. *See also* Berkeley, University of California at; Santa Cruz, University of California at; University of California, Los Angeles

lack of demographic diversity in, 210

Policy on Sexual Violence and Sexual Harassment, 85–86

sexual harassment grievance procedures in, 214

University of Maryland, 90

University of Virginia, 93, 103, 250

Unwanted Advances (Kipnis), 105–107, 226, 228

US. *See* United States

Veep, 33

verbal abuse, 75, 102–103

verbal coercion, 220

Vescio, Theresa K., 248

violence. *See also* domestic violence; homicide; intimate partner violence; physical abuse and assault; self-abuse

gender-based, 205

Robespierre on, 30

virtue and, 30

virtue, 29–30

virtue signaling, 9

Voice of the Women's Liberation Movement, 209

Voltaire, 195

Wanjuki, Wagatwe, 227

"Warrior Queen of Matamba." *See* Nzingha

Washington Post, 234, 244

We (Zamiatin), 124

Weber, Max, 24–25

Weinstein, Harvey

arrest of, 115

legal settlements by, 238

sexual harassment claims against, 112, 159

Wentworth, Blake, 89, 94, 227–228

White, Hayden, 128–129, 188–190

whiteness, of UC Berkeley History Department, 8

Why Does He Do That? Inside the Minds of Angry and Controlling Men (Bancroft), 66, 73

Wilhelm II (Kaiser), 11

"With Hegel to Salvation," 49

witnesses, witness interviews and lack of witnesses for sexual assault claims, 110

nonexistent, 99

in Office for the Prevention of Harassment and Discrimination claims, 132–143

WOASH. *See* Women Organized Against Sexual Harassment

women. *See also* #MeToo movement; misogyny

gender-based violence against, 205

silencing of, 82

in Soviet Union, 122

under Stalinist rule, 122

Women on the Margins (Davis), 201, 216–217

Women Organized Against Sexual Harassment (WOASH), 212–215

Women's Equity Action League, 90

women's liberation movement, 210–211, 214–215. *See also* feminism

Wood, Carmita, 212–213

Wood, Deborah (graduate student), 222–225

"Workers' Marseillaise," 31

World War I, 11, 31

World War II, 56. *See also* Holocaust

X. *See* Twitter

Yale University, 166, 245–246

Yekaterinburg, Russia, 181–182

Yiannopoulos, Milo, protests
    against, 45

Yoffe, Emily, 105

YouTube, 245

Yuon, Konstantin, 32

Zamiatin, Yevgeny, 124

Zelensky, Volodymyr, 233

Zoom, 171

Meridith De Avila Khan

Joy Neumeyer is a writer and historian of Russia and Eastern Europe whose essays have appeared in publications including the *New York Times*, *Nation*, *Atlantic*, and *New Left Review*. She was a Fulbright fellow in Russia and has lived and worked as a reporter in Moscow and Warsaw. She received her PhD in history from the University of California, Berkeley, in 2020.

PublicAffairs is a publishing house founded in 1997. It is a tribute to the standards, values, and flair of three persons who have served as mentors to countless reporters, writers, editors, and book people of all kinds, including me.

I. F. STONE, proprietor of *I. F. Stone's Weekly*, combined a commitment to the First Amendment with entrepreneurial zeal and reporting skill and became one of the great independent journalists in American history. At the age of eighty, Izzy published *The Trial of Socrates*, which was a national bestseller. He wrote the book after he taught himself ancient Greek.

BENJAMIN C. BRADLEE was for nearly thirty years the charismatic editorial leader of *The Washington Post*. It was Ben who gave the *Post* the range and courage to pursue such historic issues as Watergate. He supported his reporters with a tenacity that made them fearless and it is no accident that so many became authors of influential, best-selling books.

ROBERT L. BERNSTEIN, the chief executive of Random House for more than a quarter century, guided one of the nation's premier publishing houses. Bob was personally responsible for many books of political dissent and argument that challenged tyranny around the globe. He is also the founder and longtime chair of Human Rights Watch, one of the most respected human rights organizations in the world.

·   ·   ·

For fifty years, the banner of Public Affairs Press was carried by its owner Morris B. Schnapper, who published Gandhi, Nasser, Toynbee, Truman, and about 1,500 other authors. In 1983, Schnapper was described by *The Washington Post* as "a redoubtable gadfly." His legacy will endure in the books to come.

Peter Osnos, *Founder*